ABUSE OF PROCESS
AND JUDICIAL STAYS
OF CRIMINAL PROCEEDINGS

Abuse of Process and Judicial Stays of Criminal Proceedings

ANDREW L.-T. CHOO

Clarendon Press · Oxford
1993

Oxford University Press, Walton Street, Oxford OX2 6DP
Oxford New York Toronto
Delhi Bombay Calcutta Madras Karachi
Kuala Lumpur Singapore Hong Kong Tokyo
Nairobi Dar es Salaam Cape Town
Melbourne Auckland Madrid
and associated companies in
Berlin Ibadan

Oxford is a trade mark of Oxford University Press

Published in the United States
by Oxford University Press Inc., New York

British Library Cataloguing in Publication Data
Data available

Library of Congress Cataloging in Publication Data
Choo, Andrew L.-T.
Abuse of process and judicial stays of criminal proceedings/
Andrew L.-T. Choo.
p.   cm.—(Oxford monographs on criminology, law, and
justice)
Includes bibliographical references and index.
1. Criminal procedure—Great Britain.   2. Judicial discretion—
Great Britain.   I. Title.   II. Series.
KD8362.C46   1993
345.41'05—dc20
[344.1055]   93–5501
ISBN 0–19–825801–1

1 3 5 7 9 10 8 6 4 2

Typeset by Cambrian Typesetters
Frimley, Surrey
Printed in Great Britain
on acid-free paper by
Bookcraft Ltd., Midsomer Norton, Avon

*To my parents
and to Kelvin and Sharon,
with my love*

General Editor's Introduction

IN recent years the doctrine of abuse of process has been invoked with increasing frequency in cases of police impropriety, prosecutorial delay and other conduct thought to detract significantly from procedural fairness. The doctrine has developed from case to case in a characteristic common law manner, and this makes it ripe for the kind of detailed and searching review provided here by Dr Andrew Choo. Many of the questions raised—such as, whether abuse of process should ever lead to an automatic stay of process or always to judicial discretion; when, if there is evidence of police malpractice, this doctrine should apply rather than the court's discretion to exclude evidence—are of interest to practitioners as well as to academic lawyers. This monograph seeks to advance the cause of legality and 'judicial integrity' by proposing new parameters for the doctrine of abuse of process. It is a most welcome contribution to the series.

Andrew Ashworth

Preface

THE judicial discretion to stay criminal proceedings has attracted considerable attention in recent times. In 1964 the House of Lords confirmed the ability of a criminal court to stay proceedings which are an abuse of the process of the court. Since then, the number of reported cases on the abuse of process discretion in criminal litigation has increased dramatically. However, these are, in the main, decisions of Queen's Bench Divisional Courts, and most of the decisions are concerned with the single issue of the extent to which proceedings may be stayed on account of police or prosecutorial delay. The fact that very few cases on the abuse of process discretion in criminal litigation reach the Court of Appeal or House of Lords means that there has been relatively little theoretical discussion of the topic by the highest courts in the jurisdiction. Nevertheless, much interest is being shown in the topic by academic commentators, as evidenced by the rapidly growing number of journal articles and commentaries being published. To date, however, nobody in England has produced a full-length monograph on the judicial discretion to stay criminal proceedings as an abuse of process.

The chief concern of this book is to provide answers to two important, and closely related, questions which remain unresolved. First, on precisely what basis, or bases, should the judicial discretion to stay criminal proceedings be exercised? Secondly, what is the scope of the discretion? For example, it is clear that, in England, the discretion may be exercised in 'double-jeopardy' situations and in cases where there has been delay in bringing the defendant to trial. However, it appears that the discretion is not exercisable in England in cases where the defendant has been brought to trial as a result of an 'illegal extradition', or in cases of entrapment. By contrast, in certain other Commonwealth jurisdictions the discretion has been held to be exercisable in *all* of the above situations. Obviously, widely differing views on the scope of the discretion exist, and we shall see that the reasons for this difference of opinion provide an important clue to an understanding of the topic.

The present work presents a fresh perspective on the abuse of process discretion by setting the discretion against the general backdrop of the law of criminal evidence. In recent times, a number of evidence scholars have demonstrated persuasively that every exclusionary rule and exclusionary discretion in the law of criminal evidence can be explained by reference to the protection of the innocent from wrongful conviction and/or the protection of the moral integrity of the criminal process. I seek to demonstrate that the abuse of process discretion can, and should, be viewed in the same way. In this light, therefore, the present work can be seen as complementing the large volume of literature available on criminal evidence.

Whilst the main focus of this book is on English law, there are, at various points, discussions of the ways in which particular issues are dealt with in other jurisdictions, especially Canada, Australia, New Zealand, Ireland, and the United States. As will be demonstrated, there has emerged in these jurisdictions a less conservative approach to many issues than has been the case in England.

Some of my earlier thoughts on matters relevant to the topic of the present monograph have been published in journals, and I am grateful for the permission which I have received to draw on this material.

My interest in the topic began while I was a doctoral research student at the University of Oxford from 1986 until 1990, and the development of my ideas was greatly assisted by the guidance provided by Peter Mirfield (Jesus College) and Adrian Zuckerman (University College). I am very grateful also to Jill Hunter of the Faculty of Law of the University of New South Wales for her advice and encouragement over the years. Andrew Ashworth of King's College, London, has, as series editor, provided much encouragement and read the final draft on behalf of Oxford University Press. The friends I made during my time at Oxford have helped greatly in more indirect ways, and particular thanks are due to Annelies Dogterom, Guang Geng, Eifion Phillips, Ian Scott, Kathy Wedell, Ann Wright, and Leeka Xu for their support near the time of the completion of my studies at Oxford. I have also benefited from discussions with my colleagues at the Faculty of Law at the University of Leicester. The Faculty provided me with a grant in aid of my research, for which I am very grateful.

The law as stated in the book is based generally on materials available at the Bodleian Law Library, Oxford, in November 1992. Listed in the Bibliography are not only the references cited in the text or footnotes of the book, but all works to which general reference was made in the writing of the book. It is hoped that this extended bibliography will provide a useful research resource for any reader wishing to pursue individual topics in greater depth.

Andrew L.-T. Choo

University of Leicester
December 1992

Addendum

THIS is a fast-moving area of the law. Unfortunately, the important decisions of the House of Lords in *R. v. Manchester Crown Court, ex p. DPP (In re Ashton)* [1993] 2 WLR 846 (May 1993) and *R. v. Horseferry Road Magistrates' Court, ex p. Bennett* [1993] 3 WLR 90 (June 1993) have arrived too late for me to take account of them. This book, and in particular Chapters 4 and 5, should be read in the light of these decisions.

In *In re Ashton*, the House of Lords held that the decision of a Crown Court judge on whether a prosecution should be stayed is *not* amenable to judicial review by the Queen's Bench Divisional Court. Thus the cases of *R. v. Central Criminal Court, ex p. Randle and Pottle* (1990) 92 Cr. App. R. 323 and *R. v. Norwich Crown Court, ex p. Belsham* [1992] 1 WLR 54, mentioned in Chapter 5, have been overruled. I criticize the decision of the House of Lords in *In re Ashton* in a forthcoming note in the *Law Quarterly Review*.

In *Bennett*, the House of Lords has held definitively that proceedings made possible by an illegal extradition can be stayed as an abuse of the process of the court. It will be obvious from my discussions in Chapter 4 that I regard this development as a very welcome one.

A. L.-T. Choo
July 1993

Contents

Table of Cases

Australia

Canada

European Court of Human Rights

Ireland

United States

Table of Statutory Material

United States

1

The Abuse of Process Discretion and Criminal Justice

In this monograph, the power of a court to stay proceedings which are an 'abuse of the process of the court' will be generally referred to, for convenience, as the abuse of process discretion. The chief concern of this work is with the operation of the discretion in criminal cases. It seeks to identify and evaluate the situations in which criminal prosecutions may be stayed. To put it more simply, what is it that makes a criminal prosecution an abuse of process and hence liable to be stayed? On occasion, valiant attempts have been made by judges to engage in theoretical discussion of the meaning of 'abuse of process'. Consider, for example, the following two statements made in the Supreme Court of Canada:

A stay should be granted where 'compelling an accused to stand trial would violate those fundamental principles of justice which underlie the community's sense of fair play and decency' . . . or where the proceedings are 'oppressive or vexatious' . . .[1]

The doctrine is one of the safeguards designed to ensure 'that the repression of crime through the conviction of the guilty is done in a way which reflects our fundamental values as a society' . . . It acknowledges that courts must have the respect and support of the community in order that the administration of criminal justice may properly fulfil its function. Consequently, where the affront to fair play and decency is disproportionate to the societal interest in the effective prosecution of criminal cases, then the administration of justice is best served by staying the proceedings.[2]

However, such formulations when examined closely do not prove particularly helpful. What are these fundamental principles of justice and fundamental values? What precisely do the terms oppressiveness and vexatiousness mean in this context? And what are these concepts of fair play and decency? Such high-sounding phrases may highlight the paramountcy and fundamentality of the abuse of process discretion, but they do not take us much further than the phrase 'abuse of process' itself. It is, therefore, the aim of this study to provide a clearer explanation and rationalization of the discretion, and, in doing so, to put forward some proposals as to how the English law in the area might be reformed.

---

[1] *Keyowski* v. *R.* (1988) 62 CR (3d) 349, 350 per Wilson J.
[2] *R.* v. *Conway* (1989) 70 CR (3d) 209, 222–3 per L'Heureux-Dubé J.

The Origins and Development of the Abuse of Process Discretion

A very brief examination of the origins of the discretion and of its use in civil litigation may help illuminate the present-day scope of the discretion in the criminal sphere.[3] The discretion would appear to be one with a long history. In 1885 Lord Blackburn stated in the civil case of *Metropolitan Bank* v. *Pooley* that

from early times (I rather think, though I have not looked at it enough to say, from the earliest times) the Court had inherently in its power the right to see that its process was not abused by a proceeding without reasonable grounds, so as to be vexatious and harassing—the Court had the right to protect itself against such an abuse; but that was not done upon demurrer, or upon the record, or upon the verdict of a jury or evidence taken in that way, but it was done by the Court informing its conscience upon affidavits, and by a summary order to stay the action which was brought under such circumstances as to be an abuse of the process of the Court; and in a proper case they did stay the action.[4]

This power to stay proceedings was one of two powers exercisable by a court in its inherent jurisdiction, the other power being the power to punish for contempt of court and of its process. The offences to which this power to punish for contempt applied were contempt in the face or presence of the court, disobedience to the process of the court, and irregularities and misfeasances of the officers of the court. From the earliest times the superior courts assumed, in relation to these offences, the power to attach and summarily punish the offender and to release him subsequently on the payment of a fine.[5]

As Jacob explains, the jurisdiction to exercise the powers of staying proceedings and punishing for contempt is 'inherent' in the sense that such jurisdiction did not derive from any statute or rule of law, but 'from the very nature of the court as a superior court of law'. The jurisdiction is 'intrinsic in a superior court; it is its very life-blood, its very essence, its immanent attribute'. In the absence of such a jurisdiction,

the court would have form but would lack substance. The jurisdiction which is inherent in a superior court of law is that which enables it to fulfil itself as a court of law. The juridical basis of this jurisdiction is therefore the authority of the judiciary

[3] See generally R. G. Fox, 'Criminal Delay as Abuse of Process' (1990) 16 *Monash University Law Review* 64, 74 ff.; I. H. Jacob, 'The Inherent Jurisdiction of the Court' (1970) 23 *Current Legal Problems* 23; J. A. Jolowicz, 'Abuse of the Process of the Court: Handle with Care' (1990) 43 *Current Legal Problems* 77; K. Mason, 'The Inherent Jurisdiction of the Court' (1983) 57 *Australian Law Journal* 449; P. H. Winfield, *The History of Conspiracy and Abuse of Legal Procedure* (1921); P. H. Winfield, *The Present Law of Abuse of Legal Procedure* (1921).   [4] (1885) LR 10 App. Cas. 210, 220–1.
[5] Jacob, 'The Inherent Jurisdiction of the Court', 25–6.

to uphold, to protect and to fulfil the judicial function of administering justice according to law in a regular, orderly and effective manner.[6]

It has been stated in the High Court of Australia that

'inherent jurisdiction' is the power which a court has simply because it is a court of a particular description. Thus the Courts of Common Law without the aid of any authorizing provision had inherent jurisdiction to prevent abuse of their process and to punish for contempt. Inherent jurisdiction is not something derived by implication from statutory provisions conferring particular jurisdiction; if such a provision is to be considered as conferring more than is actually expressed that further jurisdiction is conferred by implication according to accepted standards of statutory construction and it would be inaccurate to describe it as 'inherent jurisdiction', which, as the name indicates, requires no authorizing provision.[7]

Castro v. *Murray*,[8] decided in 1875, provides an early illustration of the exercise of the judicial discretion to stay an action as an abuse of process. Having been convicted of a misdemeanour, the plaintiff prepared a writ of error, and requested the appropriate clerk to seal it. The clerk refused to do so on the ground that the Attorney-General had not issued his fiat. (It was, in fact, the duty of the clerk not to seal a writ of error in cases of misdemeanour until the Attorney-General had issued his fiat.) The plaintiff brought an action against the clerk claiming damages for the refusal, and mandamus to compel the clerk to seal the writ. It was held by the Court of Exchequer that, being 'absolutely groundless',[9] this action was one which the Court, in the exercise of its discretion, should stay as an abuse of process.

In 1883 the judicial discretion to stay civil proceedings found expression in Order 25, rule 4, of the Supreme Court Rules, which authorized the stay of an action which was shown by the pleadings to be 'frivolous or vexatious'. The term 'abuse of the process of the court' did not appear until the Rules were revised in 1962. Order 25, rule 4, became Order 18, rule 19, which provides:

The Court may at any stage of the proceedings order to be struck out or amended any pleading or the indorsement of any writ in the action, or anything in any pleading or in the indorsement, on the ground that—
    (*a*) it discloses no reasonable cause of action or defence, as the case may be; or
    (*b*) it is scandalous, frivolous or vexatious; or
    (*c*) it may prejudice, embarrass or delay the fair trial of the action; or
    (*d*) it is otherwise an abuse of the process of the Court;
and may order the action to be stayed or dismissed or judgment to be entered accordingly, as the case may be.

---

[6] Ibid. 27–8.
[7] *R.* v. *Forbes, ex p. Bevan* (1972) 127 CLR 1, 7 per Menzies J. This passage was cited approvingly by Gibbs J. in *Taylor* v. *Taylor* (1979) 143 CLR 1, 6.
[8] (1875) LR 10 Ex. 213.   [9] Ibid. 218 per Bramwell B.

The wording of this rule implies, therefore, that the term 'abuse of process' may be used in civil litigation to refer to a number of different situations, of which those spelt out in (*a*), (*b*), and (*c*) are only specific examples. Indeed, a glance at the relevant section of the *White Book*[10] reveals just how diverse these situations can be. The Court of Appeal has stated: 'A litigant has a right to have his claim litigated, provided it is not frivolous, vexatious or an abuse of the process. What may constitute such conduct must depend on all the circumstances of the case; the categories are not closed and considerations of public policy and the interests of justice may be very material.'[11] A helpful attempt has, however, been made by Jacob to distil the various categories of civil proceedings which may constitute an abuse of process into a manageable list:

(*a*) proceedings which involve a deception on the court, or are fictitious or constitute a mere sham;

(*b*) proceedings where the process of the court is not being fairly or honestly used but is employed for some ulterior or improper purpose or in an improper way;

(*c*) proceedings which are manifestly groundless or without foundation or which serve no useful purpose;

(*d*) multiple or successive proceedings which cause or are likely to cause improper vexation or oppression.[12]

In sum, the development of the abuse of process discretion in civil litigation has been one which has been taking place gradually for over 100 years. On the criminal side, however, the discretion received relatively little attention until the 1964 decision of the House of Lords in *Connelly* v. *DPP*,[13] and thus the development of the discretion has been confined in the main to the last three decades.

THE ABUSE OF PROCESS DISCRETION IN CRIMINAL LITIGATION

ENTRENCHMENT OF THE DISCRETION IN THE CRIMINAL SPHERE

The ability of a trial judge to stay a criminal prosecution[14] was confirmed by the House of Lords in *Connelly* in the context of a consideration of the rule against double jeopardy. I shall canvass very briefly the views of the five Law Lords.

Lord Reid acknowledged the ability of a court 'to prevent a trial from

---

[10] *The Supreme Court Practice 1993* (1992).

[11] *Ashmore* v. *British Coal Corporation* [1990] 2 QB 338, 348.

[12] Jacob, 'The Inherent Jurisdiction of the Court', 43.   [13] [1964] AC 1254.

[14] See generally R. Pattenden, 'Abuse of Process in Criminal Litigation' (1989) 53 *Journal of Criminal Law* 341; R. Pattenden, 'The Power of the Courts to Stay a Criminal Prosecution' [1985] *Criminal Law Review* 175; R. Pattenden, *Judicial Discretion and Criminal Litigation* (2nd edn., 1990), 32–8.

taking place' in the exercise of its 'residual discretion to prevent anything which savours of abuse of process'.[15] He also expressed agreement with the speeches of Lords Devlin and Pearce.[16]

Lord Devlin referred in his speech to the judgment of Lord Goddard CJ in *R. v. Chairman, County of London Quarter Sessions, ex p. Downes*.[17] Lord Goddard CJ had said that once an indictment was before a court it had to be tried except (1) if it was defective; (2) if a plea in bar (*autrefois acquit* or *autrefois convict*) was available; (3) if a *nolle prosequi* was entered by the Attorney-General; or (4) if the court had no jurisdiction.[18] Lord Devlin considered, however, that a fifth ground should be added: a court could also refuse to allow an indictment to go to trial in the case of 'a gross abuse of process'.[19]

Are the courts [he asked] to rely on the Executive to protect their process from abuse? Have they not themselves an inescapable duty to secure fair treatment for those who come or are brought before them? To questions of this sort there is only one possible answer. The courts cannot contemplate for a moment the transference to the Executive of the responsibility for seeing that the process of law is not abused.[20]

Thus, Lord Devlin considered that proceedings which put a defendant in double jeopardy could be stayed as an abuse of process even if the pleas in bar, *autrefois acquit* and *autrefois convict*, were unavailable.[21] Lord Devlin was not impressed by the argument that the pleas in bar gave accused persons all the protection against double jeopardy to which they were entitled. He thought that, if this argument were to be accepted,

it might equally well have been argued that the well-established rule that [a] confession must be voluntary gave the accused all the protection to which he was entitled against unfair questioning. If that argument had prevailed, there would have been no Judges' Rules.[22]

Lord Pearce took an approach similar to that of Lord Devlin, holding that 'it is clear from several cases that the court in its criminal jurisdiction retained a power to prevent a repetition of prosecutions, even when it did not fall within the exact limits of the pleas in bar'.[23] The main cases which Lord Pearce had in mind were *Wemyss* v. *Hopkins*,[24] *R. v. Miles*,[25] and *R. v. King*.[26] In *Wemyss* the defendant was tried with the offence that, being a driver of a carriage, he had struck a horse ridden by the prosecutor causing hurt and damage to the prosecutor. He was convicted of this offence, and later convicted of unlawfully assaulting, striking, and otherwise abusing the

---

[15] [1964] AC 1254, 1296.
[16] See, however, Lord Reid's qualification in *Atkinson* v. *USA Government* [1971] AC 197, 232. [17] [1954] 1 QB 1. [18] Ibid. 6.
[19] [1964] AC 1254, 1355. [20] Ibid. 1354. [21] Ibid. 1360.
[22] Ibid. 1348. [23] Ibid. 1362. [24] (1875) LR 10 QB 378.
[25] (1890) 24 QBD 423. [26] [1897] 1 QB 214.

prosecutor. The second conviction was quashed, Blackburn J. stating that

the defence does not arise on a plea of autrefois convict, but on the well-established rule at common law, that where a person has been convicted and punished for an offence by a Court of competent jurisdiction, transit in rem judicatam, that is, the conviction shall be a bar to all further proceedings for the same offence, and he shall not be punished again for the *same matter* . . .

This defence was described as a plea 'in the nature of a plea of autrefois convict'.[27]

In contrast to Lords Reid, Devlin, and Pearce, Lord Morris expressed agreement with what was said by Lord Goddard CJ in *Downes*. Thus,

if a charge is preferred which is contained in a perfectly valid indictment which is drawn so as to accord with what the court has stated to be correct practice and which is presented to a court clothed with jurisdiction to deal with it and if there is no plea in bar which can be upheld the court cannot direct that the prosecution must not proceed.[28]

Mere regret that a prosecution was taking place would not enable the judge to suppress the prosecution.[29]

Like Lord Morris, Lord Hodson adopted the statement of Lord Goddard CJ in *Downes*[30] and doubted the existence of a discretion to stay a prosecution where the pleas in bar were unavailable.[31]

Dicta on the staying of proceedings occur in the speeches of three of the five members of the House of Lords in *DPP v. Humphrys*.[32] Lord Salmon, in recognizing the existence of a judicial power to intervene 'if the prosecution amounts to an abuse of the process of the court and is oppressive and vexatious',[33] found himself in agreement with Lords Devlin and Pearce in *Connelly*.[34] Lord Edmund-Davies took a similar view: 'While judges should pause long before staying proceedings which on their face are perfectly regular . . . [i]n my judgment, *Connelly* . . . established that they are vested with the power to do what the justice of the case clearly demands.'[35] However Viscount Dilhorne thought that proceedings should be stayed only in situations where the trial was improperly split.[36] A strong

---

[27] (1875) LR 10 QB 378, 381 (emphasis added).   [28] [1964] AC 1254, 1300.
[29] Ibid. 1304.   [30] Ibid. 1335–6.
[31] Ibid. 1337. 'If there were such a discretion, I do not understand why so many cases have been decided and so much learning has been expended in considering the doctrine of autrefois convict and autrefois acquit. Has all this been waste of judicial time? It would seem so, if all the judge had to do was to exercise his discretion as to whether or not a second indictment in such a case as this should be allowed to proceed.'   [32] [1977] AC 1.
[33] Ibid. 46.   [34] Ibid. 45.   [35] Ibid. 55.
[36] 'If at the time of *Connelly* v. *Director of Public Prosecutions* it had been possible to try the murder and robbery charges together, then it might well have been held unfair, oppressive and an abuse of process for them to be tried separately, each charge being based on the same evidence' (ibid. 24). See also ibid. 26: it may be right to stay proceedings 'in cases where there could be one trial for more than one offence and it is sought without good reason to have two trials on the same facts'.

statement was made by Viscount Dilhorne underlining the traditional distinction between the functions of the executive and the judiciary:

A judge must keep out of the arena. He should not have or appear to have any responsibility for the institution of a prosecution. The functions of prosecutors and of judges must not be blurred. If a judge has power to decline to hear a case because he does not think it should be brought, then it soon may be thought that the cases he allows to proceed are cases brought with his consent or approval.[37]

In sum, it would appear that a majority of the House of Lords in both *Connelly* and *Humphrys* has recognized the ability of a trial judge to stay proceedings outside the four categories identified by Lord Goddard CJ in *Downes*. Certainly there does not appear any longer to be any doubt in relation to the *existence* of a judicial discretion to stay criminal proceedings as an abuse of process. The *scope* of the discretion, however, is far from clear, and it is this which will be our chief concern in the remainder of the monograph.

THE NATURE OF A STAY

A stay typically takes the form of an order that an indictment remain on file with the instruction that it not be proceeded with.[38] A stay is not technically an acquittal,[39] although for all practical purposes it may have the same effect. The revival of a stayed prosecution, without the leave of the court, is likely itself to be considered an abuse of process and to be stayed accordingly.[40]

BROADER PERSPECTIVES

As will be apparent from the comments of Lord Devlin in *Connelly*, the abuse of process discretion raises important questions concerning the relation of the judiciary *vis-à-vis* the executive. In determining whether a criminal prosecution should be stayed, a court is effectively reviewing the exercise of prosecutorial discretion by the executive. The validity of such

---

[37] Ibid.
[38] *Connelly* v. *DPP* [1964] AC 1254, 1347 per Lord Devlin. See also *R.* v. *Moxon-Tritsch* [1988] Crim. LR 46.
[39] See *R.* v. *Griffiths* (1980) 72 Cr. App. R. 307, in which a strict distinction is drawn between a stay of proceedings and the direction of a verdict of not guilty. The latter, it was said, was possible only if s. 17 of the Criminal Justice Act 1967 was satisfied. S. 17 provides: 'Where a defendant arraigned on an indictment or inquisition pleads not guilty and the prosecutor proposes to offer no evidence against him, the court before which the defendant is arraigned may, if it thinks fit, order that a verdict of not guilty shall be recorded without the defendant being given in charge to a jury, and the verdict shall have the same effect as if the defendant had been tried and acquitted on the verdict of a jury.'
[40] Pattenden, 'Abuse of Process in Criminal Litigation', 353.

judicial action has traditionally not been universally accepted.[41] The traditional notion was that the decision to bring a prosecution was the prerogative of the executive, and that, once a case came to court, the concern of the trial judge with the conduct of Crown officers was confined to what occurred within the four walls of the courtroom. Thus it has always been accepted that a trial judge possesses an inherent power to regulate court proceedings,[42] and that this power may be exercised to control prosecutorial improprieties occurring at the trial itself.[43] Suppose that, in the course of cross-examining a defence witness, counsel for the prosecution puts to the witness questions which are needlessly offensive and insulting. It has been held that in this situation the judge clearly has a duty to admonish counsel and to inform the witness that the questions need not be answered. If counsel persists, it may be necessary to exclude her from the court and to adjourn the proceedings. The judge may also instruct the taxing officer of the court that the misconduct should be reflected in what is properly allowed on taxation.[44] To take another example, it has been held that, if the prosecution appears to be exercising its discretion with respect to the calling of a witness improperly, the trial judge may intervene and invite the prosecution to call the witness. If the prosecution refuses to do so, the judge herself may call the witness without the consent either of the prosecution or of the defence, if in her opinion this is necessary in the interests of justice.[45] I am not suggesting that the law relating to judicial control of executive misconduct in the courtroom is completely satisfactory at present; rather, the point is that the general responsibility of trial judges to deal with such misconduct is not doubted. More controversial is the determination by a court of the propriety of the executive in bringing a prosecution in the first place. However, the acknowledgement of the availability of the abuse of process discretion in criminal litigation means that it is now well within the province of a court to determine in appropriate circumstances that a prosecution should not have been brought, and to stay the proceedings accordingly. The crucial question is what these circumstances are.

Until relatively recently, responsibility for both the investigation and the prosecution of offences lay in the hands of the police. The Prosecution of Offences Act 1985 has changed this. There now exists in England and Wales

[41] See e.g. the views of Viscount Dilhorne in *DPP* v. *Humphrys* [1977] AC 1, discussed above.   [42] *Collier* v. *Hicks* (1831) 2 B. & Ad. 663, 668, 670, 672.

[43] For US discussion on prosecutorial misconduct in the courtroom, see A. W. Alschuler, 'Courtroom Misconduct by Prosecutors and Trial Judges' (1972) 50 *Texas Law Review* 629; Note, 'The Nature and Consequences of Forensic Misconduct in the Prosecution of a Criminal Case' (1954) 54 *Columbia Law Review* 946; R. G. Singer, 'Forensic Misconduct by Federal Prosecutors—and How it Grew' (1968) 20 *Alabama Law Review* 227.

[44] See generally *R.* v. *Kalia* (1974) 60 Cr. App. R. 200, 211; *R.* v. *Maynard* (1979) 69 Cr. App. R. 309, 317–18.

[45] See generally *R.* v. *Oliva* (1965) 49 Cr. App. R. 298; *R.* v. *Tregear* [1967] 2 QB 574; *R.* v. *Cleghorn* [1967] 2 QB 584; *R.* v. *Roberts* (1984) 80 Cr. App. R. 89.

a salaried service of public prosecutors, known as the Crown Prosecution Service, which is generally responsible for conducting criminal proceedings after the initial decision to proceed has been taken by the police.[46] Whether or not this separation of functions has resulted in better filtering of potential prosecutions is an issue deserving of thorough empirical research which is outside the scope of the present monograph. Our concern here is with the extent to which a court can halt a prosecution which has passed successfully through the relevant filters and actually been brought.

The Prosecution of Offences Act 1985 also provides, in section 23, that the Director of Public Prosecutions may, at any time during the 'preliminary stages' of the proceedings, order that the proceedings be discontinued. 'Preliminary stage' is defined as any stage before committal, or, in the case of summary trial, before the court has begun to hear evidence for the prosecution.[47] In paragraph 10 of the Code for Crown Prosecutors issued under section 10 of the Prosecution of Offences Act 1985, it is provided that

the use by the Crown Prosecutor of his power to terminate proceedings, whether by using the procedure under Section 23 . . . or the continuing power to withdraw or offer no evidence, is in many ways the most visible demonstration of the [Crown Prosecution] Service's fundamental commitment towards ensuring that only fit and proper cases are taken to trial. . . . the discretion to discontinue is a continuing one, and even when proceedings are under way Crown Prosecutors should continue to exercise their reviewing function. . . . It is important that cases should be kept under continuous review, not least because the emergence of evidence or information hitherto unknown to the Crown Prosecutor may sometimes cast doubt on the propriety of the initial decision to proceed.[48]

It is to be noted that a further way in which executive discontinuation of proceedings may be achieved is provided by the *nolle prosequi* (no bill) mechanism. 'The Attorney-General . . . may stop any prosecution on indictment by entering a *nolle prosequi*. He merely has to sign a piece of paper saying that he does not wish the prosecution to continue. He need not give any reasons.'[49] Thus the power of the Attorney-General to issue a *nolle*

---

[46] S. 3(2)(*a*) provides that a duty of the Director of Public Prosecutions (the head of the Crown Prosecution Service) is 'to *take over* [emphasis added] the conduct of all criminal proceedings, other than specified proceedings, instituted on behalf of a police force . . .'. See generally F. Bennion, 'The New Prosecution Arrangements: (1) The Crown Prosecution Service' [1986] *Criminal Law Review* 3; K. W. Lidstone, 'The Reformed Prosecution Process in England: A Radical Reform?' (1987) 11 *Criminal Law Journal* 296. It has been held that only the Crown Prosecution Service can take over a prosecution when a defendant has been arrested and charged by the police; a private prosecutor may not do so: *R.* v. *Ealing JJ, ex p. Dixon* [1990] 2 QB 91. But see *R.* v. *Jackson* [1990] Crim. LR 55 and *R.* v. *Stafford Justices, ex p. Customs and Excise Commissioners* [1990] 3 WLR 656 (Customs and Excise Commissioners may conduct prosecution even though defendant charged by police).
[47] S. 23(2).
[48] See also *Cooke* v. *DPP and Brent JJ* (1991) 156 JPR 497, 504–5.
[49] *Gouriet* v. *UPW* [1978] AC 435, 487 per Viscount Dilhorne.

prosequi can be seen as complementary to the power of the DPP to discontinue proceedings under section 23. It would seem that the exercise of the power to enter a *nolle prosequi* is not subject to judicial control.[50]

Thus there are, in theory at least, a number of ways in which an *executive* stay of criminal proceedings may be achieved. The chief concern of the present work, however, is with the extent to which *judicial* stays may be ordered.

ASPECTS OF CRIMINAL JUSTICE

Any serious discussion of the abuse of process discretion in criminal litigation must take place against the background of an acceptance of certain principles of criminal justice.[51] One accepted function of the criminal justice system is the conviction of the guilty, and, correspondingly, the protection of the innocent from conviction. In relation to the non-conviction of the innocent, Ronald Dworkin has pointed out that 'people have a profound right not to be convicted of crimes of which they are innocent'.[52] The conviction of an innocent person, Dworkin points out, involves a special moral harm which is to be distinguished from, and which transcends, the bare harm which a person suffers through punishment. For instance, 'when someone old, sick, and feeble is executed by a community that wrongly believes him guilty of treason, the bare harm, considered in cold utilitarian terms, might be very little, but the moral harm very great'.[53]

However, it is too simplistic merely to assume that the sole function of the criminal justice system is the conviction of those who commit criminal offences (and the protection from conviction of the innocent). There is also a consideration which has force *independently* of considerations pertaining to guilt and innocence. This is the consideration of the public interest in the moral integrity of the criminal justice system.

It is necessary to have regard to a number of aspects of criminal justice in order to achieve a proper understanding of why the public has an interest in the moral integrity of the criminal justice system. The first matter which deserves attention in this context may be termed the behavioural aspect of criminal justice. The aim of making certain behaviour criminal is, in the words of H. L. A. Hart, 'to announce to society that these actions are not to be done and to secure that fewer of them are done'.[54] It is only by

[50] R. v. *Comptroller-General of Patents* [1899] 1 QB 909, 914 per A. L. Smith LJ; *Turner* v. *DPP* (1978) 68 Cr. App. R. 70, 76.

[51] See generally P. Arenella, 'Rethinking the Functions of Criminal Procedure: The Warren and Burger Courts' Competing Ideologies' (1983) 72 *Georgetown Law Journal* 185; I. H. Dennis, 'Reconstructing the Law of Criminal Evidence' (1989) 42 *Current Legal Problems* 21.

[52] R. Dworkin, *A Matter of Principle* (1986), 72.   [53] Ibid. 83.

[54] H. L. A. Hart, *Punishment and Responsibility: Essays in the Philosophy of Law* (1968), 6.

subscribing to the notion that the criminal law sets up standards of behaviour to encourage certain forms of conduct and discourage others that one can distinguish a punishment in the form of a fine from a tax on a course of conduct.[55] Thus a crime may be viewed generally as a public, rather than a private, wrong. In the words of Blackstone, writing as far back as 1765:

Private wrongs, or civil injuries, are an infringement or privation of the civil rights which belong to individuals, considered merely as individuals; public wrongs, or crimes and misdemeanours, are a breach and violation of the public rights and duties, due to the whole community, considered as a community, in its social aggregate capacity.[56]

A second noteworthy point relates to the consequences of a criminal conviction. Conviction carries 'a formal and solemn pronouncement of the moral condemnation of the community' as well as the threat of unpleasant physical consequences in the form of punishment.[57] The crucial difference between the situation of a prison inmate and that of a patient committed to a mental hospital, it has been pointed out, is that the former has incurred the moral condemnation of her community, while the latter has not.[58] A convicted offender may become more likely to be suspected of subsequent offences, particularly offences resembling her original one, and may be ostracized by family and friends. She may also find it more difficult to obtain or to retain employment.[59] This, indeed, is borne out by empirical research: in two experiments, one conducted in the Netherlands and the other in New Zealand, fictitious job applications which 'admitted' convictions for theft prompted significantly fewer favourable responses than those which did not.[60]

The punishment meted out to an offender following her conviction has a certain symbolic significance, or what Feinberg has termed an expressive function. 'Punishment is a conventional device for the expression of attitudes of resentment and indignation, and of judgments of disapproval and reprobation, on the part either of the punishing authority himself or of those "in whose name" the punishment is inflicted.'[61] By punishing a criminal offender, the State is effectively condemning and disavowing her act. It is telling the community that the offender had no right to do as she did, and that it does not condone her actions. As a State has a kind of 'power of attorney' for its citizens, it is, by punishing a criminal offender,

---

[55] Ibid. 6–7.

[56] W. Blackstone, *Commentaries on the Laws of England (Vol. 4)* (A Facsimile of the First Edition of 1765–9) (1979), 5. (I have updated the spelling.)

[57] H. M. Hart, jun., 'The Aims of the Criminal Law' (1958) 23 *Law and Contemporary Problems* 401, 405.   [58] Ibid. 405–6.

[59] N. Walker, *Punishment, Danger and Stigma: The Morality of Criminal Justice* (1980), 142.   [60] Ibid. 146.

[61] J. Feinberg, *Doing and Deserving: Essays in the Theory of Responsibility* (1970), 98.

expressing effective public denunciation and, through it, symbolic non-acquiescence in the crime.[62]

Another important feature of criminal justice is the notion that human dignity must be respected when the power of the State is ranged against an individual, as in a criminal prosecution.[63] The social stigma which may attach to conviction and punishment (discussed above) has prompted recognition by the law of the concepts of freedom of action and the ability of an individual to exercise self-determination in her choice of actions. As Lord Simon put it in *DPP* v. *Lynch*:

> The law ... accepts generally as an axiom the concept of the free human will—that is, a potentiality in the conscious mind to direct conscious action—specifically, the power of choice in regard to action. ... The general basis of criminal responsibility is the power of choice involved in the axiomatic freedom of the human will.[64]

And in the words of Packer:

> Very simply, the law treats man's conduct as autonomous and willed, not because it is, but because it is desirable to proceed as if it were. It is desirable because the capacity of the individual human being to live his life in reasonable freedom from socially imposed external constraints (the only kind with which the law is concerned) would be fatally impaired unless the law provided a *locus poenitentiae*, a point of no return beyond which external constraints may be imposed but before which the individual is free—not free of whatever compulsions determinists tell us he labors under but free of the very specific social compulsions of the law.[65]

Thus the doctrine of mens rea is founded on the principle that freedom of action is not to be interfered with unless it has been *knowingly* abused; the criminal law usually does not predicate criminal liability on acts alone. If it did, the State's power to interfere in the lives of its citizens would be greatly increased. In a discussion of mens rea, H. L. A. Hart imagines the consequence of a hypothetical abandonment of the mens rea requirement in the crime of assault. Every blow, even if it was clearly a purely accidental or careless one, would become a matter to be investigated. Official interferences with the life of the individual would consequently become more frequent, and their incidence less predictable.[66]

---

[62] See generally ibid. 102–5, in which elements of the expressive function of punishment are discussed.

[63] See generally H. Gross, *A Theory of Criminal Justice* (1979), 32–3; P. Stein and J. Shand, *Legal Values in Western Society* (1974), 130 ff.

[64] [1975] AC 653, 689.

[65] H. L. Packer, *The Limits of the Criminal Sanction* (1969) 74–5. See also Stein and Shand, *Legal Values in Western Society*, 137: 'The requirement of personal responsibility for the application of the sanctions of the criminal law gives the individual the power to determine by his choice what is to happen to him ... Even if things go wrong and his acts cause harm to others, he will not suffer the penalties which the law would impose on those whose acts are voluntary. If he has done his best and made the right choices, and it is through accident or mistake that harm has been done, the law will excuse him.'

[66] H. L. A. Hart, *Punishment and Responsibility*, 206.

The above discussion of various aspects of criminal justice has brought out clearly the public dimension as well as the moral dimension of criminal justice. We have seen that the criminal process may be viewed as a medium of communication with the public at large. The conviction of an offender for her criminal actions has the effect of warning the public against engaging in such actions. Conviction thus imposes upon the offender a special moral stigma of community condemnation; it serves as an expression of moral condemnation of the defendant, emphasizing the criminal law's behavioural message and pointing to the defendant as an example to reinforce this message. Punishment, similarly, expresses attitudes of resentment and indignation as well as judgments of disapproval and reprobation. It is precisely because of this public dimension of criminal justice that criminal justice has also acquired a moral dimension.[67] This suggests that it should not be too much to expect criminal proceedings to have moral authority and a verdict of guilty moral force. Thus, an offender should not be exposed to the stigmatic effects of conviction and punishment unless the values attached to dignity and freedom have been respected in the course of bringing the offender to conviction. It is for this reason, we have seen, that the doctrine of mens rea plays a central role in the criminal law.

Yet the moral dimension of criminal justice requires much more than just recognition of the substantive doctrine of mens rea. Also required, for example, is a recognition that the judge in a criminal trial should not be concerned solely with the conviction of the guilty and the acquittal of the innocent. The public interest does not simply require the conviction of the guilty at all costs. Rather, what the public interest demands is that offenders are brought to conviction in a civilized and publicly acceptable manner. Thus the public has an interest not only in the conviction of the guilty and the acquittal of the innocent, but also an interest in the moral integrity, or, to put it more simply, the *quality*, of criminal proceedings.[68]

It is my thesis that, in determining whether a particular criminal prosecution is to be stayed, the court should apply what will be referred to, for convenience, as the principle of judicial legitimacy.[69] This principle is premised on the idea that a court does not behave legitimately unless it fulfils its public duty of protecting the innocent from wrongful conviction and protecting the moral integrity of the criminal process, while at the same

---

[67] To say that criminal justice has a moral dimension is certainly not to suggest that the criminal process functions for the sake of morality. In fact, I would wish to disassociate myself strongly from such a view. As has been put by H. Gross, *A Theory of Criminal Justice* (1979), 33: 'Moral matters . . . are of the greatest importance in carrying on the business of criminal justice, though it is not for the sake of moral matters that it is carried on. And one may include among the many ironies of criminal justice that it is least likely to be morally sound when it is carried on most moralistically.'

[68] See generally Dennis, 'Reconstructing the Law of Criminal Evidence', 36–8.

[69] See A. A. S. Zuckerman, 'Illegally-Obtained Evidence—Discretion as a Guardian of Legitimacy' (1987) 40 *Current Legal Problems* 55, 59.

time keeping in mind the public interest in bringing offenders to conviction. In simple terms, this means that a court, in determining whether a particular prosecution should be stayed, must take into account, and in no particular order of priority, (1) the need to bring criminal offenders to conviction; (2) the need to protect the innocent from wrongful conviction; and (3) the need to protect the moral integrity of the criminal process. A prosecution may therefore be stayed because (1) there is a sufficient danger of an innocent person being convicted, and/or (2) the continuation of the proceedings would compromise the moral integrity of the criminal justice system to such an extent that the prosecution should be stayed notwithstanding the public interest in the conviction of the guilty. I seek to defend and elaborate upon this thesis in the chapters that follow.

It is worthy of note that in recent times a number of commentators have rationalized the law of criminal evidence in a similar way. They have demonstrated that an item of prosecution evidence may be excluded either because of its potential unreliability (and hence its possible contribution to the conviction of an innocent person) or because of reasons of public policy which do not relate to reliability. Thus Galligan has written that

there are two distinct issues: (i) one concerns rules about the probative value of evidence; (ii) the other concerns rules about the exclusion of evidence for reasons other than reasons of evidentiary value. The question in (i) is how to deal with evidence the probative value of which is in doubt, or which, although of probative value, contains a degree of risk that it will be used improperly. . . . The guiding objective in these cases is rectitude of outcome; the question is, given some such uncertainty or defect, how best is rectitude achieved; what is the most rational procedure for obtaining an accurate outcome. These are issues *internal* to proof. In (ii) the issue is whether certain kinds of evidence, which are likely to be of probative value and therefore relevant in achieving rectitude, should be excluded, in order to advance other values or policies . . . These are issues *external* to proof; they are based on values which compete with rectitude. The exclusion of evidence in order to uphold those values may mean the loss of probative evidence and thus a lower level of accuracy. The distinction between (i) and (ii) is fundamental, since (i) is concerned with the rationality of proof, while (ii) is concerned with the conflict of values.[70]

Zuckerman's monograph on the principles of criminal evidence[71] provides a clear exposition of this dichotomy. Zuckerman points out that principles like the hearsay rule and the similar-facts rule are best viewed as being concerned primarily with the protection of the innocent from wrongful conviction, while the principles relating to competence and compellability and the admissibility of improperly obtained evidence are best seen as being directed to the protection of the moral integrity of the criminal process.

[70] D. J. Galligan, 'More Scepticism about Scepticism' (1988) 8 *Oxford Journal of Legal Studies* 249, 255 (emphasis in original).
[71] A. A. S. Zuckerman, *The Principles of Criminal Evidence* (1989).

CONTENT AND STRUCTURE OF WORK

The structure of the remainder of this work is as follows. Chapters 2 and 3 are concerned with specific situations in which the abuse of process discretion is available at present in England, while Chapter 4 examines a situation in which the English courts have shown reluctance to invoke the discretion. Chapter 2 deals with double jeopardy and other instances of prosecutorial manipulation or misuse of process, and Chapter 3 is about the extent to which pre-trial police or prosecutorial delay should lead to a stay of the proceedings. In Chapter 4 we explore the unwillingness of English courts to stay proceedings on account of police impropriety at the investigatory stage, adopting illegal extradition as an example of such impropriety. Chapter 5 explores various procedural issues associated with the exercise of the abuse of process discretion, including the concept of judicial discretion itself. Chapter 6 deals with a topic in relation to which English law is still relatively undeveloped, that of entrapment. Chapter 7 attempts to synthesize the discussions in the preceding six chapters into a proposal for the rationalization and reform of the law relating to the abuse of process discretion in criminal litigation.

Trials on indictment in the Crown Court will typically be adopted as a paradigm for the purposes of exegesis. In Chapter 5 the applicability of the abuse of process discretion to proceedings in magistrates' courts will be discussed in detail. For the present, however, it should be noted that, where appropriate, all discussions in this work apply *mutatis mutandis* to proceedings in magistrates' courts. Lord Scarman said in *R. v. Sang* in relation to the judicial discretion to exclude evidence to ensure a fair trial:

The development of the discretion has, of necessity, been largely associated with jury trial. In the result, legal discussion of it is apt to proceed in terms of the distinctive functions of judge and jury. No harm arises from such traditional habits of thought, provided always it be borne in mind that the principles of the criminal law and its administration are the same, whether trial be (as in more than 90 per cent of the cases it is) in the magistrates' court or upon indictment before judge and jury. The magistrates are bound, as is the judge in a jury trial, to ensure that the accused has a fair trial according to law; and have the same discretion as he has in the interests of a fair trial to exclude legally admissible evidence.[72]

The *raison d'être* of the abuse of process discretion (protection of the innocent from wrongful conviction and protection of the moral integrity of the criminal justice system) is surely as applicable to proceedings in magistrates' courts as to trials on indictment.

---

[72] [1980] AC 402, 456.

2

Prosecutorial Manipulation or Misuse of Process

In this chapter it is proposed to examine situations in which, in the words of the Divisional Court in R. v. *Derby Crown Court, ex p. Brooks*, 'the prosecution have manipulated or misused the process of the court so as to deprive the defendant of a protection provided by the law or to take unfair advantage of a technicality'.[1]

DOUBLE JEOPARDY

In very crude terms, the rule against double jeopardy seeks to prevent the reprosecution of someone who has already been prosecuted for the same matter. As will have been seen from the brief discussion in the preceding chapter of the decision of the House of Lords in *Connelly* v. *DPP*,[2] double-jeopardy protection in English law is afforded not only by the pleas in bar (autrefois acquit and autrefois convict), but also by the judicial discretion to stay proceedings as an abuse of process. A further possible protection, the doctrine of issue estoppel, was held by the House of Lords in 1976 to be unavailable in English criminal law.[3] It is now proposed to consider the rule against double jeopardy in greater detail, and, in particular, to consider the precise scope of the abuse of process discretion in the double-jeopardy context.

THE RATIONALE

In his monograph on *Double Jeopardy*, Professor M. L. Friedland regards[4] the rationale for double-jeopardy protection as having been summed up in the following passage from the decision of the US Supreme Court in *Green* v. *US*:

The underlying idea, one that is deeply ingrained in at least the Anglo-American system of jurisprudence, is that the State with all its resources and power should not

---

[1] (1984) 80 Cr. App. R. 164, 168–9.　　　　[2] [1964] AC 1254.
[3] *DPP* v. *Humphrys* [1977] AC 1.
[4] M. L. Friedland, *Double Jeopardy* (1969), 4.

be allowed to make repeated attempts to convict an individual for an alleged offense, thereby subjecting him to embarrassment, expense and ordeal and compelling him to live in a continuing state of anxiety and insecurity, as well as enhancing the possibility that even though innocent he may be found guilty.[5]

Immediately apparent from this, then, is the fact that there are two independent aspects to the double-jeopardy principle. First, to put a defendant in double jeopardy may increase her chances of being found guilty even if innocent. Secondly, regardless of the first consideration, it is in any event morally questionable to subject someone to the embarrassment, expense, and ordeal of a second prosecution. Thus, in short, the double-jeopardy principle can be viewed, at least in contemporary circumstances,[6] as being directed to the protection of the innocent from wrongful conviction and the protection of the moral integrity of the criminal justice system. Both aspects will now be discussed in greater detail.

(a) Protection of the Innocent from Wrongful Conviction

This first aspect is rooted in intrinsic rather than extrinsic policy: the double-jeopardy principle assists in preventing the possibility that an innocent person may be convicted. In many cases an innocent person may not have the resources or the stamina to defend a second charge effectively. Even if she has, she may be at a greater disadvantage than she was at her first trial, since she will normally have disclosed her complete defence at that trial. If she testified at the previous trial, the prosecution will be able to study the transcript to find apparent defects and inconsistencies in the defence evidence for use at the second trial. As Lord Devlin pointed out in *Connelly*: 'The Crown might, for example, begin with a minor accusation so as to have a trial run and test the strength of the defence.'[7]

(b) Protection of Moral Integrity

It is in the public interest that members of the public should not be subjected by the State to embarrassment, expense, and anxiety through repeated

---

[5] 355 US 184, 187–8 (1957).

[6] For a perceptive discussion of the history of double jeopardy, see J. Hunter, 'The Development of the Rule against Double Jeopardy' (1984) 5 *Journal of Legal History* 3.

[7] [1964] AC 1254, 1353. See also *Grady* v. *Corbin* 110 S. Ct. 2084, 2092 (1990). In fact the issue has been the subject of considerable discussion in the US Supreme Court. See *Ashe* v. *Swenson* 397 US 436, 447 (1970) (after the defendant's acquittal at his first trial, the prosecutor 'did what every good attorney would do—he refined his presentation in light of the turn of events at the first trial'); *Tibbs* v. *Florida* 457 US 31, 41 (1982) (the rule against double jeopardy 'prevents the State from honing its trial strategies and perfecting its evidence through successive attempts at conviction'). Note also *Hoag* v. *New Jersey* 356 US 464 (1958): after an acquittal in the first trial, the State altered its presentation of proof in the second trial, calling only the witnesses who testified most favourably the first time, and obtained a conviction.

Note that the possibility that putting a defendant in jeopardy for a second time may increase the possibility of his being convicted even if innocent seems to have been overlooked by Lord Morris in *Connelly*, who states ([1964] AC 1254, 1300): 'He will not be convicted unless his guilt of the charge is established so that a jury are quite sure of it.'

attempts to convict them for the same offence—even if they are in fact guilty of it. The strain of a second criminal prosecution is in many cases greater than that of a second civil action, and the accused is often kept in custody while awaiting the second prosecution.[8] By preventing harassment and inconsistent results and by conserving judicial resources and court facilities, the double-jeopardy principle serves to maintain the moral integrity of the criminal process.

The issue of inconsistent verdicts appears to be treated by the courts as an especially cogent one. It assumes particular significance where a second prosecution is brought following an acquittal: even if there are doubts about the soundness of the acquittal, it is considered inappropriate to expose the accused to the possibility of a conviction which will be inconsistent with that acquittal. Lord Devlin had this to say on the issue in *Connelly*:

> Human judgment is not infallible. Two judges or two juries may reach different conclusions on the same evidence, and it would not be possible to say that one is nearer than the other to the correct. Apart from human fallibility the differences may be accounted for by differences in the evidence. No system of justice can guarantee that every judgment is right, but it can and should do its best to secure that there are not conflicting judgments in the same matter. . . . every system of justice is bound to insist upon the finality of the judgment arrived at by a due process of law. It is quite inconsistent with that principle that the Crown should be entitled to reopen again and again what is in effect the same matter.[9]

Another issue which may be mentioned in this context is the fact that, in the words of Friedland, 'sound penal policy requires that all aspects of a given course of illegal conduct be determined, if possible, at one time; for example, the threat of a further prosecution may well interfere with rehabilitation'.[10] Such possible interference with rehabilitation surely cannot enhance the moral integrity of the criminal process.

THE SCOPE OF THE PLEAS IN BAR

The rule against double jeopardy has as some of its offspring the pleas of 'autrefois acquit' and 'autrefois convict', or to use another language and a lot more words, 'Nemo debet bis vexari pro eadem causa' and 'Nemo debet bis puniri pro uno delicto'. These are special pleas in bar in trials on indictment . . .[11]

Although the pleas can technically be invoked only in trials on indictment, it

---

[8] M. L. Friedland, *Double Jeopardy*, 162.
[9] [1964] AC 1254, 1353. See also *R. v. Cwmbran JJ, ex p. Pope* (1979) 143 JPR 638; *R. v. Roberts* [1979] Crim. LR 44; *Dewhurst v. Foster & Foster* [1982] Crim. LR 582; *R. (Smith) v. Birch and Harrington* [1983] Crim. LR 193; *R. v. Intervision Ltd. and Norris* [1984] Crim. LR 350; *R. v. Noe* [1985] Crim. I R 97. Cf. *R. v. Smyth* [1986] Crim. LR 46.
[10] M. L. Friedland, *Double Jeopardy*, 162–3.
[11] *R. v. Humphrys* [1977] AC 1, 52 per Lord Edmund-Davies.

is accepted that analogous defences which are 'the same in all but name' are available in summary trials.[12]

The pleas in bar of trial constitute the main part of the rule against double jeopardy, and provide protection against a reprosecution for the same offence.[13] The plea of *autrefois acquit* protects a defendant from a second prosecution for an offence of which she has previously been acquitted, while the plea of *autrefois convict* protects a defendant from a second prosecution for an offence of which she has previously been convicted.[14] However, the notion of the 'same offence' is not to be taken perfectly literally. For instance, a prosecution of X for the murder of Y will bar a subsequent prosecution of X not only for the murder of Y, but for some other related offences as well. The difficulty lies in determining the precise outer limits of the scope of the pleas—an issue on which differing views exist. In particular, there is no consensus as to whether certain situations are accommodated by the pleas in bar or are more appropriately viewed as being within the scope of the judicial discretion to stay proceedings as an abuse of process. The advantage of being able to rely on a plea in bar as opposed to the abuse of process discretion is that the former 'gives the defendant an absolute right to relief and the other only a qualified right'.[15]

A plea in bar can be pleaded at any stage of the proceedings.[16] In the recent case of *Cooper* v. *New Forest District Council*[17] it was held that the Crown Court had power to consider a plea in bar even though the defendant had pleaded guilty. The rule against double jeopardy was so fundamental that, when it was contended after a plea of guilty that grounds for a plea in bar existed, it was incumbent on the court to inquire into the circumstances to see whether such grounds did exist. On a plea of *autrefois acquit* or *autrefois convict* the defendant 'is not restricted to a comparison between the later indictment and some previous indictment or to the records

[12] *Williams* v. *DPP* [1991] 3 All ER 651, 654 per Rougier J. See also *R.* v. *Truro and South Powder JJ, ex p. McCullagh* [1991] RTR 374, 377–8.
[13] Cf. art. 14.7 of the International Covenant on Civil and Political Rights: 'No one shall be liable to be tried or prosecuted again for an offence for which he has already been finally convicted or acquitted in accordance with the law and penal procedure of each country.'
[14] According to the Court of Appeal in the recent case of *R.* v. *Green (Bryan)*, *The Times*, 14 July 1992, the previous proceedings must have been *criminal* proceedings; the plea of autrefois convict cannot 'jump the boundary' between civil and criminal proceedings. Note also the recent case of *Richards* v. *R.* [1992] 3 WLR 928. The Privy Council held that a plea of autrefois convict cannot 'be sustained by anything less than evidence that the offence with which the defendant stands charged has already been the subject of a complete adjudication against him by a court of competent jurisdiction comprising both the decision establishing his guilt (whether it be the decision of the court or of the jury or the entry of his own plea) *and* the final disposal of the case by the court by passing sentence or making some other order such as an order of absolute discharge' (ibid. 931 (emphasis added)). A plea of autrefois convict cannot be supported by a finding of guilt alone.
[15] *Connelly* v. *DPP* [1964] AC 1254, 1358 per Lord Devlin.
[16] Ibid. 1331 per Lord Hodson; 1341 per Lord Devlin. See also Friedland, *Double Jeopardy*, 114. [17] *The Times*, 19 Mar. 1992.

of the court', but may prove by evidence 'such questions as to the identity of persons, dates and facts as are necessary'.[18] Previously, a plea in bar was tried by the jury rather than by the trial judge, even though it would appear that a judge typically exercised considerable control over the jury when such a plea was being determined.[19] Further, a new jury would be used if a plea failed and there was any danger of prejudice.[20] However, section 122 of the Criminal Justice Act 1988 now provides: 'Where an accused pleads autrefois acquit or autrefois convict it shall be for the judge, without the presence of a jury, to decide the issue.'[21]

The scope of the pleas in bar has benefited (and in some instances suffered) from extensive judicial and academic discussion.[22] Accordingly, nothing more than a very general overview will be attempted here, under a number of headings.

(a) The 'In Peril' Test

This is the basic test of *autrefois acquit* and *autrefois convict*. On this test, the second prosecution is barred if the defendant has previously been 'in peril' of conviction of the offence charged. This is the case if the second prosecution is (1) for precisely the same offence as the one of which the defendant has been already acquitted or convicted (as the case may be), or (2) for an offence of which the defendant *could have been* convicted. Prosecutions for precisely the same offence are, of course, practically never brought.[23]

The second aspect of the 'in peril' test (which bars the trial of an offence of which the defendant could have previously been convicted) is the result of the power of juries to return alternative verdicts.[24] Apart from statutory provisions which enable particular alternative verdicts to be returned in specific situations, there is a provision of general application, section 6(3) of the Criminal Law Act 1967, which provides:

Where, on a person's trial on indictment for any offence except treason or murder, the jury find him not guilty of the offence specifically charged in the indictment, but the allegations in the indictment amount to or include (expressly or by implication) an allegation of another offence falling within the jurisdiction of the court of trial,

---

[18] *Connelly* v. *DPP* [1964] AC 1254, 1305 per Lord Morris. See also ibid. 1331–2 per Lord Hodson.   [19] *R.* v. *Thomas* [1950] 1 KB 26.

[20] *R.* v. *Kendrick and Smith* (1931) 144 LT 748.

[21] This provision would also appear to reflect the practice in Canada: Friedland, *Double Jeopardy*, 114–15.

[22] For judicial discussions, see especially *Connelly* v. *DPP* [1964] AC 1254 and *R.* v. *O'Loughlin, ex p. Ralphs* (1971) 1 SASR 219; for academic discussions Friedland, *Double Jeopardy*, and J. B. Hunter, 'Multiple Incriminations and Criminal Justice' (Ph.D. thesis, 1982). Friedland and Hunter provide extensive references to the other academic literature.

[23] But see *R.* v. *Emden* (1808) 9 East 437, 103 ER 640; *R.* v. *Clark* (1820) 1 Brod. & B. 473, 129 ER 804.

[24] See the observations of Lord Morris in *Connelly* v. *DPP* [1964] AC 1254, 1311–12.

the jury may find him guilty of that other offence or of an offence of which he could be found guilty on an indictment specifically charging that other offence.

Magistrates, by contrast, do not have a general power to return alternative verdicts.

It would seem that a defendant can be considered to have been 'in peril'[25] of conviction at the first trial only if a jury had been sworn and the defendant put in its charge, or, in the case of a summary trial, a plea had been taken.[26]

(*b*) Substantially the Same Offence

On occasion the basic 'in peril' test has been extended to cover offences which are 'in effect the same' or 'substantially the same'[27] in a legal sense.[28] Thus, a trial is barred if the crime charged 'is in effect the same, or is substantially the same, as either the principal or a different crime in respect of which [the defendant] has been acquitted or could have been convicted or has been convicted'.[29] Unfortunately, there is no consensus among those who take this view as to how it is to be determined whether two offences are substantially the same, and thus the precise scope of this notion of 'substantial sameness' is extremely uncertain.[30]

(*c*) Prosecution for a Lesser Included Offence

What is the position where a trial is followed by a subsequent prosecution for a lesser offence which is wholly included in the offence for which the defendant was previously tried? For the purposes of illustration, the example of a prosecution for common assault after a trial for aggravated assault in relation to the same factual circumstances will be employed.

---

[25] Note that in *Connelly* Lord Devlin said (ibid. 1353) that 'the doctrine of autrefois protects an accused in circumstances in which he has actually been in peril. It cannot, naturally enough, protect him in circumstances in which he could have been put in peril but was not.'

[26] *Williams* v. *DPP* [1991] 3 All ER 651. See also *R.* v. *Dabhade*, *The Times*, 14 Aug. 1992; noted by S. Gilchrist, 'Crime Reporter' (1992) 136 *Solicitors' Journal* 888. The Court of Appeal said that, where a charge was dismissed because it was defective (either as a matter of law, or because the evidence was insufficient to sustain a conviction, or because of a rationalization or reorganization of the prosecution case), the plea of autrefois acquit was unavailable.   [27] *Connelly* v. *DPP* [1964] AC 1254, 1305 per Lord Morris.

[28] 'That the facts in the two trials have much in common is not a true test of the availability of the plea of autrefois acquit' (ibid. 1310 per Lord Morris). See also ibid. 1322 per Lord Morris and ibid. 1340 per Lord Devlin: 'My noble and learned friend [Lord Morris] in his statement of the law, accepting what is suggested in some dicta in the authorities, extends the doctrine to cover offences which are in effect the same or substantially the same. I entirely agree with my noble and learned friend that these dicta refer to the legal characteristics of an offence and not to the facts on which it is based.'

[29] Ibid. 1305 per Lord Morris.

[30] See Friedland, *Double Jeopardy*, 108, who points out that, apart from the problems of vagueness, lack of predictability, and so on, 'a more serious consequence is the fact that a decision in one case that two offences are "substantially the same" may compel the same result in another case involving the same two offences where the circumstances may be such that a second prosecution should be permissible'.

(i) Prior Acquittal

There is no logical bar to a subsequent prosecution for a lesser included offence following an acquittal (unless, of course, the 'in peril' test applies). The fact that the defendant is not guilty of aggravated assault does not imply that she is not guilty of common assault: it could be precisely the aggravating circumstances which were not proved at the first trial so that an acquittal resulted. An illustration of this type of situation may be found in *R. v. Barron*[31] where the defendant, having been acquitted of sodomy on appeal owing to wrongly admitted evidence, was then convicted in relation to the same factual circumstances of gross indecency with another male person. It was held that the plea of *autrefois acquit* would have been unavailable to the defendant:

The graver charge of sodomy involves gross indecency and something else, and . . . an acquittal of the whole of an offence does not involve an acquittal of every part of it. There has, therefore, been no verdict that the appellant was not guilty of gross indecency . . .[32]

(It is to be noted that the 'in peril' test was inapplicable since the defendant apparently could not have been convicted of the lesser offence at the first trial.[33])

(ii) Prior Conviction

Obviously, a conviction of aggravated assault must logically bar a subsequent prosecution for common assault. The conviction implies that all the elements of the common assault, plus the aggravating circumstances, were proved. Thus the defendant has in effect been convicted already of common assault.

(d) Prosecution for a Greater Encompassing Offence

The converse situation will now be considered: a trial for common assault followed by a subsequent prosecution for aggravated assault in relation to the same factual circumstances.

(i) Prior Acquittal

'Where there is acquittal of a lesser offence which is in law an essential ingredient in a greater it is plainly not possible to convict on the greater without in effect reversing the acquittal on the other and lesser offence.'[34] Thus an acquittal of common assault must logically bar a subsequent prosecution for aggravated assault: the common assault 'core' of the aggravated assault offence has already not been proved.

---

[31] [1914] 2 KB 570.   [32] Ibid. 576.   [33] Ibid. 571.
[34] *Connelly v. DPP* [1964] AC 1254, 1332 per Lord Hodson.

The facts of *R. v. De Salvi*[35] illustrate the importance of determining carefully whether an offence of which a defendant was acquitted previously is indeed an offence which is wholly included in the offence for which she is now being prosecuted.[36] In *De Salvi*, an acquittal of unlawful wounding with intent to kill was followed by a prosecution for murder. At first sight the second prosecution may appear to be for a greater encompassing offence and therefore logically barred, but a closer examination reveals that this is not the case. The first offence was not wholly included in the second, as, although intent to kill is an essential element of the offence of which the defendant was acquitted, it is not an essential element of murder, for which intent to cause grievous bodily harm is sufficient.

(ii) Prior Conviction

A prosecution for aggravated assault following a conviction of common assault is not logically barred, since an acquittal of aggravated assault could still result if the aggravating circumstances are not proved. However, this is an area in which, in the words of Bray CJ in *R. v. O'Loughlin, ex p. Ralphs*, 'the courts have followed the path of mercy rather than the path of logic'.[37] Thus in many instances the courts have not allowed a person who has been convicted of an offence to be tried for a greater encompassing offence. An example is *R. v. Miles*,[38] where a conviction of common assault was held to preclude a subsequent trial for aggravated assault. However, there are limits to this concession of the courts to mercy rather than logic. In particular, the concession does not seem to apply where a defendant is convicted of a non-fatal offence against the person but the victim subsequently dies and the defendant is then charged with murder or manslaughter.[39] In such cases strict logic will prevail, and the prosecution for murder or manslaughter will not be barred.

What is unclear, however, is the precise basis on which this 'path of mercy' has been followed in preference to the path of logic. Is it (1) achieved through an expansion of the scope of the plea of *autrefois convict*, thus providing defendants with a legal right to relief in such circumstances, or (2) merely an illustration of the exercise of the judicial discretion to stay proceedings? It is possible to find judicial (and academic) support for either proposition.[40] A good illustration of judicial support for the first proposition

---

[35] (1857) 10 Cox CC 481 n.

[36] See the discussion of this case by Bray CJ in *R. v. O'Loughlin, ex p. Ralphs* (1971) 1 SASR 219, 223.   [37] Ibid.   [38] (1890) 24 QBD 423.

[39] See *R. v. Morris* (1867) LR 1 CCR 90; *R. v. Friel* (1890) 17 Cox CC 325; *R. v. Tonks* [1916] 1 KB 443; *R. v. Thomas* [1950] 1 KB 26. See also the comments made in *Connelly* v. *DPP* [1964] AC 1254, 1319 per Lord Morris; 1332 per Lord Hodson; 1365 per Lord Pearce.

[40] e.g., Lord Devlin in *Connelly* thought that *R. v. Miles* (1890) 24 QBD 423 was decided on the basis of the abuse of process discretion ([1964] AC 1254, 1357–8), while Bray CJ in *R. v. O'Loughlin, ex p. Ralphs* thought that the same case was decided on the basis of an expanded version of the plea of autrefois convict ((1971) 1 SASR 219, 223).

is to be found in the recent decision of the New South Wales Court of Criminal Appeal in *R. v. Dodd and Dodd*.[41] At issue here was a prosecution for supplying heroin (in the sense of having the heroin in possession for supply) following a conviction of possessing heroin. It was held that the prosecution for the greater encompassing offence was barred on an application of the expanded version of the *autrefois convict* plea. Gleeson CJ said: 'the matter should be dealt with as one of right rather than as depending upon an exercise of discretion. The right is one recognised by the common law as a protection of the subject against the executive and it should not be watered down.'[42]

(e) The 'Vandercomb Test'

This test had its origins in the statement of Buller J. in *R. v. Vandercomb and Abbott* that 'unless the first indictment were such as the prisoner might have been convicted upon by proof of the facts contained in the second indictment, an acquittal on the first indictment can be no bar to the second'.[43] In other words, a trial is barred if the evidence which is *necessary* to secure a conviction would have secured a conviction of an offence of which the defendant was in peril of conviction in the previous trial.[44] In the words of Lord Morris in *Connelly* v. *DPP*, it is necessary to determine

> whether the evidence which is necessary to support the second indictment, or whether the facts which constitute the second offence, would have been sufficient to procure a legal conviction upon the first indictment either as to the offence charged or as to an offence of which, on the indictment, the accused could have been found guilty.[45]

Thus, in the circumstances of *Connelly*, where a murder trial was followed by a prosecution for robbery with aggravation, the test was not satisfied because 'it was in no way necessary to prove that anyone had been killed in order to prove a charge of robbery with aggravation'.[46] However, in line with (d)(ii) above, the 'Vandercomb test' is 'subject to the proviso that the offence charged in the second indictment had in fact been committed at the time of the first charge; thus if there is an assault and a prosecution and conviction in respect of it there is no bar to a charge of murder if the assaulted person later dies'.[47]

(f) The Draft Criminal Code

Specific reference to double jeopardy is made in the Law Commission's

---

[41] (1991) 56 A. Crim. R. 451.   [42] Ibid. 457.
[43] (1796) 2 Leach 708, 720; 168 ER 455, 461.
[44] See generally *Connelly* v. *DPP* [1964] AC 1254, 1305 per Lord Morris; *R. v. O'Loughlin, ex p. Ralphs* (1971) 1 SASR 219, 227–8 per Bray CJ; Friedland, *Double Jeopardy*, 97–101.   [45] [1964] AC 1254, 1305.
[46] Ibid. 1311 per Lord Morris.   [47] Ibid. 1305 per Lord Morris.

Draft Criminal Code of 1989, but it should be noted that the prospects for the introduction in England and Wales of a Criminal Code remain extremely uncertain. The provision of the 1989 Draft Criminal Code dealing with double jeopardy is clause 11, of which the key subclauses are the following:

(1) A person shall not be tried for an offence ('the offence now charged')—
    (*a*) of which he has been convicted or acquitted; or
    (*b*) of which he might (on sufficient evidence being adduced) have been convicted on an indictment or information charging him with another offence of which he has been convicted or acquitted; or
    (*c*) which includes—
        (i) an offence of which he has been acquitted; or
        (ii) an offence of which he might (on sufficient evidence being adduced) have been convicted on an indictment or information charging him with another offence of which he has been acquitted; or
    (*d*) which includes—
        (i) an offence of which he has been convicted; or
        (ii) an offence of which he might (on sufficient evidence being adduced) have been convicted on an indictment or information charging him with another offence of which he has been convicted, except where an element of the offence now charged is alleged to have occurred after the day of the conviction . . .
(7) This section does not limit any power of a court to stay proceedings on the ground that they constitute an abuse of the process of the court.

In short, this provision combines the 'in peril' test with a policy of barring trials for greater encompassing offences.[48] Significantly, the words 'on sufficient evidence being adduced' make it clear that a defendant could have been in peril for the purposes of this provision even if an acquittal was directed by the judge because of insufficient evidence. As mentioned earlier, a trial for a greater encompassing offence after an acquittal is, in any event, barred on logical grounds. But this is not the case in relation to a trial for a greater encompassing offence after a conviction, where, however, the policy of mercy generally applies. What is uncertain at the moment, as we have seen, is whether this policy of mercy has crystallized into a principle of law or whether it is relevant only in the exercise of the judicial discretion to stay proceedings as an abuse of process. The Draft Criminal Code incorporates the policy as a principle of law, subject to the usual exception to accommodate cases where, for example, the prosecution wishes to

---

[48] See generally the discussion in Law Commission, *Criminal Law: Codification of the Criminal Law—A Report to the Law Commission* (1985), 46–50. The 1989 Draft Code makes provision as to alternative verdicts in cl. 8, and contains, in column 6 of Schedule 1, a full list of specified alternative verdicts. Thus the determination of precisely what offences the defendant might have been convicted of on the first occasion should be relatively straightforward.

prosecute for murder or manslaughter because of the subsequent death of the victim.

Just as a trial for a greater encompassing offence following a conviction is not logically barred, so too a trial for a lesser included offence following an acquittal, but the Draft Code does not specifically bar such a trial. However, it may be expected that such a trial would typically be barred on the basic 'in peril' test in any event.

Thus, while clause 11 clarifies one or two uncertain aspects of the double-jeopardy principle, it introduces no new or novel concepts, and does not move away from the traditional stance of focusing on the legal similarity between offences rather than on their factual relationship as well. A purely factual relationship would still need to be taken into account in the exercise of the abuse of process discretion, which discretion is specifically preserved by clause 11.

(g) The US Position

In the United States, the rule against double jeopardy is enshrined in the Fifth Amendment to the US Constitution, which provides that no person shall 'be subject for the same offence to be twice put in jeopardy of life or limb'. The most recent pronouncements of the US Supreme Court on the US equivalent of the pleas in bar[49] are to be found in *Grady* v. *Corbin*[50] and *US* v. *Felix*.[51] In *Grady* v. *Corbin*, the Court stated that there are two situations in which a trial may be barred on double-jeopardy grounds.[52]

(1) The first situation is one where the traditional *Blockburger*[53] test applies—that is, where the offences have identical elements, or where one is a lesser included offence of the other.[54] In the case of *Harris* v. *Oklahoma*,[55] a conviction of felony murder was followed by a prosecution for robbery with a firearm. The *Blockburger* test was not satisfied, 'since, as a statutory matter, felony murder could be established by proof of any felony, not just robbery, and robbery with a firearm did not require proof of a death'.[56] Similarly, the test was not satisfied in *Illinois* v. *Vitale*,[57] where a conviction of failure to reduce speed to avoid an accident was followed by a prosecution for involuntary manslaughter, because, 'although involuntary

---

[49] On issue estoppel (generally termed collateral estoppel in the US) see *Ashe* v. *Swenson* 397 US 436 (1970) and *Dowling* v. *US* 110 S. Ct. 668 (1990).

[50] 110 S. Ct. 2084 (1990). See J. M. Herrick, 'Double Jeopardy Analysis Comes Home: The "Same Conduct" Standard in *Grady* v. *Corbin*' (1991) 79 *Kentucky Law Journal* 847; T. J. Hickey, 'Double Jeopardy after *Grady* v. *Corbin*' (1992) 28 *Criminal Law Bulletin* 3; L. A. McGinnis, '*Grady* v. *Corbin*: Doubling the Scope of the Double Jeopardy Clause?' (1991) 17 *Ohio Northern University Law Review* 873; G. C. Thomas III, 'A Modest Proposal to Save the Double Jeopardy Clause' (1991) 69 *Washington University Law Quarterly* 195; C. J. Webre, '*Grady* v. *Corbin*: Successive Prosecutions Must Survive Heightened Double Jeopardy Protection' (1991) 36 *Loyola Law Review* 1171.

[52] 110 S. Ct. 2084, 2087 (1990).   [53] *Blockburger* v. *US* 284 US 299 (1932).

[54] 110 S. Ct. 2084, 2090 (1990).   [55] 433 US 682 (1977).

[56] *Grady* v. *Corbin* 110 S. Ct. 2084, 2092 (1990).   [57] 447 US 410 (1980).

manslaughter required proof of a death, failure to reduce speed did not. Likewise, failure to slow was not a statutory element of involuntary manslaughter.'[58]

(2) The second situation is one where, to establish an essential element of the offence charged in the second prosecution, the prosecution will prove conduct which constitutes an offence for which the defendant has already been prosecuted.[59] The US Supreme Court in *Grady* v. *Corbin* felt that this additional protection was necessary in view of the narrowness of the *Blockburger* test.

The relevant facts of *Grady* v. *Corbin* are as follows. The defendant, having pleaded guilty to driving while intoxicated and failing to keep right of the median, was subsequently charged in respect of the same incident with, *inter alia*, reckless manslaughter, criminally negligent homicide, and third-degree reckless assault. The Supreme Court[60] held that the *Blockburger* test did not afford relief: that test would allow the defendant to be tried, in four separate trials, for failure to keep right of the median, driving while intoxicated, assault, and homicide.[61] Turning to the second possible ground of relief, the Court observed that the prosecution had, by its own pleadings, admitted that it would prove the entirety of the conduct for which the defendant had been convicted (driving while intoxicated and failing to keep right of the median) to establish essential elements of the homicide and assault offences. Thus the second trial of the defendant was barred. It would have been different, however, if the bill of particulars had indicated that the prosecution would not be relying on conduct for which the defendant had already been convicted (for example, if sole reliance were to be placed on driving too fast in heavy rain to establish recklessness or negligence).[62]

The Court conceded that there may be an exception to the application of the rule against double jeopardy where the prosecution was unable to proceed on the more serious charge on the previous occasion because the additional facts necessary to sustain that charge had not yet occurred or had not yet been discovered despite the exercise of due diligence. The primary purpose of such an exception is, of course, to facilitate a trial for homicide where the death of the victim occurred after the first prosecution, and we have seen earlier that a similar principle is recognized in English law. The exception was, however, inapplicable in *Grady* v. *Corbin* since the assistant

---

[58] *Grady* v. *Corbin* 110 S. Ct. 2084, 2090 (1990).
[59] Herrick, 'Double Jeopardy Analysis Comes Home', 855–6 explains this succinctly: 'if conduct *x* constitutes Offense I, for which a defendant has been prosecuted, he cannot thereafter be prosecuted for Offense II (with elements A, B, and C) if the government relies on proof of conduct *x* to establish A, B, or C.'
[60] Brennan J. delivered the opinion of the Court, in which White, Marshall, Blackmun, and Stevens JJ joined. The other four judges dissented. The decision was reached, therefore, on a slender 5 : 4 majority.   [61] 110 S. Ct. 2084, 2093 (1990).   [62] Ibid. 2094.

district attorney had been informed of the victim's death on the night of the accident itself.[63]

In sum, the decision in *Grady* v. *Corbin* endorses a welcome expansion of double-jeopardy protection in the United States, shifting the focus away from the constituent elements of an offence to the *conduct* relied upon by the prosecution to prove these elements. However, the potential reach of this principle has been already curtailed by the Supreme Court in a subsequent decision. In *US* v. *Felix* it was held that 'prosecution of a defendant for conspiracy, where certain of the overt acts relied upon by the Government are based on substantive offenses for which the defendant has been previously convicted, does not violate the Double Jeopardy Clause'.[64] Thus Felix's double-jeopardy claim failed even though, of the nine overt acts supporting the conspiracy charge against him, two were based on conduct for which he had been previously prosecuted.[65] The Court's reasoning was that this notion that a substantive offence and a conspiracy to commit that offence are not the 'same offence' for double-jeopardy purposes had been long established by a line of authorities which were not questioned in *Grady* v. *Corbin*.[66]

THE ABANDONMENT OF ISSUE ESTOPPEL

The difference between issue estoppel and the autrefois principle is that, while the latter prevents the prosecution from impugning the validity of the verdict as a whole, the former prevents it from raising again any of the separate issues of fact which the jury have decided, or are presumed to have decided, in reaching their verdict in the accused's favour.[67]

It has been argued that, if it is accepted that a *verdict* should be protected from challenge in a later case involving the same parties, then there is a good prima-facie case for a decision on a particular *issue* to be similarly protected.[68] This consideration notwithstanding, the doctrine of criminal issue estoppel was held by the House of Lords in *DPP* v. *Humphrys*[69] to be unavailable in England. By contrast, the doctrine is a recognized part of a defendant's double-jeopardy protection in the United States,[70] where it is

---

[63] 110 S. Ct. 2090 n. 7.　　　　　　　　[64] 112 S. Ct. 1377, 1380 (1992).
[65] Ibid. 1383.　　　　　　　　　　　　[66] See generally ibid. 1383–5.
[67] *Connelly* v. *DPP* [1964] AC 1254, 1343–4 per Lord Devlin.
[68] P. Mirfield, 'Shedding a Tear for Issue Estoppel' [1980] *Criminal Law Review* 336, 338.
[69] [1977] AC 1.
[70] *Ashe* v. *Swenson* 397 US 436, 443 (1970) ('when an issue of ultimate fact has once been determined by a valid and final judgment, that issue cannot again be litigated between the same parties in any future lawsuit'); *Dowling* v. *US* 110 S. Ct. 668, 672 (1990) ('unlike the situation in *Ashe* v. *Swenson*, the prior acquittal did not determine an ultimate issue in the present case. . . . We decline to extend *Ashe* v. *Swenson* and the collateral estoppel component of the Double Jeopardy Clause to exclude in all circumstances . . . relevant and probative evidence that is otherwise admissible under the Rules of Evidence simply because it relates to alleged criminal conduct for which a defendant has been acquitted').

generally known as collateral estoppel, and in Canada.[71] A simple illustration of the application of the doctrine of criminal issue estoppel is to be found in the recent decision of the Canadian Supreme Court in *R*. v. *Grant*.[72] It was held in this case that, because the Crown had failed to appeal against the accused's acquittal of operating a motor vehicle while disqualified, it was estopped from appealing against his acquittal of failing or refusing to comply with a demand to provide a breath sample. This was because a conviction of failure to comply would require a prior finding of fact that it was the accused who was driving the vehicle in question at the relevant time. But the acquittal of driving while disqualified constituted a finding of fact on this very issue in favour of the accused. To allow the appeal on the charge of failure to comply 'would result in an impermissible co-existence of inconsistent verdicts in respect of charges arising out of the same transaction'. Put another way, a conviction on the charge of failure to comply could be obtained only by undermining a determination already made in favour of the accused on the charge of driving while disqualified. The acquittal on the charge of driving while disqualified must be taken as a conclusive finding in favour of the accused that he was not driving a motor vehicle at the relevant time, and this precluded a finding that he was in fact driving the vehicle for the purposes of the charge of failure to comply.[73]

In short, three main reasons were given by the House of Lords in *Humphrys* for its conclusion that it was inappropriate to recognize the doctrine of criminal issue estoppel.[74]

(*a*) Mutuality

It was said that, if the doctrine were to apply in criminal cases, then 'it must apply equally to both parties, to the Crown and the defendant, as it does to the parties to civil litigation'.[75] For the Crown always to be able to invoke the doctrine against an accused would clearly be unfair.[76]

However, it is not at all obvious that, if the doctrine of criminal issue estoppel were part of English law, it *must* be equally available to both parties. To determine the nature of criminal issue estoppel in the light of its civil counterpart is misguided. Criminal issue estoppel should be viewed as part and parcel of the double-jeopardy principle, and the basis of this principle (protection of the innocent from wrongful conviction and protection of the moral integrity of the criminal process) does not obtain in civil proceedings.

---

[71] *R*. v. *Grant* (1991) 7 CR (4th) 388.   [72] Ibid.
[73] Ibid. 399–400.
[74] For much more detailed discussions, see Mirfield, 'Shedding a Tear for Issue Estoppel'; Hunter, 'Multiple Incriminations and Criminal Justice', ch. 7.
[75] [1977] AC 1, 20 per Viscount Dilhorne.
[76] Ibid. 33 per Lord Hailsham; 51–2 per Lord Edmund-Davies.

(*b*) Identification and isolation of issues

It was also stated that, in contrast to the position in civil proceedings, the identification and isolation of an 'issue' in criminal litigation may be difficult or even impossible:

The doctrine of [civil] issue estoppel has developed to its present degree of sophistication by a relatively sensitive and precise system of pleadings and, in the great majority of modern cases, by a reasoned judgment delivered by a judge sitting alone. In modern criminal procedure, the indictment is jejune to the extreme, and, except in the rarest cases, the only pleading is the oral plea of not guilty on arraignment. The jury delivers an unreasoned verdict of 'guilty' or 'not guilty'. It can only be in the rarest case that an issue can be identified and isolated in such a way as to give rise to issue estoppel as understood in civil proceedings, and such a case depends not at all upon the merits or danger of double jeopardy but upon the course which the previous proceedings adventitiously happened to take. If it were desired to apply this doctrine to criminal as to civil law it would become necessary to alter the whole system on which the criminal law is administered.[77]

Additionally, 'the difficulty may be enormously increased in relation to decisions in the magistrates' courts, unless they state the reasons for their decisions, which they are not generally obliged to do'.[78]

As an illustration it was pointed out that a subsequent trial for perjury would seldom be barred on the basis of issue estoppel, since it would seldom be possible to isolate the issue upon which the jury at the first trial had decided to acquit.[79]

Even if the application of a particular doctrine may present practical difficulties, it seems strange to use the fact that the doctrine may be able to be invoked successfully in only a few cases to deny its availability *in toto*. On the contrary, one might argue that the difficulty experienced by accused persons in invoking the doctrine should constitute a good reason for attempting to *liberalize* the doctrine. The difficulty of identifying and isolating issues does not appear to have perturbed US courts to the same extent that it did the House of Lords. A broad view of the evidence which a court may consider in performing the task has been taken by the US Supreme Court. It has endorsed the view that, where a prior acquittal was based on a general verdict, the court must 'examine the record of [the] prior proceeding, taking into account the pleadings, evidence, charge, and other relevant matter, and conclude whether a rational jury could have grounded its verdict upon an issue other than that which the defendant seeks to foreclose from consideration'.[80] The burden of demonstrating that the issue

---

[77] [1977] AC 1, 34 per Lord Hailsham. See also ibid. 43 per Lord Salmon; 49 per Lord Edmund-Davies.   [78] Ibid. 49 per Lord Edmund-Davies.
[79] Ibid. 31 per Lord Hailsham.
[80] *Ashe* v. *Swenson* 397 US 436, 444 (1970).

in question was actually decided in the prior proceeding falls on the defendant.[81]

(c) Artificiality and unfairness

In *Humphrys* it was said that, even in cases where an 'issue' could be identified and isolated,

issue estoppel would often be artificial and unfair. Take the not infrequent case in which the jury decides an issue in the defendant's favour not because they are satisfied that their solution is correct but because they are left in doubt as to whether the contrary had been proved. In such a case, surely it would be artificial and unjust if the defendant, who, quite rightly in my view, enjoys many advantages, should be given the added bonus that that issue should thereafter be presumed for ever to have been irrevocably decided in his favour as between himself and the Crown. This might mean that upon a totally different charge against the same defendant, supported by overwhelming evidence against him, he might quite unjustly escape conviction because of the issue estoppel.[82]

The answer to this is obvious. Why should speculation about the thought processes of the jury suddenly assume legitimacy and importance in this context when, for example, any attempt to question the validity of a verdict of not guilty is typically viewed as a challenge to jury autonomy and the sanctity of the acquittal? The jury, after all, forms the basis of our criminal justice system, at least in so far as trials on indictment are concerned. Even convictions are difficult to appeal against on factual grounds.[83] Accordingly, to regard a determination of a jury in favour of an accused as being, in a sense, something to be taken less than seriously goes right through the heart of English criminal justice.

(d) Conclusion

While, as has been demonstrated, the arguments raised by the House of Lords in *Humphrys* against the availability of criminal issue estoppel are not especially persuasive, it would seem that the decision that the doctrine is unavailable is unlikely to be reconsidered in the near future. This can be attributed, at least in part, to a perception that the doctrine is unnecessary in view of the availability of the abuse of process discretion in the double-jeopardy context. As will now be demonstrated, the courts do not generally

---

[81] *Dowling* v. *US* 110 S. Ct. 668, 673 (1990).

[82] [1977] AC 1, 43–4 per Lord Salmon.

[83] In *R.* v. *Cooper (Sean)* [1969] 1 QB 267, the Court of Appeal remarked (ibid. 271) that where the case is one 'in which every issue was before the jury and in which the jury was properly instructed . . . this court will be very reluctant indeed to intervene. It has been said over and over again throughout the years that this court must recognise the advantage which a jury has in seeing and hearing the witnesses, and if all the material was before the jury and the summing-up was impeccable, this court should not lightly interfere.' See also *R.* v. *McIlkenny* [1992] 2 All ER 417, 425.

appear to shy away from staying proceedings as an abuse of process where they consider that the double-jeopardy principle is being infringed.

APPLICATION OF THE ABUSE OF PROCESS DISCRETION

In the preceding chapter it was argued that, in determining whether proceedings should be stayed, the court should apply what was termed the principle of judicial legitimacy. This principle is rooted in the responsibility of a court to have regard to the public interest in the fair administration of criminal justice. The principle requires a consideration of the need to protect the innocent from wrongful conviction and the need to protect the moral integrity of the criminal process, against the background of the need to convict the guilty. In this chapter we have seen that the rule against double jeopardy is also premised on 'protection of the innocent' and 'moral integrity' concerns. It is not surprising, therefore, that there have been, since the decision of the House of Lords in *Connelly*, a plethora of reported cases in which applications for the exercise of the abuse of process discretion on double-jeopardy grounds have been made.

(a) *Connelly* v. *DPP*

Connelly itself concerned a relatively simple, but specialized, factual situation. The defendant participated in an armed robbery in the course of which a man was shot and killed. He was tried and convicted of murder, but this conviction was quashed by the Court of Criminal Appeal owing to a misdirection. The plea of autrefois acquit being unavailable, the question therefore was whether the prosecution of the defendant for armed robbery would constitute an abuse of the process of the court.

The House of Lords had little hesitation in holding that it would not, and that it was accordingly quite in order for Connelly to be tried for armed robbery. In so holding, the House of Lords was influenced by the existence of the rule of practice based on *R.* v. *Jones*,[84] now abolished,[85] that a second charge could never be joined with a charge of murder in the same indictment. The House of Lords said that a prosecutor should generally join in one indictment all the charges which it is intended to prefer, but where it would have been improper to do so a second indictment should be permitted.[86] By framing two indictments in the present case, 'the prosecution were not at fault and were only doing what they were obliged to do'.[87] 'It cannot be oppressive for the prosecution to do what the court has told it that it must do.'[88]

---

[84] [1918] 1 KB 416.
[85] *Practice Direction (Homicide: Indictment)* [1964] 1 WLR 1244.
[86] [1964] AC 1254, 1296 per Lord Reid.   [87] Ibid. 1301 per Lord Morris.
[88] Ibid. 1346 per Lord Devlin.

The decision in *Connelly* is thus best viewed as confined to its own specialized facts. More guidance on the way in which courts deal with applications for a stay of proceedings on double-jeopardy grounds may be gleaned from an examination of the subsequent cases.

(*b*) Prosecution Subsequent to Prosecution for Conspiracy

In *R. v. Riebold*,[89] two accused were indicted on twenty-nine counts, the first two being counts of conspiracy which would either stand or fall together. The remaining twenty-seven related to overt acts which were relied on by the prosecution to establish one or other of the conspiracy counts. The prosecution initially proceeded only on the second count of conspiracy, and an application for leave to proceed on the remaining counts was subsequently made. It was held that leave should be refused. The prosecution was effectively seeking to secure a retrial of the whole case, and such retrial would amount to a complete reproduction of the earlier trial. There would be no different issues of fact at all, since the subject-matter of counts 3–29 'did in fact constitute the whole of the overt acts of the conspiracy on which the prosecution relied, and there were no additional factors or evidence on which the prosecution relied in order to secure a conviction on the conspiracy charge'.[90]

In the more recent case of *R. v. Payne and Marshall*,[91] however, a different conclusion was reached by the Court of Appeal. The appellants and others were charged with conspiracy to burgle and with twenty counts of burglary and handling stolen goods. The prosecution proceeded on the conspiracy count only, and at the close of the prosecution case an acquittal was directed. Leave was then sought by the prosecution to proceed on the substantive counts before a new jury. On appeal, it was held that the judge had been right to grant leave: it was not impermissible to proceed on a substantive count after a prosecution for conspiracy which had been tried separately had ended with a direction to acquit. Unfortunately, the brevity of the report of the case does not make it possible to analyse the decision in any detail or to discern any compelling grounds for distinction between this case and *Riebold*. Was the Court of Appeal in *Payne and Marshall* effectively regarding as crucial the fact that the conspiracy trial had not proceeded to a jury verdict? If so, would it have made any difference if the trial had run its full course but resulted in an acquittal anyway? In any event, why should it matter that an acquittal has resulted from a direction from the judge rather than deliberation by the jury?

(*c*) Same Activity/Transaction/Course of Conduct

It seems quite common for a prosecution to be stayed on the basis that it relates to an offence which occurred as part of the same activity,

[89] [1965] 1 All ER 653.　　　　[90] Ibid. 656.　　　　[91] [1982] Crim. LR 684.

transaction, or course of conduct as an offence for which the defendant has already been tried. In *R.* v. *Roberts*[92] the defendant was charged in 1978 with, *inter alia*, stealing an outboard motor from his landlord, A, between May 1975 and May 1976. He had previously (in 1977) been charged with stealing certain hydraulic jacks from A during the same period. His defence in 1977 was that the items were not wanted, and that A had told him that he could do what he liked with them as they were old and in poor condition. A did not give evidence in 1977 but his two sons did, and the defendant was acquitted. The defendant's defence would have been the same in 1978, when A was available to give evidence. The court held, however, that the prosecution should be stayed since the matter was stale, and any conviction would be illogical in the light of the earlier acquittal. It would appear, therefore, that the court was placing considerable reliance on the possibility of an inconsistent verdict being handed down if the proceedings were allowed to continue.

To a similar effect is *Dewhurst* v. *Foster and Foster*.[93] The first defendant worked for a firm of butchers, and the second defendant, his wife, was served by him with a package of meat. The prosecution contended that she did not hand any money over, but that her husband rang up 10p on the till and handed 90p to her. They were both tried for theft of the meat and argued in their defence that a £1 note had in fact been handed over; the meat cost only 10p because the husband had a free meat allowance. Both defendants were acquitted, and the employers then brought a private prosecution against them for theft of the 90p. Not surprisingly, it was held that this prosecution should be stayed: if not, precisely the same issues would be tried again, and the jury in the first trial would have been unlikely to acquit if they were of the view that no £1 note had been handed over.

In *R. (Smith)* v. *Birch and Harrington*[94] S alleged that B and H entered his back garden one night and damaged washing hanging on a line, a roof of a lean-to extension to the house, and a fence. The police, however, charged B and H with criminally damaging the roof and the washing only. The defendants agreed to consent to being bound over to keep the peace, and thus the prosecution offered no evidence and the charge was dismissed by the magistrates. S then commenced a private prosecution against B and H alleging, *inter alia*, criminal damage to the fence. B and H elected jury trial and appeared on an indictment containing a count alleging damage to the fence, and one other count. An application for a stay of the prosecution in relation to the first count was successful.

(d) The Road Traffic Cases

The following cases provide an illustration of the operation of the 'same

[92] [1979] Crim. LR 44.   [93] [1982] Crim. LR 582.
[94] [1983] Crim. LR 193.

activity/transaction/course of conduct' notion in the specific context of road traffic prosecutions.

The applicant in *R. v. Cwmbran JJ, ex p. Pope*,[95] having been acquitted by a jury in the Crown Court of driving with excess alcohol, was to face a charge of driving without due care and attention in a magistrates' court. The Divisional Court held that the proceedings should be stayed

not because that last charge gives rise to the same issue as that which was canvassed before the jury at the Crown Court but because it would be a little, at least, unfair to require him to stand his trial before the justices upon what does involve the self-same issue, and because also it would not be entirely in the interests of public policy that one tribunal might be in a situation in which it feels itself driven to a decision directly in conflict with what was the finding of a jury, who after all form the basis of our administration of common law justice . . .[96]

In *R. v. Moxon-Tritsch*[97] the defendant pleaded guilty in a magistrates' court to driving without due care and attention and driving with excess alcohol. A private prosecution was then instituted against her for causing death by reckless driving. The defendant's application for a stay of the proceedings was successful. The report in the Criminal Law Review of the decision of Faulks J. is couched in the following terms:

The proposed prosecution arose from the same facts as those upon which she had been convicted . . . It would be oppressive to let her face a second trial for a more aggravated form of the same offence to which she had already pleaded guilty. If this matter were allowed to proceed . . . it would have very wide ramifications for any citizens who pleaded guilty to road traffic offences in the magistrates' courts. The learned judge said he could well understand the private prosecutors' desire that the defendant should face the more serious charge before a jury. But the learned judge considered that her ordeal must be brought to an end. The judge said he was satisfied that the two offences were substantially similar . . . Accordingly, he ruled in his inherent jurisdiction, that it would be an abuse of the process of the court to allow the private prosecution to continue.

This decision is worthy of deeper analysis,[98] as the judgment, as least as reported, is rather unclear. It is to be noted that the defendant was convicted previously of not one, but *two*, offences (driving without due care and attention and driving with excess alcohol), and it is unclear which of these two offences Faulks J. is referring to at any particular point. The case is, however, susceptible of analysis in the following manner. Dealing first with the previous conviction of driving without due care and attention, it is clear that this is a lesser offence included in the offence with which the defendant was subsequently charged, that of causing death by reckless driving. This is because recklessness is, in effect, an aggravated form of carelessness: driving which is reckless is necessarily careless. Thus the situation is one of a

---

[95] (1979) 143 JPR 638.   [96] Ibid. 640.   [97] [1988] Crim. LR 46.
[98] See the very helpful discussion of the case by J. C. Smith in [1988] Crim. LR 47.

conviction followed by a prosecution for a greater encompassing offence—a situation in relation to which, as we have seen, the courts will generally follow the 'path of mercy'. Turning now to the conviction of driving with excess alcohol, it is clear that this offence is not a lesser offence included in the offence subsequently charged: a driver may cause death by reckless driving without being in excess of the alcohol limit. The '*Vandercomb* test' would also not be satisfied, in the sense that, in proving the offence of causing death by reckless driving, it is not *necessary* for the prosecution to prove that the defendant was driving with excess alcohol. Indeed, the circumstances in which evidence of consumption of alcohol is admissible on a charge of causing death by reckless driving are narrowly circumscribed.[99] Thus, if the only previous charge had been the charge of driving with excess alcohol, any protection from a trial for causing death by reckless driving would have to be purely discretionary.[100]

Precisely such a situation was considered in *R. v. Forest of Dean JJ, ex p. Farley*,[101] where it was held that a prosecution for causing death by reckless driving following a summary acquittal or conviction of driving with excess alcohol would constitute an abuse of process. Rather, 'the prosecution should . . . proceed on the greater charge of reckless driving, and, if the applicant is acquitted, then consider whether to continue the lesser summary prosecution for excess alcohol. Alternatively, they could proceed with the excess alcohol charge alone.'[102]

(e) Miscellaneous Situations

Deserving of mention are three decisions which turn very much on their own particular facts. In *Mills* v. *Cooper*[103] an information preferred against the defendant, alleging that he on 22 December 1965 being a gypsy did without lawful authority or excuse encamp on a highway, was dismissed on the basis that there was insufficient evidence that he was a gypsy. Later, a similar information was preferred alleging that he was a gypsy on 13 March 1966. It was held that the proceedings did not constitute an abuse of process since,

once . . . one approaches this matter on the basis of the meaning of 'gipsy' as a man leading a nomadic life, it is I think impossible to say that there were any circumstances here which entitled the justices to say that proceedings brought some two-and-a-half months later on the issue whether he was a gipsy could in any sense of the word be said to be oppressive and an abuse of the process of the court.[104]

---

[99] See generally *R. v. Clarke (Andrew)* [1990] RTR 248; *Hand* v. *DPP* [1991] RTR 225; *R. v. Downes* [1991] RTR 395; *R. v. Bennett* [1991] Crim. LR 788; *R. v. Welburn* [1992] Crim. LR 203.

[100] Even if the 'substantially-the-same-offence' test were applied, causing death by reckless driving would not be considered substantially the same offence, in a legal sense, as driving with excess alcohol.   [101] [1990] RTR 228.   [102] Ibid. 237 per Garland J.

[103] [1967] 2 QB 459.   [104] Ibid. 467 per Lord Parker CJ.

Another case in which the nature of the particular statutory offence was regarded as crucial is *R. v. Thomson Holidays Ltd.*[105] In 1972 the defendants pleaded guilty under section 14(1)(*b*) of the Trade Descriptions Act 1968 to recklessly making false statements in a travel brochure that, *inter alia*, a particular hotel in Greece had certain amenities. In 1973 they were charged under the same provision with recklessly making false statements in the same edition of the brochure in respect of the same hotel and the same amenities. Both prosecutions arose from separate complaints made by people who, relying on the brochure, had booked separate holidays at the hotel. The Court of Appeal held that the second prosecution was permissible, because the Trade Descriptions Act 1968 itself contemplated that more than one prosecution could be brought in respect of the same course of conduct. This was to be inferred from section 30, which provided that local prosecuting authorities must inform the Department of Trade and Industry of their intentions to start proceedings, and provide the Department with a summary of the facts on which the charges were to be founded. This was aimed at facilitating some measure of co-ordination of prosecutions in order that they did not become oppressive. Because the object of the Act was to protect members of the public as individuals, two prosecutions in respect of false statements in the same brochure could not be said to constitute an abuse of process.[106]

The chronology of the relevant events in *R. v. Griffiths*[107] is as follows. The defendant was tried for conspiracy to supply cocaine and possession of cocaine with intent to supply on or before 14 January 1988, but the jury failed to agree on a verdict. The defendant was later brought to trial on the same indictment and acquitted as no evidence was offered by the Crown. Later still, the defendant was charged with conspiracy to import cocaine between November 1987 and February 1988. The trial judge held that the plea of autrefois acquit was inapplicable, but that the proceedings should be stayed as an abuse of process because the Crown was seeking to reopen an earlier decision which had resulted in the defendant's acquittal. The Crown was not proposing to use any new evidence discovered since the acquittal, the material before the court having been available to the Crown on the day no evidence was offered.

(*f*) Prosecution of a Different Defendant

It is to be noted that the courts have considered that the need to prevent inconsistent results may extend in appropriate circumstances to the staying of proceedings where a trial of substantially the same question against a *different defendant* has resulted in acquittal. This is, of course, not technically a double-jeopardy situation, since the defendant in the second

---

[105] [1974] 1 QB 592.

[106] Ibid. 598. A petition for leave to appeal was dismissed by the Appeal Committee of the House of Lords.   [107] [1990] Crim. LR 181.

prosecution cannot be said to have been previously 'in jeopardy'. None the less, it does highlight the issue of inconsistent results and of the adverse effect which such results can have upon the moral integrity of the criminal justice system.

In *R. v. Intervision Ltd. and Norris*[108] raids under the Obscene Publications Act 1959 were carried out almost simultaneously on the premises of Intervision Ltd., from which one video 'master tape' was seized, and on the premises of A Ltd., from which were seized 454 copies of the master tape seized from the premises of Intervision Ltd. It was clear that Intervision Ltd. had assigned to A Ltd. all rights of distribution, sale, hire, etc. of copies of the master tape. Informations which alleged possession of obscene articles for publication for gain were laid against Intervision Ltd. and Norris, its general manager, while similar informations were laid against A Ltd. and its directors at a different magistrates' court, A Ltd. being situated in a different petty sessional area. A Ltd. and its directors consented to summary trial. At the hearing the only issue was whether the articles were obscene, and all summonses were dismissed by the magistrate. Intervision Ltd. and Norris elected Crown Court trial at a later date, and applied to the court for a stay of the proceedings on the grounds that (1) the assignment by Intervision Ltd. to A Ltd. of distribution and other rights meant that the likely audience in the case against the defendants was the same as that considered by the magistrate, and that the issues to be determined were therefore identical; (2) all the matters could have been brought before the same magistrates' court in order that adjudication could be by the same tribunal; and (3) by seeking to relitigate an issue which had already been decided by a competent court, the Crown was effectively impugning the finding of that court, and a conviction, if obtained, would be irreconcilable with that finding. The Crown Court held that the proceedings should be stayed.

A similar case is *R. v. Noe*.[109] On 8 October 1982 a number of video tapes were seized from a video hire shop belonging to DN, the defendant's husband. DN was charged with having obscene articles for publication for gain, and elected jury trial. The sole issue at his trial on 2 October 1984 was whether the tapes were obscene, and he was acquitted on four of the charges. On 17 December 1982 another video hire shop belonging to DN, which was situated less than a mile from the shop raided two months earlier, was raided, and tapes seized. The defendant was charged with having obscene publications for gain, and at her trial on 12 November 1984 one of the issues to be determined was whether the tapes were obscene. An application for a stay of the proceedings on the counts relating to the titles in respect of which DN had earlier been acquitted was successful, for the same reasons as in *Intervision*. It was held that the DPP had a duty to have

---

[108] [1984] Crim. LR 350.   [109] [1985] Crim. LR 97.

all matters brought before the same Crown Court pursuant to the powers conferred by the Indictment Act 1915 and rule 9 of the Indictment Rules 1971.[110] In her commentary on the case, Birch rightly points out that in such a case the fact that the distance between the two shops was small is not necessarily decisive: 'if one branch is next to a large comprehensive school and another in the backstreets of a town the fact that they are only one mile apart may not be of very great weight.'[111]

In *R. v. Smyth*,[112] however, the opposite conclusion was reached. The defendant was charged with possession of obscene video tapes for publication for gain. The distributors had been acquitted earlier of possession of two of those tapes. It was argued that the proceedings in relation to these two tapes should be stayed, since the issue of obscenity in relation to them had already been decided by a jury. This argument was rejected by Hyam J. The present case, it was said, could be distinguished from *Intervision* and *Noe* on the basis that there was here no indication of what evidence had been put before the jury at the trial of the distributors. Hyam J. appeared also to suggest, as an alternative ground for his decision, that *Intervision* and *Noe* were wrongly decided, since a 'repeat prosecution' does not constitute an abuse of process so long as the indictment is proper in form and there is no element of oppression in the bringing of the prosecution. The test of obscenity was, Hyam J. thought, bound to lead to conflicting decisions on the same material.

It would be unfair on the basis of the brief report of *Smyth* to pass judgment on the correctness of Hyam J.'s decision not to stay the proceedings. What is clear is that Hyam J.'s apparent alternative ground for his decision—that a stay should not be ordered if the indictment is proper in form and the prosecution is not behaving oppressively in bringing the proceedings—cannot be supported. This line of reasoning is reminiscent of the narrow views expressed by the minority of the House of Lords in *Connelly*. However, whether *Intervision* and *Noe* can legitimately be distinguished from *Smyth* on factual grounds is difficult to ascertain in the absence of a fuller report of all three cases. Whether a stay of proceedings should be ordered is always very much a question of fact and degree to be determined by the trial judge in the circumstances of each particular case.[113] In cases like *Intervision*, *Noe*, and *Smyth*, the crucial question is whether the danger of an inconsistent result is great enough to justify a stay of the proceedings, in the interest of safeguarding the moral integrity of the criminal justice system.

---

[110] R. 9 states: 'Charges for any offences may be joined in the same indictment if those charges are founded on the same facts, or form or are a part of a series of offences of the same or a similar character.'

[111] [1985] Crim. LR 98.

[112] [1986] Crim. LR 46.

[113] See also *R. v. Newham JJ, ex p. C, The Times*, 26 Aug. 1992.

(g) *Hui Chi-ming* v. R.

In the light of the apparent seriousness with which the possibility of inconsistent verdicts has been taken by some courts, the decision of the Privy Council in *Hui Chi-ming* v. R.[114] comes as somewhat of a surprise. Hui Chi-ming had gone with Ah Po and a number of other youths to a housing estate for the purpose of attacking one Ah Hung. Ah Po was carrying a length of water pipe. A man fitting the description of Ah Hung was seized and struck by the metal pipe, which was being wielded by Ah Po. The victim (who, as it turned out, was not Ah Hung at all) received bruises, wounds, and fractures, and later died from his injuries. Ah Po was tried for murder and acquitted of murder but found guilty of manslaughter. The defendant was tried for murder at a later trial. The trial judge directed the jury that the defendant would be guilty of murder if he lent himself to a criminal enterprise contemplating that, in the carrying out of the common unlawful purpose, one of his partners might act with the intention of causing death or grievous bodily harm.[115] The jury convicted the defendant of murder. He appealed to the Privy Council against his conviction on the ground, *inter alia*, that his prosecution for murder rather than for manslaughter constituted an abuse of process, and should accordingly have been stayed. This argument was rejected:

Having reviewed the facts, their Lordships find no aspect of the case which can credibly be described as an abuse of process, that is, something so unfair and wrong that the court should not allow a prosecutor to proceed with what is in all respects a regular proceeding. There can be no suggestion that the defendant was the victim of a plea bargaining situation since he did not plead guilty to the lesser offence. There was no sign of fraud or deceit and, as between the Crown and the defendant, the charge was fair.[116]

It is to be noted that after stating this conclusion Lord Lowry went on almost immediately to describe what had occurred as a 'serious anomaly', and to observe that, if the defendant had been tried jointly with Ah Po, he would undoubtedly have been acquitted of murder.[117] In the light of this, the refusal of Lord Lowry to hold that the prosecution of the defendant for murder constituted an abuse of process is to be deplored.

Equally objectionable is Lord Lowry's suggestion that any injustice to the defendant could, in any event, be mitigated by the commutation of his death sentence by the executive.[118] This is, ironically, just the type of attitude which the abuse of process discretion is meant to counteract. It seems to fly completely in the face of the oft-quoted words of Lord Devlin in *Connelly* v.

---

[114] [1992] 1 AC 34. For a general discussion of all aspects of the case, see A. L.-T. Choo, 'Joint Unlawful Enterprises and Murder' (1992) 55 *Modern Law Review* 870.

[115] This is a classic direction in relation to joint unlawful enterprises and murder, in accordance with the principles articulated in *Chan Wing-Siu* v. R. [1985] AC 168.

[116] [1992] 1 AC 34, 57. See also R. v. *Breen* (1990) 99 FLR 474.

[117] [1992] 1 AC 34, 57.   [118] Ibid.

DPP: 'Are the courts to rely on the Executive to protect their process from abuse? Have they not themselves an inescapable duty to secure fair treatment for those who come or are brought before them?'[119]

IS REFORM NECESSARY?

The question of whether any major reforms are necessary in this area of the law must be seen in the light of the apparent willingness of the courts to stay proceedings on double-jeopardy grounds—an apparent willingness which is perhaps unsurprising in view of the fact that it was in the context of double jeopardy that the House of Lords in *Connelly*, by a majority, confirmed the availability in criminal proceedings of the abuse of process discretion. Thus, if the courts are already cognizant of the importance of double-jeopardy protection, and in fact are already providing such protection, is there any real need for reform?

The central issue concerns the relationship between the pleas in bar, which provide a legal right to relief, and the abuse of process discretion, which provides discretionary relief only. A legal system may not dispute the need for double-jeopardy protection, but it still has to determine whether this is better achieved by expanding the scope of the pleas in bar or by using the abuse of process discretion to 'plug the gaps'. The latter approach appears to represent the prevailing approach in England. Thus Lord Pearce in *Connelly* v. *DPP* thought that 'instead of attempting to enlarge the pleas beyond their proper scope, it is better that the courts should apply to such cases an avowed judicial discretion based on the broader principles which underly the pleas'.[120] A number of academic commentators, notably Friedland,[121] take a similar view.

On the other hand, some have advocated the alternative approach of expanding the scope of the pleas in bar. In particular, it has been suggested that the pleas should incorporate *factual* considerations as well as legal ones.[122] Thus, one should look not only at whether the two offences are the same (or substantially the same) in a legal sense, but also at the degree of factual overlap between the two. This, then, raises the crucial question of how it is to be determined whether a sufficient degree of factual overlap exists between two offences in order for the trial of the second to be barred. Hunter recommends that the principles of sentencing relating to concurrent sentences be drawn upon here for guidance. It is an accepted principle that, if a defendant has committed two or more offences arising from the same set of facts, she should be sentenced concurrently rather than consecutively if certain criteria are satisfied. It is precisely the same criteria, Hunter

---

[119] [1964] AC 1254, 1354.   [120] [1964] AC 1254, 1364.

[121] Friedland, *Double Jeopardy*, 93.

[122] R. v. *O'Loughlin, ex p. Ralphs* (1971) 1 SASR 219 per Bray CJ. See also *Travers* v. *Wakeham* (1991) 54 A. Crim. R. 205.

contends, which should dictate whether a second trial is to be *legally* barred on double-jeopardy grounds.[123]

It is submitted that this approach of strengthening the protection to which a defendant is entitled as of right is the preferable one. Further, it is desirable that the doctrine of criminal issue estoppel (which also provides legal, rather than discretionary, relief) be revived. It was seen earlier that there is a good prima-facie case for recognition of the doctrine, and that the arguments against its existence are not strong. The abuse of process discretion should be reserved for deployment in exceptional cases which fall outside the expanded scope of the pleas in bar, and the scope of the issue estoppel doctrine. To consider the pleas in bar in the light only of the legal similarity between offences is unduly narrow. The number of offences which exist in contemporary criminal law makes it possible to carve out even of a single, simple set of facts a large number of legally distinct offences. Furthermore, as will be seen in greater detail in Chapter 5, it is much easier for a defendant to appeal successfully against a determination reached as a matter of law rather than in the exercise of judicial discretion. Ease of appeal should surely be a key feature of a principle as fundamental as the double-jeopardy principle.

There appears, however, to be little prospect at present of a reform of the law along these lines, and the Draft Criminal Code essentially maintains the status quo. It is accordingly fortunate that, since the decision of the House of Lords in *Connelly*, courts have apparently not shied away from utilizing the abuse of process discretion as a means of compensating for the inadequacies of the pleas in bar and for the unavailability of the doctrine of criminal issue estoppel. It is to be hoped that this trend will continue, and that courts will keep in mind in every case the underlying rationale for the abuse of process discretion: protection of the innocent from wrongful conviction and protection of the moral integrity of the criminal justice system.

FURTHER INSTANCES OF MANIPULATION OR MISUSE

There are a number of other situations in which prosecutorial manipulation or misuse of the process of the court, aimed at depriving the defendant of a legal protection or at taking unfair advantage of a technicality, has led to a stay of the proceedings.

CIRCUMVENTION OF STATUTORY TIME LIMIT FOR LAYING AN INFORMATION

Section 127(1) of the Magistrates' Courts Act 1980 (formerly section 104 of

---

[123] Hunter, 'Multiple Incriminations and Criminal Justice'.

the Magistrates' Courts Act 1952) provides that an information is to be laid within six months of the commission of the offence. In *R. v. Brentford JJ, ex p. Wong*[124] the prosecution, without having reached a decision as to whether to prosecute, laid an information just before the expiry of the six-month limit. The summonses were finally served on the defendant eleven months after the commission of the offence. It was held that the proceedings should be stayed:

It is open to justices to conclude that it is an abuse of the process of the Court for a prosecutor to lay an information when he has not reached a decision to prosecute. ... [The purpose of the six-month statutory time limit] is wholly frustrated if it is possible for a prosecutor to obtain summonses and then, in his own good time and at his convenience, serve them. Of course there may be delays in service of the summonses due perhaps to the evasiveness of the defendant. There may be delays due to administrative reasons which are excusable, but that is not so in this case. ... Here, as I understand it, there was a deliberate attempt to gain further time in which to reach a decision.[125]

In *R. v. Newcastle-upon-Tyne JJ, ex p. Hindle*,[126] summonses were issued alleging that the defendant had driven with excess alcohol, and obstructed a police officer in the execution of his duty. The breathalyser summons proceeded on the basis that the defendant had not, contrary to what he had told the constable, consumed alcohol after ceasing to drive. Thus further particulars were sought to discover whether the obstruction summons proceeded on the basis that the defendant had lied to the constable (which would be consistent with the breathalyser summons), or on the basis that the defendant had deliberately consumed alcohol after the accident to frustrate the breathalyser test (which would be inconsistent with the breathalyser summons). The prosecution refused to provide these particulars. It was held that the hearing of the obstruction summons should be stayed:

By laying a charge which was ambiguous in the sense that it could be read as referring to one or other of two inconsistent offences, and by failing to give the requisite particulars when asked to do so, the effect was that the prosecution were preserving an opportunity to advance their case on the basis of either of these two offences under the one summons when it came on for hearing. In our judgment, this is at least as objectionable a course as the laying of an information where no decision has been taken to prosecute, for, if permitted, it would allow a prosecution to postpone, until after the expiry of the six-month period, their decision whether to prosecute for a particular offence. If the decision had been properly taken before the expiry of the six-month period, there should have been no difficulty in formulating the particulars requested.[127]

[124] (1980) 73 Cr. App. R. 67.　　[125] Ibid. 70.　　[126] [1984] 1 All ER 770.
[127] Ibid. 781. Cf. *Sherwood and Hart* v. *Ross* [1989] Crim. LR 576. See also *R. v. Wirral District Magistrates' Court, ex p. Meikle* (1990) 154 JPR 1035 and *R. v. Great Yarmouth Magistrates, ex p. Thomas* [1992] Crim. LR 116 on the circumvention of custody time limits.

REPEATED COMMITTAL PROCEEDINGS

Just as a subsequent trial for the same matter may be stayed in the exercise of the abuse of process discretion, so too may subsequent committal proceedings for the same matter. In *R. v. Manchester City Stipendiary Magistrate, ex p. Snelson*,[128] the prosecutor offered no evidence in committal proceedings, with the result that the defendant was discharged. Instead of applying for a voluntary bill, the prosecution instituted fresh committal proceedings for the same offence. It was held that these subsequent proceedings did not constitute an abuse of process. By contrast, in *R. v. Horsham JJ, ex p. Reeves*,[129] the justices found that the defendant had no case to answer after committal proceedings which lasted three days, and the prosecution then sought to prefer fresh charges against the defendant which were based on the original charges, but shortened and simplified. It was held that the second committal proceedings should be stayed as an abuse of process. The prosecution should not have been entitled to treat the first committal proceedings as a 'dummy run' and, having concluded that they had over-complicated them, to bring virtually the same proceedings in the form in which they should have been brought in the first place. The defendant had already been put to considerable anxiety and expense during the three-day proceedings, and there had been the passage of time between the defendant's arrest in May 1977 and January 1979, when the second committal proceedings were to take place. To allow the second proceedings would

encourage poor representation with resultant waste of time and money. . . . The prosecution must direct its energies to the simplification of cases they desire to present. All too often juries, and to a lesser extent magistrates, are treated like computers into whom superfluous and ill-digested material is fed in the over-optimistic hope that somehow or another they will produce the right result.[130]

'DEPRIVATION' OF RIGHT TO A PARTICULAR TYPE OF TRIAL

The courts appear to be somewhat unwilling to stay proceedings on the basis that the actions of the prosecution have 'deprived' the defendant of her right to a particular type of trial (for example, jury trial or summary trial). In *R. v. Canterbury and St Augustine JJ, ex p. Klisiak*,[131] the defendants elected jury trial on charges triable either on indictment or summarily. The prosecution offered no evidence on those charges at the committal proceedings, preferring instead charges triable only summarily. It was held that the trials of these charges should not be stayed: if the lesser charges had

---

[128] (1977) 66 Cr. App. R. 44.   [129] (1980) 75 Cr. App. R. 236.
[130] Ibid. 240 per Ackner LJ.   [131] [1982] 1 QB 398.

been preferred at the outset, the defendants would have had no cause for complaint about being deprived of the right to elect jury trial, and there was no reason why they should have such cause now, given that there was nothing oppressive or unjust about the procedural course adopted by the prosecution to achieve the same result.[132]

In *R. v. Liverpool Stipendiary Magistrate, ex p. Ellison*,[133] a charge of attempted theft of property from a motor vehicle, an offence triable either way, was replaced with a charge of vehicle interference, an offence triable summarily only. It was held that, 'in the absence of bad faith on the part of the prosecutor or of unfairness or prejudice to the accused, the prosecutor's motive in making the substitution was irrelevant'. Here there was no suggestion of bad faith on the part of the prosecutor or of unfairness or prejudice to the applicant. The fact that the substitution was made in order to have the case tried summarily did not involve any manipulation or misuse of process; although it was desirable that the charge ultimately brought against a defendant should be correct in the first place, this could not always occur.[134]

In *R. v. Rotherham JJ, ex p. Brough*,[135] the prosecutor ensured that the return date of the summons was fixed for the day after Brough's seventeenth birthday, so that jurisdiction would be removed from the juvenile court. It was held that the proceedings did not constitute an abuse of process as it was not possible to attribute any element of misconduct or, still less, mala fides to anyone involved on the Crown side. There was at most a lack of judgment. The prosecutor was entitled to take the view that the case was likely to go to the Crown Court in any event, whether it commenced in the juvenile court or in the magistrates' court. While prosecutors should allow the juvenile court to take the decision which the law entrusted to them, in this case the Crown had not manipulated or misused the process so as to deprive Brough of the protection provided by the law. And, although Brough had lost the protective jurisdiction of the juvenile court to determine his place of trial, it was probable that the juvenile court would in any event have judged committal to the Crown Court to be appropriate, and not accepted jurisdiction to try him. Furthermore, if Brough were convicted, the trial judge would undoubtedly take his age at the time of the offence, and the circumstances of his committal, into account in determining sentence.

Similarly, no abuse of process was found in *R. v. Redbridge JJ and Fox, ex p. Whitehouse*,[136] where the defendant was charged with an offence triable either way. The prosecutor wanted the case to be heard in the Crown Court but the defendant did not agree, and the prosecutor then preferred an

---

[132] Ibid. 412. It is to be noted that the Appeal Committee of the House of Lords dismissed petitions by the defendants for leave to appeal.   [133] [1990] RTR 220.
[134] Ibid. 226 per Leggatt J.   [135] [1991] Crim. LR 522.

additional charge triable only on indictment. An application for a stay of the proceedings in respect of both charges failed.[137]

It is to be hoped, notwithstanding these decisions, that courts in the future will not refrain from examining carefully the facts of individual cases in order to determine the degree of culpability of the prosecution in each case. Of course, the mere fact that the prosecution has effectively 'deprived' the defendant of a particular type of trial is not a sufficient justification for a stay of the proceedings. There may, however, be situations where some element of misconduct, mala fides, or improper motive on the part of the prosecution can be shown. In such cases a stay of the proceedings may be appropriate in the interest of protecting the moral integrity of the criminal justice system, even if there is no suggestion that the ability to launch a proper defence has been hampered in any way by the conduct of the prosecution.

[136] (1991) 156 JPR 293.

[137] Cf. *R.* v. *Brooks* [1985] Crim. LR 385. The defendant was charged with wounding contrary to s. 20 of the Offences Against the Person Act 1861, and elected summary trial. The prosecutor, however, sought trial on indictment. The magistrates decided to try the defendant summarily but the prosecuting solicitor, dissatisfied with this decision, preferred a charge of wounding contrary to s. 18 of the 1861 Act. The defendant was consequently tried on indictment. On his appeal against sentence, the Court of Appeal stated that such action by the prosecuting solicitor was plainly unjust and wrong.

3
Delay

THE ENGLISH POSITION

In this chapter it is proposed to examine the second major area in relation to which the discretion to stay criminal proceedings as an abuse of process has been acknowledged as available in England. This is the area of pre-trial police or prosecutorial delay.[1] The problem of delay in criminal procedure is one which in recent times has been a matter of continuing concern, and which has therefore had a lot of airing, both in England and in other jurisdictions. Broadly, delay may occur in either of two parts of the pre-trial stage: before charge, or between the date of charge and the date of trial. The past decade or so has seen a plethora of decisions in which English courts have acknowledged that criminal proceedings may be stayed on account of pre-trial delay. Indeed, the abuse of process discretion probably remains the chief mechanism protecting English defendants from the consequences of undue delay, at least so far as prosecutions for serious offences are concerned.

The scheme of this chapter is as follows. First, brief mention will be made of a number of mechanisms, apart from the abuse of process discretion, which have been developed for the purpose of dealing with the problem of pre-trial delay: specific statutory provisions (including clause 29 of the Magna Carta), article 6(1) of the European Convention on Human Rights, and paragraph 8(ii) of the Code for Crown Prosecutors. We then proceed to the main focus of the chapter: the extent to which proceedings may be stayed on account of pre-trial delay. The English position will be examined, and this will be followed by a discussion of the way in which the issue has been addressed in the United States and Canada. In the light of this discussion, some recommendations for reform of the English position will then be made.

STATUTORY PROVISIONS

There do exist, in England, statutory provisions which are of relevance to the issue of delay in criminal proceedings. As has been seen in the preceding

---

[1] See A. L.-T. Choo, 'Abuse of Process and Pre-Trial Delay: A Structured Approach' (1989) 13 *Criminal Law Journal* 178, which is based on an earlier version of this chapter.

chapter, section 127 of the Magistrates' Courts Act 1980 provides that a magistrates' court is not to try an information unless it was laid within six months of the commission of the offence. Further, individual statutory provisions may prescribe time limits for particular summary proceedings.[2]

In recent years there have emerged a number of general provisions which are of relevance to trials on indictment.[3] Section 22(1) of the Prosecution of Offences Act 1985 provides:

The Secretary of State may by regulations make provision, with respect to any specified preliminary stage of proceedings for an offence, as to the maximum period—

(a) to be allowed to the prosecution to complete that stage;

(b) during which the accused may, while awaiting completion of that stage, be—

(i) in the custody of a magistrates' court; or

(ii) in the custody of the Crown Court;

in relation to that offence.

'Preliminary stage' is defined as any stage of the proceedings before arraignment in the Crown Court or, in the case of summary proceedings, before the magistrates' court has begun to hear evidence for the prosecution at the trial.[4] Extension of a time limit may be granted by the appropriate court if it is satisfied 'that there is good and sufficient cause for doing so'[5] *and* 'that the prosecution has acted with all due expedition'.[6] Non-compliance with a time limit will result in the accused being 'treated, for all purposes, as having been acquitted of that offence'.[7]

---

[2] e.g., Road Traffic Offenders Act 1988, s. 6(1): 'Subject to subsection (2) below, summary proceedings for an offence to which this section applies may be brought within a period of six months from the date on which evidence sufficient in the opinion of the prosecutor to warrant the proceedings came to his knowledge.' S. 6(2) provides: 'No such proceedings shall be brought by virtue of this section more than three years after the commission of the offence.' See generally J. Wadham, 'Abuse of Process through Delay in the Criminal Courts' [Feb. 1991] *Legal Action* 15.

[3] For proposals for further reform, see E. Gilvarry, 'Speeding Up Crime Cases' (1991) 88(8) *Law Society's Guardian Gazette* 3, 5.   [4] S. 22(11).   [5] S. 22(3)(a).

[6] S. 22(3)(b).

[7] S. 22(4). The Prosecution of Offences (Custody Time Limits) Regulations 1987, the Prosecution of Offences (Custody Time Limits) (Amendment) Regulations 1988, the Prosecution of Offences (Custody Time Limits) (Amendment) Regulations 1989, the Prosecution of Offences (Custody Time Limits) (Amendment) (No. 2) Regulations 1989, and the Prosecution of Offences (Custody Time Limits) (Amendment) Regulations 1991 have been made by the Secretary of State pursuant to s. 22(1). These regulations now apply throughout England and Wales, and make provision as to the maximum period during which a person accused of an indictable offence other than treason may be kept in custody while awaiting trial or committal for trial. See *White* v. *DPP*, *The Times*, 20 Oct. 1988 (a *defence* request for more time can in certain circumstances constitute 'good and sufficient cause' for allowing an extension of the time a defendant may be held in custody); R. v. *Governor of Canterbury Prison, ex p. Craig* [1990] 3 WLR 126; R. v. *Birmingham Crown Court, ex p. Ricketts* [1991] RTR 105; R. v. *Sheffield Justices, ex p. Turner* [1991] 1 All ER 858; *In re Ward, Ward and Bond (Application for Writ of Habeas Corpus)* (1990) 155 JPR 181 (an application for extension of the custody time limit must be made 'clearly and unmistakably' and the defence must be given the opportunity to object to the application and make appropriate representations; any order for extension of the limit must be announced in the clearest possible

It is to be noted that field trips were conducted in selected Crown Courts and magistrates' courts prior to the implementation of these provisions, so as 'to examine the practical implications of limits for the parties and the courts and to assist in identifying deadlines which were realistic yet tight enough to act as a discipline, thereby minimising time spent awaiting trial'.[8] In particular, the field trips examined the levels of compliance with test limits; case factors associated with long interval to trial; the proportion of elapsed time attributable to courts, prosecution, and defence; the intervals between key events or decisions and the reasons given; the difficulties experienced by the prosecution in complying with the test limits; and the views of prosecutors as to the possible grounds for extension under statutory limits.[9] The results of the study are set out in detail in a report,[10] and need not be repeated here.

Also relevant is section 77 of the Supreme Court Act 1981, which provides that 'Crown Court Rules shall prescribe the minimum and the maximum period which may elapse' between a person's committal for trial and the beginning of the trial (that is, arraignment). These periods are prescribed by rule 24(1) of the Crown Court Rules 1982, which provides that

the trial of a person committed by a magistrates' court—(*a*) shall not begin until the expiration of 14 days beginning with the date of his committal, except with his consent and the consent of the prosecution, and (*b*) shall, unless the Crown Court has otherwise ordered, begin not later than the expiration of 8 weeks beginning with the date of his committal.

However it has been held that the prescribed maximum period of eight weeks is, in effect, directory and not mandatory. Thus a properly conducted

terms and the relevant details given; the clerk in the court must ensure that a proper and permanent record is made of the order); *R.* v. *Governor of Winchester Prison, ex p. Roddie* [1991] 1 WLR 303 (neither the seriousness of the offence charged nor the shortness of the extension sought constituted 'good and sufficient cause' for extending the limit, and 'the test of due expedition must be measured against some objective yardstick'); *R.* v. *Governor of Winson Green Prison, ex p. Trotter* (1991) 155 JPR 671; *R.* v. *Norwich Crown Court, ex p. Parker and Ward* (1992) 156 JPR 818; *R.* v. *Norwich Crown Court, ex p. Stiller* (1992) 156 JPR 624 (the fact that no judge or courtroom was available for the case to be tried did not constitute 'good and sufficient cause' in circumstances where there was no clear indication as to when the trial could proceed); *R.* v. *Luton Crown Court, ex p. Neaves, The Times*, 9 June 1992 (the protection of a member of the public from violence was capable of constituting 'good and sufficient cause'); *R.* v. *Norwich Crown Court, ex p. Cox, The Times*, 3 Nov. 1992 (the words 'good and sufficient cause' were neither constrained nor defined in the Act, and the phrase was not suitable for judicial definition; neither the seriousness of the offence nor the shortness of the time sought for the extension could fall within the phrase; however, there was no reason why the lack of a court or the non-availability of a judge should not be capable of coming within the phrase).

See also C. Corbett and Y. Korn, 'Custody Time Limits in Serious and Complex Cases: Will they Work in Practice?' [1987] *Criminal Law Review* 737.

[8] P. Morgan and J. Vennard, *Pre-Trial Delay: The Implications of Time Limits* (Home Office Research Study, No. 110; 1989), 1.   [9] Ibid. 7.   [10] Ibid.

trial commencing after that period, without the court having granted an extension of time, is not a nullity.[11] Indeed it would appear that the time limit is commonly exceeded in practice.[12]

Finally, it should be noted that, perhaps surprisingly, the Magna Carta may count as a relevant statute in the present context. In *A-G's Reference (No. 1 of 1990)*[13] the respondent's primary submission to the Court of Appeal was that the delay which had occurred was prohibited by statute, the 'statute' in question being the Magna Carta. Clause 29 of the 1225 (Henry III) and 1297 (Edward I) versions of the Magna Carta guarantees, *inter alia*, that 'we will not deny, or defer, to any man, either justice or right'. The respondent argued that the word 'defer' in this context meant 'put off', 'postpone', or 'delay', and that, accordingly, a finding of delay would justify a stay of the proceedings irrespective of whether the defendant could prove prejudice.

This argument did not find favour with the Court of Appeal: 'it seems clear to us that the delay or deferment means, at its lowest, wrongful delay or deferment, such as is not justified by the circumstances of the case.'[14] Thus it would seem that the respondent's argument was rejected on factual grounds. This implies that, in the view of the Court of Appeal, *wrongful* delay or deferment must lead automatically to a stay of the proceedings because such delay is prohibited by the Magna Carta. What would constitute wrongful delay or deferment for the purposes of this principle was, however, left unclarified by the Court.

In *Tan* v. *Cameron* the Privy Council referred to the argument raised in *A-G's Reference (No. 1 of 1990)* in relation to clause 29, and remarked: 'No such argument has been advanced in the present case, and their Lordships need say nothing about it.'[15]

In Australia, by contrast, the effect of clause 29 has received a substantial amount of judicial consideration. In a number of New South Wales cases the view was put forward by McHugh JA that clause 29 embodied the right to a speedy trial.[16] Reliance was placed by McHugh JA on Coke's declaration, at page 22 of volume 1 of his *First Institute*, that Magna Carta was 'but a confirmation or restitution of the common law'. McHugh JA considered it irrelevant whether Coke's view of Magna Carta was in fact correct: 'more than once the alleged errors of Coke have changed the face of the common law.'[17] The fact that there was at the time of Coke no means of enforcing the right to a speedy trial was not, McHugh JA thought, a conclusive factor against its existence. Furthermore, McHugh JA considered

[11] R. v. *Spring Hill Prison Governor, ex p. Sohi* [1988] 1 All ER 424.
[12] See Corbett and Korn, 'Custody Time Limits in Serious and Complex Cases', 737.
[13] [1992] 3 WLR 9.   [14] Ibid. 16.   [15] [1992] 3 WLR 249, 262.
[16] *Herron* v. *McGregor* (1986) 6 NSWLR 246, 252; *Aboud* v. *A–G (NSW)* (1987) 10 NSWLR 671, 691; *Jago* v. *District Court (NSW)* (1988) 12 NSWLR 558, 583 ff.
[17] Ibid. 584.

that the fact that people were until comparatively recently given speedy trials accounted for the paucity of authority on the speedy trial right.[18]

The views of McHugh JA have been, however, rejected by the High Court of Australia in *Jago* v. *District Court (NSW)*.[19] Brennan J. thought that, had there been a common-law right to a speedy trial recognized by the Magna Carta which could be enforced by staying the prosecution, the commissions of general gaol delivery would hardly have taken the form which they did, section 6 of the Habeas Corpus Act 1679 might not have been necessary, and the idea that time did not run against the King would not have gained currency. It was also strange, Brennan J. thought, that there was no reported case of a stay having been granted on account of mere delay in the commencement of a prosecution.[20] Brennan J. further opined that Coke was merely

describing the qualities of justice to which the courts aspire—free, full and speedy—but he did not assert the existence of a legal right giving effect to that aspiration. Coke did not claim for the courts a power to refuse to exercise their jurisdiction if, in the exercise of its powers, the Crown impaired the freedom, fulness or speed of administering criminal justice.[21]

Toohey J. was of a similar mind to Brennan J., pointing out that Coke's view of Magna Carta had been generally discredited and that, even if clause 29 could be regarded as declaratory of some fundamental law, it was not possible to find in the clause any principle evidencing the right to a speedy trial.[22] Toohey J. drew attention to McKechnie's comment that clause 29 'has had much read into it that would have astonished its framers: application of modern standards to ancient practice has resulted in complete misapprehension'. Toohey J. observed that, whilst the apparent intention of clause 29 was to correct the worst abuses associated with the practice of charging heavy fees for writs, this was in order to ensure the pre-eminence of royal justice.[23]

EUROPEAN CONVENTION ON HUMAN RIGHTS

Article 6(1) of the European Convention on Human Rights provides: 'In the determination of his civil rights and obligations or of any criminal charge against him, everyone is entitled to a fair and public hearing within a reasonable time . . .' In the important case of *X* v. *Austria* the European Commission of Human Rights decided that 'the words "within a reasonable time" . . . refer to the period that elapses between the charge and sentence, and not that between the offence and the charge, as is quite clear from the English text as well as the French'.[24]

---

[18] Ibid. 585.   [19] (1989) 168 CLR 23.   [20] Ibid. 41.
[21] Ibid. 42.   [22] Ibid. 67.   [23] Ibid. 66.
[24] Case 1545/62: 5 Yearbook 270, 276.

CODE FOR CROWN PROSECUTORS

It is also worthy of note that the Code for Crown Prosecutors issued under section 10 of the Prosecution of Offences Act 1985 provides, in paragraph 8(ii):

Regard must be had not only to the date when the last known offence was committed, but also the length of time which is likely to elapse before the matter can be brought to trial. The Crown Prosecutor should be slow to prosecute if the last offence was committed three or more years before the probable date of trial, unless, despite its staleness, an immediate custodial sentence of some length is likely to be imposed. Less regard will be paid to staleness, however, if it has been contributed to by the accused himself, the complexity of the case has necessitated lengthy police investigation or the particular characteristics of the offence have themselves contributed to the delay in its coming to light. Generally, the graver the allegation, the less significance will be attached to the element of staleness.

STAY OF PROCEEDINGS

The issue of the circumstances in which proceedings may be stayed on account of pre-trial delay has been considered in a large number of reported Queen's Bench Divisional Court, and even first instance, decisions.[25] For a long time the issue did not receive consideration by the Court of Appeal, but there are now two relevant judgments of that court.[26] Additionally, there have been a number of considerations of the issue by the Privy Council.[27]

---

[25] *R. v. Oxford City JJ, ex p. Smith* [1982] RTR 201; *R. v. Watford JJ, ex p. Outrim* [1983] RTR 26; *R. v. Grays JJ, ex p. Graham* [1982] 3 WLR 596; *R. v. Magnaload and Greenham Premises* [1984] CLY 572; *R. v. Canterbury and St Augustine JJ, ex p. Turner* (1983) 147 JPR 193; *R. v. Guildhall JJ and DPP, ex p. Carson-Selman* (1983) 148 JPR 392; *R. v. West London Stipendiary Magistrate, ex p. Anderson* (1984) 148 JPR 683; *R. v. Derby Crown Court, ex p. Brooks* (1984) 80 Cr. App. R. 164; *R. v. Bow Street Magistrates' Court, ex p. Van der Holst* (1985) 83 Cr. App. R. 114; *R. v. Colwyn JJ, ex p. DPP* (1988) 154 JPR 989; *R. v. Sunderland Magistrates' Court, ex p. Z* [1989] Crim. LR 56; *R. v. Bow Street Stipendiary Magistrate, ex p. DPP and Cherry* (1989) 91 Cr. App. R. 283; *Daventry District Council, v. Olins* (1990) 154 JPR 478; *R. v. Newham (West) JJ, ex p. Sandhu* [1991] COD 55; *R. v. LPB* (1990) 91 Cr. App. R. 359; *R. v. Liverpool Deputy Stipendiary Magistrate, ex p. Devereux* [1991] COD 236; *R. v. Bow Street Magistrates' Court, ex p. Watts* [1991] COD 87; *R. v. Central Criminal Court, ex p. Randle and Pottle* (1990) 92 Cr. App. R. 323; *R. v. Telford JJ, ex p. Badhan* [1991] 2 WLR 866; *R. v. Clerkenwell Stipendiary Magistrate, ex p. Bell* (1991) 155 JPR 669; *R. v. Norwich Crown Court, ex p. Belsham* [1992] 1 WLR 54; *R. v. Crawley JJ, ex p. DPP* (1991) 155 JPR 841; *R. v. Cheltenham JJ, ex p. Millin* [1992] COD 108; *R. v. JAK* [1992] Crim. LR 30; *R. v. Bow Street Metropolitan Stipendiary Magistrate, ex p. DPP* (1992) 95 Cr. App. R. 9; *R. v. Sheffield Stipendiary Magistrate, ex p. Stephens* (1992) 156 JPR 555; *R. v. Newham JJ, ex p. C, The Times*, 26 Aug. 1992.

[26] *R. v. Buzalek and Schiffer* [1991] Crim. LR 115; *A-G's Reference (No. 1 of 1990)* [1992] 3 WLR 9.

[27] *Bell v. DPP* [1985] AC 937 (re s. 20(1) of the Jamaican Constitution, which provides that 'whenever any person is charged with a criminal offence he shall, unless the charge is withdrawn, be afforded a fair hearing within a reasonable time . . .'); *Mungroo v. R.* [1991] 1 WLR 1351 (re s. 10(1) of the Constitution of Mauritius, which provides that 'where any

The judgment of the Court of Appeal (delivered by Lord Lane CJ) in *A-G's Reference (No.1 of 1990)*[28] is likely to be treated as the leading authority in the foreseeable future, and it is therefore appropriate to proceed directly to an examination of this judgment.

The chronology of events giving rise to this *Reference* is as follows. On 16 August 1987 the respondent, a police officer, attended an incident involving two brothers named Murphy, who were arrested and charged with public order offences. A number of complaints were made by members of the public about the conduct of some of the police officers who attended the incident, and the respondent was informed the day after the incident that such a complaint had been made against him. On 1 September 1987 a notice was served on him pursuant to regulation 7 of the Police (Discipline) Regulations 1985, and on 7 September 1987 an interim police report was submitted. In accordance with police procedure, further investigation of the complaint was deferred until the conclusion of the criminal proceedings against the Murphys. The Murphys were acquitted on 19 January 1988 and the investigation of the complaint against the respondent was resumed, with a further notice under regulation 7 being served on him on 22 March 1988. He was interviewed under caution in May and June 1988, and in September 1988 a final police report was submitted. This report consisted of 235 paragraphs and was supported by 112 pages of statements and 366 pages of documents, and in November 1988 it was submitted to the DPP for consideration. Summonses were sought in respect of the respondent on 2 March 1989, and on 20 March 1989 papers were served on him. It was then that he consulted a solicitor for the first time. On 8 May 1989 the case was adjourned for committal proceedings, which commenced on 21 September 1989 and were concluded on 13 October 1989. On 2 November 1989 the case was listed for Crown Court trial, and at the commencement of the trial on 11 December 1989 the respondent submitted that the proceedings constituted an abuse of the process of the court and should accordingly be stayed. This submission was accepted by the trial judge.

The following point of law arising from the case was referred by the Attorney-General, under section 36 of the Criminal Justice Act 1972, to the Court of Appeal for a ruling:

(i) whether proceedings upon indictment may be stayed on the grounds of prejudice resulting from delay in the institution of those proceedings even though that delay has not been occasioned by any fault on the part of the prosecution; (ii) if the answer to (i) above is in the affirmative, what is the degree of: (*a*) the likelihood and (*b*) the seriousness of any prejudice which is required to justify a stay of such proceedings.[29]

---

person is charged with a criminal offence, then, unless the charge is withdrawn, the case shall be afforded a fair hearing within a reasonable time . . .'); *Tan* v. *Cameron* [1992] 3 WLR 249.

[28] [1992] 3 WLR 9; noted by A. L.-T. Choo, 'Delay and Abuse of Process' (1992) 108 *Law Quarterly Review* 565.   [29] [1992] 3 WLR 9, 13.

Because, as mentioned earlier, the Magna Carta was held not to afford the respondent relief, and because 'there is no statutory limitation period for criminal proceedings such as those in the instant case',[30] the Court of Appeal proceeded to a consideration of abuse of process.[31] The Court observed that the earlier and stricter judicial views on abuse of process, enunciated in cases such as *R. v. Heston-Francois*[32] and *R. v. Derby Crown Court, ex p. Brooks*,[33] had given way to the broader views enunciated in cases such as *R. v. Bow Street Stipendiary Magistrate, ex p. DPP and Cherry*[34] and *R. v. Telford JJ, ex p. Badhan*.[35] In the light of this liberalization, the Court felt compelled to answer the first certified question in the affirmative, but it went on to caution that:

1. It was only in exceptional circumstances that proceedings should be stayed either on account of delay or for any other reason. If stays were to become a matter of routine, the public would, understandably, soon view the criminal process with suspicion and mistrust.

2. Even in cases where the delay in question could be considered unjustifiable, a permanent stay of the proceedings should be the exception rather than the rule.

3. 'Still more rare should be cases where a stay can properly be imposed in the absence of any fault on the part of the complainant or prosecution.'[36]

4. Proceedings should never be stayed on account of delay due merely to the complexity of the case, or contributed to by the actions of the defendant herself.

With respect to the second certified question, the Court stated that the defendant had to be able to show on the balance of probabilities that she would suffer serious prejudice to the extent that no fair trial could take place. In determining whether the defendant had discharged this onus, the judge should keep in mind that there were two mechanisms, other than a stay of the proceedings, by which prejudice could be mitigated or eliminated. First, the judge had the power both at common law and under the Police and Criminal Evidence Act 1984 (hereafter PACE) to regulate the admissibility of evidence. Secondly, the judge could ensure that the jury had for its consideration all relevant factual issues arising from the delay, and that the jury received appropriate directions before considering its verdict.

Turning to the facts of the case, the Court held that the decision of the judge to stay the proceedings had been wrong:

The delay, such as it was, was not unjustifiable; the chances of prejudice were remote; the degree of potential prejudice was small; the powers of the judge and the

---

[30] [1992] 3 WLR 9, 16.   [31] Ibid. 16 ff.   [32] [1984] 1 All ER 785.
[33] (1984) 80 Cr. App. R. 164.   [34] (1989) 91 Cr. App. R. 283.
[35] [1991] 2 WLR 866.   [36] [1992] 3 WLR 9, 19.

trial process itself would have provided ample protection for the respondent; there was no danger of the trial being unfair; in any event the case was in no sense exceptional so as to justify the ruling.[37]

Unfortunately, no explanation was provided by the Court as to how it reached each of these conclusions. While it is true that there was little reason for the Court to do so in the context of what was, after all, an academic appeal, it would nevertheless have been instructive to have been told precisely why the delay was not unjustifiable, why the chances of prejudice were remote, and so on. Such explanation would be of considerable assistance to trial judges in future cases.

The Court expressed the hope that its judgment would result in a significant reduction in the number of applications to stay proceedings on account of delay.[38] There is reason to believe that this may indeed be a consequence of the judgment, as the guide-lines provided by the Court, such as they are, are likely to be treated as authoritative in the future. Perhaps the merit of the judgment lies in the (admittedly somewhat reluctant) decision of the Court to accept the broader views on abuse of process expressed in later cases in preference to the narrower views expressed in earlier ones. What is disappointing about the judgment, however, is that it contains no discussion of the *rationales* behind the guide-lines laid down. The judgment suggests, for example, that judges should be slower to stay proceedings on account of delay if there has been no fault on the part of the complainant or prosecution than if there has been such fault, but we are not told why this is so. And why is it that delay due merely to the complexity of the case can never lead to a stay, even if it can be demonstrated that the defendant will be seriously prejudiced in her defence as a result of the delay? Is it the conduct of the prosecution rather than prejudice to the defence which is the crucial consideration? Perhaps the Court meant its judgment to be read in the light of the discussions undertaken in the large number of earlier Divisional Court decisions. Be that as it may, the Court should surely, at the very least, have addressed the fundamental issue of principle: what is the actual basis for a stay of proceedings on the ground of delay? It is to be hoped that this and other important issues of principle will receive detailed consideration by the Court of Appeal or House of Lords in the future.

It should be noted, however, that there are a number of relevant decisions of the Privy Council. *Bell* v. *DPP*[39] and *Mungroo* v. *R.*[40] involved considerations of whether there had been infringements of section 20(1) of the Constitution of Jamaica and section 10(1) of the Constitution of Mauritius respectively. Both provisions are essentially similar and provide that a person charged with a criminal offence must, unless the charge is withdrawn, be afforded a fair hearing within a reasonable time. In *Bell* the

---

[37] Ibid.   [38] Ibid.   [39] [1985] AC 937.   [40] [1991] 1 WLR 1351.

Privy Council observed that, even prior to the enactment of the written Constitution, Jamaican courts, applying the common law of England, would have been capable of dealing with the problem of pre-trial delay by exercising the discretion to stay proceedings.[41] Their Lordships expressly acknowledged the 'relevance and importance' to their inquiry of the criteria laid down by the US Supreme Court in the case of *Barker* v. *Wingo*.[42] 'The desirability of applying the same or similar criteria to any constitution, written *or unwritten*, which protects an accused from oppression by delay in criminal proceedings'[43] was also acknowledged. As we shall see later, the US law has also been relied and elaborated upon in Canada. Given that this area of the law represents a rare instance of the willingness of the English judiciary to borrow directly from the US law in the area, it is appropriate to proceed later in the chapter to an examination of the US position on the procedural implications of pre-trial executive delay.

In *Tan* v. *Cameron*,[44] the latest relevant Privy Council pronouncement, the judgment of the Court of Appeal in *A-G's Reference (No. 1 of 1990)* was endorsed. The Privy Council then proceeded to clarify the following passage from the judgment of the Divisional Court in *R.* v. *Bow Street Stipendiary Magistrate, ex p. DPP and Cherry*:

Obviously, what has to be demonstrated to the court is that the delay complained of has produced genuine prejudice and unfairness. In some circumstances as the cases show, Mr Lawson referred to them in his skeleton argument, prejudice will be presumed from substantial delay. Where that is so it will be for the Prosecution to rebut, if it can, the presumption. ... He contended that in the absence of a presumption where there is substantial delay it will be for the prosecution to justify it. He went further and said that the prosecution bore that burden whenever the issue of prejudice through delay was raised. We have no difficulty in accepting the former . . .[45]

The Privy Council in *Tan* observed that this passage had apparently led Barnett J. in the High Court of Hong Kong

to conclude that the district judge should have approached the inquiry on the footing that (i) the burden of showing that the continuance of the prosecution would be a misuse of the process of the court rested upon the applicant, but (ii) this burden could prima facie be discharged by demonstrating an inexcusably long delay, unless the prosecution could in turn discharge the burden of showing that prejudice did not in fact follow from the delay.

Their Lordships do not agree with this appreciation of the law. Naturally, the longer the delay the more likely it will be that the prosecution is at fault, and that the delay has caused prejudice to the defendant; and the less that the prosecution has to offer by explanation, the more easily can fault be inferred. But the establishment of these

---

[41] [1985] AC 937, 950.   [42] 407 US 514 (1972).
[43] [1985] AC 937, 953 (emphasis added).   [44] [1992] 3 WLR 249.
[45] (1989) 91 Cr. App. R. 283, 296–7.

facts is only one step on the way to a consideration of whether, in all the circumstances, the situation created by the delay is such as to make it an unfair employment of the powers of the court any longer to hold the defendant to account. This is a question to be considered in the round, and nothing is gained by the introduction of shifting burdens of proof, which serves only to break down into formal steps what is in reality a single appreciation of what is or is not unfair.[46]

OTHER JURISDICTIONS

THE UNITED STATES

(a) The Sixth Amendment Right to a Speedy Trial

The Sixth Amendment of the US Constitution provides: 'In all criminal prosecutions, the accused shall enjoy the right to a speedy ... trial ...' Violation of this right, the Supreme Court has held, will result in dismissal of the indictment.[47]

(i) 'Attachment' of the Right

The US Supreme Court takes the view that 'a literal reading of the Amendment suggests that this right attaches only when a formal criminal charge is instituted and a criminal prosecution begins'.[48] Thus, 'it is either a formal indictment or information or else the actual restraints imposed by arrest and holding to answer a criminal charge that engage the particular protections of the speedy trial provision of the Sixth Amendment'.[49] In *US v. Marion*[50] the defendants were indicted on 21 April 1970 on nineteen counts of fraud alleged to have been committed from 15 March 1965 until 6 February 1967. It was argued that the delay of approximately three years between the end of the criminal scheme charged and the return of the indictment violated the Sixth Amendment. The Supreme Court held, however, that

the Sixth Amendment speedy trial provision has no application until the putative defendant in some way becomes an 'accused', an event that occurred in this case only when the appellees were indicted on April 21, 1970. . . . On its face, the protection of the Amendment is activated only when a criminal prosecution has begun and extends only to those persons who have been 'accused' in the course of that prosecution. These provisions would seem to afford no protection to those not yet

---

[46] [1992] 3 WLR 249, 264.

[47] The Court observed in *Barker* v. *Wingo* 407 US 514, 522 (1972): 'The amorphous quality of the right . . . leads to the unsatisfactorily severe remedy of dismissal of the indictment when the right has been deprived. This is indeed a serious consequence because it means that a defendant who may be guilty of a serious crime will go free, without having been tried. Such a remedy is more serious than an exclusionary rule or a reversal for a new trial, but it is the only possible remedy.' See also *Strunk* v. *US* 412 US 434, 439–40 (1973).

[48] *US* v. *MacDonald* 456 US 1, 6 (1982).

[49] *US* v. *Marion* 404 US 307, 320 (1971).   [50] 404 US 307 (1971).

accused, nor would they seem to require the Government to discover, investigate, and accuse any person within any particular period of time.[51]

Also of interest is *US* v. *MacDonald*,[52] in which it was held that the time between the dismissal of military charges and a subsequent indictment on civilian criminal charges should not be considered in determining whether the delay in bringing the defendant to trial violated his rights under the Speedy Trial Clause of the Sixth Amendment. The Court pointed out that, during the intervening period, the defendant had not been under arrest, in custody, or subject to any 'criminal prosecution'. After the dismissal of the military charges the defendant was in the same position, legally and constitutionally, as he would have been had no charges been laid: 'He was free to go about his affairs, to practice his profession, and to continue with his life.'[53]

(ii) When is the Right Violated?

Given that violation of the Sixth Amendment right to a speedy trial leads automatically to dismissal of the indictment, it is not surprising that the US Supreme Court has given careful consideration to the issue of what constitutes a violation of the right. The Court has emphasized that the Speedy Trial Clause is not to be taken literally, since, if it were, it would forbid the government to delay a trial for any reason at all.[54] Instead, four factors have been identified by the Court which should be considered in determining whether a particular defendant has been deprived of her Sixth Amendment right to a speedy trial. Each of these will be examined in turn.

Length of delay. The delay in question must be of sufficient length to be 'presumptively improper': if this requirement is not satisfied, there is no need to proceed further with a determination of whether the defendant's speedy-trial right has been violated.[55] But the issue of whether delay is presumptively improper will be dependent upon the circumstances of the particular case.[56] It is necessary to take into account both the nature of the offence charged and the manner in which the prosecution case is to be proven. Thus 'the delay that can be tolerated for an ordinary street crime is considerably less than for a serious, complex conspiracy charge',[57] because genuine difficulties in preparing for trial are more likely to be encountered by the prosecution in the latter case than in the former. In a case involving serious charges the Court held a ninety-month delay to be presumptively improper,[58] and in the recent case of *Doggett* v. *US* 'the extraordinary 8½

---

[51] 404 US 307 (1971), 313.   [52] 456 US 1 (1982).
[53] 456 US 1, 10.   [54] *Doggett* v. *US* 112 S. Ct. 2686, 2690 (1992).
[55] *Barker* v. *Wingo* 407 US 514, 530 (1972); *US* v. *$8,850* 461 US 555, 565 (1983).
[56] *Barker* v. *Wingo* 407 US 514, 530–1 (1972); *US* v. *$8,850* 461 US 555, 565 (1983).
[57] *Barker* v. *Wingo* 407 US 514, 530–1 (1972).
[58] *US* v. *Loud Hawk* 106 S. Ct. 648, 655 (1986).

year lag between Doggett's indictment and arrest'[59] was similarly regarded. The manner in which the prosecution case is to be proven is relevant because documentary evidence, for example, will retain its reliability through a period of delay whereas the memories of eyewitnesses are liable to fade: in a case which depends on eyewitness testimony a delay of even nine months may be presumptively improper.[60]

The reason for the delay. 'Different weights should be assigned to different reasons.' For example, deliberate delay which is motivated by a desire to hamper the defence will weigh heavily against the Government. In comparison, 'a more neutral reason such as negligence or overcrowded courts' will weigh less heavily. Finally, it may be that there is a valid reason for the delay, such as a missing witness.[61] The Court has held that delay caused by an interlocutory appeal by the Government was justified; there was no showing of bad faith or dilatory purpose on the part of the Government.[62]

The defendant's assertion of her right. The fact that the defendant has asserted her speedy-trial right will weigh heavily in her favour, while failure to do so will make it difficult for her to establish that she was denied a speedy trial.[63] The strength of any efforts to assert the right is also a relevant consideration: 'The strength of his efforts will be affected by the length of the delay, to some extent by the reason for the delay, and most particularly by the personal prejudice, which is not always readily identifiable, that he experiences.'[64] In *US* v. *Loud Hawk*[65] the Court held that the mere fact that the defendants had repeatedly moved for dismissal on speedy-trial grounds did not of itself suffice to establish that they had appropriately asserted their rights: at the same time as making claims for a speedy trial they consumed six months by filing frivolous petitions for rehearing and for certiorari, and 'also filled the District Court's docket with repetitive and unsuccessful motions'.[66] It is clear, therefore, that a court will look at all relevant circumstances to determine the seriousness with which it should take the fact that the defendant asserted her speedy-trial right: a defendant who asserts the right while at the same time delaying matters herself is unlikely to be actually experiencing any personal prejudice as a result of the delay.

Similarly, the time at which an assertion was made is also a relevant

[59] 112 S. Ct. 2686, 2691 (1992).
[60] *Barker* v. *Wingo* 407 US 514, 531 n. 31 (1972).   [61] Ibid. 531.
[62] *US* v. *Loud Hawk* 106 S. Ct. 648, 656 (1986).
[63] *Barker* v. *Wingo* 407 US 514, 531–2 (1972).   [64] Ibid. 531.
[65] 106 S. Ct. 648 (1986).
[66] Ibid. 655–6. See also *Barker* v. *Wingo* 407 US 514, 534 (1972): 'the record shows no action whatever taken between October 21, 1958, and February 12, 1962, that could be construed as the assertion of the speedy trial right.'

consideration: the fact that the defendant asserted her speedy-trial right just prior to the trial may suggest that the assertion was merely an attempt to add weight to her speedy-trial claim rather than being motivated by any personal prejudice which she was experiencing as a result of the delay. Thus the Sixth Circuit of the Court of Appeals held in *Martin* v. *Rose* that a demand for a speedy trial five days before the trial was due to commence did not constitute an appropriate assertion,[67] and in *Takacs* v. *Engle* that an assertion thirteen days before the trial was due to commence was also insufficient.[68]

Prejudice to the defendant. The fourth factor regarded by the Court as relevant is whether the delay has resulted in 'prejudice to the defendant'. Essentially, it is considered that a defendant may be 'prejudiced' by delay in any one of three ways:

(*a*) Through oppressive pre-trial incarceration. The Court has adverted to the emotional and practical consequences for an accused of time spent in jail awaiting trial:

It often means loss of a job; it disrupts family life; and it enforces idleness. Most jails offer little or no recreational or rehabilitative programs. The time spent in jail is simply dead time. Moreover, if a defendant is locked up, he is hindered in his ability to gather evidence, contact witnesses, or otherwise prepare his defense.[69]

(*b*) Through anxiety and concern, even if the defendant is on bail and not therefore being incarcerated. She is still disadvantaged by restraints on her liberty and by the anxiety, suspicion, and probable hostility resulting from arrest and the presence of unresolved criminal charges.[70]

(*c*) Through impairment of her defence. This is regarded by the Court as the most serious of the three, 'because the inability of a defendant adequately to prepare his case skews the fairness of the entire system'. Prejudice will occur where witnesses die or disappear during a delay, or where defence witnesses are unable to recall events accurately.[71] However, the mere *possibility* of 'impairment of a fair trial that may well result from the absence or loss of memory of witnesses' would appear not to suffice.[72]

The Court has emphasized that the four factors identified by it as relevant to a determination of whether a defendant's speedy-trial right has been

[67] 744 F. 2d 1245, 1252 (6th Cir. 1984).

[68] 768 F. 2d 122, 128 (6th Cir. 1985).

[69] *Barker* v. *Wingo* 407 US 514, 532–3 (1972).

[70] Ibid. 533; *US* v. *MacDonald* 456 US 1, 8 (1982). See also *US* v. *Marion* 404 US 307, 320 (1971): 'Arrest is a public act that may seriously interfere with the defendant's liberty, whether he is free on bail or not, and that may disrupt his employment, drain his financial resources, curtail his associations, subject him to public obloquy, and create anxiety in him, his family and his friends.'   [71] *Barker* v. *Wingo* 407 US 514, 532 (1972).

[72] *US* v. *Loud Hawk* 106 S. Ct. 648, 656 (1986).

violated do not constitute an exhaustive list, but must be considered together with any other circumstances which may be relevant.[73] Given that the Court has held that violation of the right will lead automatically to dismissal of the indictment, a determination of whether the right has been violated is in effect synonymous with a determination of whether the defendant should be put on trial after the delay. A cursory examination of the four factors might suggest that there is little connection between them, but a closer examination reveals that the Court is concerned essentially with three issues. The first is that a delay in bringing a person to trial must be in some way improper before any question of protecting her from the trial can arise. Secondly, it seems that an important consideration in determining whether a person should be put on trial after a delay is whether her defence would be impaired as a result of the delay. Thirdly, it would appear that a further consideration in determining whether a delayed trial should take place is the extent to which the defendant has suffered oppression, anxiety, or concern as a result of the delay. We shall see that these three issues are precisely those which should underlie any consideration of whether a defendant should be protected from trial on account of delay by the executive.

(b) Due Process

Given that the Speedy Trial Clause of the Sixth Amendment is concerned solely with delay occurring at the postaccusation stage, the US Supreme Court has had to consider separately the problem of delay occurring prior to that stage. In doing so, the Court has acknowledged that due-process principles[74] 'would require dismissal of the indictment if it were shown at trial that the pre-indictment delay . . . caused substantial prejudice to [the defendant's right] to a fair trial *and* that the delay was an intentional device to gain tactical advantage over the accused'.[75] Thus, it is necessary to consider (1) whether the delay has caused substantial prejudice to the defendant's ability to defend herself; and (2) the reason for the delay.

As to the first of these requirements, it is clear that there must be actual prejudice to the conduct of the defence. This may, for example, be demonstrated by specific events at trial.[76] As to the second, it must be shown 'that the Government intentionally delayed to gain some tactical advantage over [the defendant] or to harass [her]'.[77] The Supreme Court pointed out in *US* v. *Lovasco*[78] that this requirement will not be satisfied by the fact that a prosecutor delayed seeking an indictment until she had probable cause to believe the suspect to be guilty; indeed, it is unprofessional

---

[73] *Barker* v. *Wingo* 407 US 514, 533 (1972).

[74] Due-process clauses are to be found in both the Fifth Amendment ('No person . . . shall . . . be deprived of life, liberty, or property, without due process of law . . .') and the Fourteenth Amendment ('No State shall . . . deprive any person of life, liberty, or property, without due process of law . . .').   [75] *US* v. *Marion* 404 US 307, 324 (1971) (emphasis added).

[76] Ibid. 326.   [77] Ibid. 325.   [78] 431 US 783 (1977).

conduct for a prosecutor to recommend an indictment on less than probable cause. Further, prosecutors are under no obligation to file charges as soon as probable cause exists. Such an obligation would have a number of undesirable consequences. First, where a criminal enterprise involves more than one person, an immediate arrest or indictment may impair the prosecutor's ability to continue her investigation and thus bring other offenders to conviction. Even if she is able to continue her investigation and obtain additional indictments, the result will be multiple trials involving the same set of facts. Secondly, a duty to prosecute as soon as probable cause is established will probably result in an increase in the number of unwarranted charges being filed, and will also add to the time during which defendants stand accused but untried. Thus, a desire to reduce preaccusation delay may lead, ironically, to increased postaccusation delay. Finally, a requirement to prosecute as soon as probable cause is established may prevent the Government from awaiting the information necessary for a proper exercise of its prosecutorial discretion to determine whether prosecution would be in the public interest.[79]

In the circumstances of *Lovasco* it was held that due process was not violated by delay caused by efforts to identify persons in addition to the defendant who may have participated in the offences in question: 'to prosecute a defendant following investigative delay does not deprive him of due process.'[80]

(c) Statutory Provisions

In addition to the Sixth Amendment Speedy Trial Clause and due-process principles, specific statutory provisions are of considerable importance when considering the US approach to the problem of delay in bringing cases to trial. As far as the preaccusation period is concerned, a statute of limitations may provide that prosecution for the offence in question must commence within a certain period after the commission of the offence. For example, 18 USC section 3282 provides that, except as otherwise expressly provided by law, a person may not be prosecuted, tried, or punished for any non-capital offence 'unless the indictment is found or the information is instituted within five years next after such offense shall have been committed'. Indeed, the attitude of the Supreme Court is that 'the applicable statute of limitations . . . is usually considered the primary guarantee against bringing overly stale criminal charges'.[81] Statutes of limitations, it is said, 'represent legislative assessments of relative interests of the State and the defendant in administering and receiving justice';[82] 'a limitation is designed

---

[79] Ibid. 790–6.
[80] Ibid. 796. See also *Clayton* v. *Ralphs and Manos* (1987) 26 A. Crim. R. 43, 84 per Legoe J.   [81] *US* v. *Ewell* 383 US 116, 122 (1966).
[82] *US* v. *Marion* 404 US 307, 322 (1971).

to protect individuals from having to defend themselves against charges when the basic facts may have become obscured by the passage of time and to minimize the danger of official punishment because of acts in the far-distant past'.[83]

In the postaccusation period, too, a defendant's speedy-trial right under the Sixth Amendment may be buttressed by relevant statutory provisions. For example, rule 48(*b*) of the Federal Rules of Criminal Procedure authorizes the dismissal of a case by a trial court on the ground of unnecessary delay.[84] Also of importance in the Federal jurisdiction is the Speedy Trial Act 1974.[85] This provides that any information or indictment charging an individual with an offence must be filed within thirty days of the date of arrest or service of summons.[86] In the event that a plea of not guilty is entered, trial must commence within seventy days from the filing date of the information or indictment, or from the date the defendant has appeared before a judicial officer of the court in which the charge is pending, whichever is the later.[87] However, unless the defendant consents to the contrary in writing, the trial must not commence less than thirty days from the date on which the defendant first appears before the court through counsel or *pro se*.[88] The Act provides that certain types of delay are to be excluded in computing the time within which an information or indictment must be filed, or within which a trial must commence.[89] To be excluded, for example, are any delay resulting from other proceedings involving the defendant;[90] any delay resulting from the absence or unavailability of the defendant or an essential witness;[91] any period resulting from the fact that the defendant is mentally incompetent or physically unable to stand trial;[92] and any period resulting from a continuance granted by a judge on the basis 'that the ends of justice served by taking such action outweigh the best interest of the public and the defendant in a speedy trial'.[93]

If an indictment or information is not filed within the time limit required by the Act, the charge must be 'dismissed or otherwise dropped'.[94] And if a defendant is not brought to trial within the time limit required by the Act, the information or indictment must be dismissed on a motion by the defendant. The defendant carries the burden of proof on the motion, and failure to move for dismissal prior to trial constitutes a waiver of the right to dismissal.[95] A case may be dismissed under the Act either with or without

---

[83] *Toussie* v. *US* 397 US 112, 114–15 (1970).

[84] 'If there is unnecessary delay in presenting the charge to a grand jury or in filing an information against a defendant who has been held to answer to the district court, or if there is unnecessary delay in bringing a defendant to trial, the court may dismiss the indictment, information or complaint.'

[85] 18 USC ss. 3161–74.

[86] 18 USC s. 3161(*b*).

[87] 18 USC s. 3161(*c*)(1).

[88] 18 USC s. 3161(*c*)(2).

[89] 18 USC s. 3161(*h*).

[90] 18 USC s. 3161(*h*)(1).

[91] 18 USC s. 3161(*h*)(3).

[92] 18 USC s. 3161(*h*)(4).

[93] 18 USC s. 3161(*h*)(8)(A).

[94] 18 USC s. 3162(*a*)(1).

[95] 18 USC s. 3162(*a*)(2).

prejudice, and in determining whether to dismiss a case with or without prejudice the court must consider, *inter alia*, the following factors: (1) the seriousness of the offence; (2) the facts and circumstances of the case which led to the dismissal; and (3) the impact of a reprosecution on the administration of the Act and on the administration of justice.[96]

(*d*) Conclusion

It is clear that the problem of delay in bringing cases to trial has received considerable attention in the United States. There appears, however, to be a divergence between US attitudes to postaccusation and preaccusation delay. Where delay occurs after a suspect has in some way become an 'accused' (for example, after arrest), protection is afforded not only by the Speedy Trial Clause of the Sixth Amendment, but also, in the Federal jurisdiction, by the detailed provisions of the Speedy Trial Act 1974. In determining whether a defendant's right to a speedy trial has been violated, trial courts are required to consider and to weigh up a number of relevant factors. It is evident that protection from prejudice to the conduct of the defence is merely one aspect of the speedy-trial right. Also relevant are such considerations as the reason for the delay, and the oppression which would inevitably be felt by an accused while awaiting trial (whether in jail or on bail).

By contrast, preaccusation delay is dealt with on a different level. The Speedy Trial Clause is inapplicable to such delay, and statutes of limitations and due process principles form the basis of the arguments available to a defendant. Where a criminal prosecution is instituted within the time limit stipulated in any relevant statute of limitations, there is some reluctance to hold that due process has been violated. For a violation of due process to be established there must exist evidence of prejudice to the conduct of the defence *as well as* proof of intent to gain a tactical advantage over or to harass the defendant. This is a far more rigid approach than that taken to a determination of whether the speedy-trial right of a defendant has been violated, and this rigidity is clearly unfounded. It is a mistake to assume that preaccusation delay cannot have serious consequences. In particular, it should be noted that the ability to defend oneself may be hampered to a greater extent by preaccusation delay than by postaccusation delay. Where a person has been accused of a specific offence, she is able at least to take steps to preserve her memory, or the memories of witnesses, of relevant details pertaining to the alleged occurrences. But a person who is unaware that criminal charges will eventually be brought against her will have no reason to do so.[97]

---

[96] See generally 18 USC s. 3162(*a*)(1) and (2).

[97] *US* v. *Marion* 404 US 307, 331 (1971); A. L. Schneider, 'The Right to a Speedy Trial' (1968) 20 *Stanford Law Review* 476, 489. Further, the view has been expressed that 'the

In sum, therefore, a shortcoming of US law in this area lies in its failure to deal with preaccusation delay in a manner commensurate with that in which it deals with postaccusation delay. This position is, of course, attributable to the fact that the Speedy Trial Clause is regarded as inapplicable to preaccusation delay, with the result that the only Constitutional protection applicable to such delay is provided by due process principles.

The Privy Council, to its credit, appears to have adopted a slightly more flexible approach in relation to the distinction between preaccusation delay and postaccusation delay. In *Mungroo* v. *R.* the issue arose as to whether section 10(1) of the Constitution of Mauritius, which provides that a person charged with a criminal offence 'shall be afforded a fair hearing within a reasonable time', had been infringed. Their Lordships remarked that 'it may be that in some cases, in considering whether a reasonable time has elapsed before the conclusion of the hearing of criminal proceedings, it would be proper to take into account the period *before* the accused was arrested'.[98] Statements made in the English cases, too, appear to suggest that, in considering whether proceedings should be stayed as an abuse of process on account of pre-trial delay, the entire period from the time of the commission of the alleged offence should be considered.[99] This is clearly the correct approach to adopt.

CANADA: CANADIAN CHARTER OF RIGHTS AND FREEDOMS, SECTION 11(*b*)

As in the United States, there exists in Canada a specific Constitutional provision directed at the problem of delay in criminal procedure. Section 11(*b*) of the Canadian Charter of Rights and Freedoms provides: 'Any person charged with an offence has the right . . . to be tried within a reasonable time . . .' This provision has been the subject of recent scrutiny by the Canadian Supreme Court in a series of cases.[100] As considerations drawn from the approach adopted by the Court will be useful in our later

---

anxiety and concern attendant on public accusation may weigh more heavily upon an individual who has not yet been formally indicted or arrested for, to him, exoneration by a jury of his peers may be only a vague possibility lurking in the distant future' (*US* v. *Marion* 404 US 307, 330–1 (1971)).

[98] [1991] 1 WLR 1351, 1354 (emphasis added).

[99] See *R.* v. *Sunderland Magistrates' Court, ex p. Z* [1989] Crim. LR 56 (the relevant period was that from the time of commission of the alleged offence, and not simply from the date of issue of the summons or warrant); *R.* v. *Telford JJ, ex p. Badhan* [1991] 2 WLR 866, 876 ('the period of the lapse is that between the date of the commission of the alleged offence and the date when the accused can first formally raise the point, that is to say immediately before the proposed opening of the committal proceedings').

[100] *Mills* v. *R.* (1986) 52 CR (3d) 1; *BC (AG)* v. *Craig Prov. J.* (1986) 52 CR (3d) 100; *Rahey* v. *R.* (1987) 57 CR (3d) 289; *R.* v. *Conway* (1989) 70 CR (3d) 209; *R.* v. *Kalanj* (1989) 70 CR (3d) 260; *R.* v. *Stensrud* (1989) 52 CCC (3d) 96; *R.* v. *Smith* (1989) 73 CR (3d) 1; *R.* v. *Askov* (1990) 79 CR (3d) 273; *R.* v. *Morin* (1992) 71 CCC (3d) 1; *R.* v. *Sharma* (1992) 71 CCC (3d) 184; *R.* v. *CIP Inc.* (1992) 12 CR (4th) 237.

discussion of how an English court should determine whether proceedings ought to be stayed on account of pre-trial delay, this approach will be sketched briefly here with reference to the most recent major pronouncement of the Court, *R. v. Morin*.[101] The main judgment in *Morin* was delivered by Sopinka J.,[102] who provided a summary of all aspects of section 11(*b*).

(*a*) Purpose of Section 11(*b*)

In the view of Sopinka J., the primary purpose of section 11(*b*)[103] is the protection of three individual rights of accused persons: (1) the right to security of the person; (2) the right to liberty; and (3) the right to a fair trial. The right to security is protected by seeking to minimize the anxiety, concern, and stigma of exposure to criminal proceedings; the right to liberty is protected by seeking to minimize exposure to restrictions on liberty resulting from pre-trial incarceration and restrictive bail conditions; the right to a fair trial is protected by seeking to ensure that proceedings take place while evidence is available and fresh.

There is also, in the view of Sopinka J., a secondary societal interest implicit in section 11(*b*). This societal interest has two aspects. First, society as a whole has an interest in seeing that citizens accused of crimes are treated humanely and fairly by being tried promptly. The second aspect is society's interest in ensuring that those who transgress the law are promptly brought to trial and dealt with in accordance with the law.

(*b*) Factors for Consideration

Sopinka J. identified four factors to be taken into account in determining whether an infringement of section 11(*b*) has occurred: the length of the delay,[104] waiver of time periods, [105] the reasons for the delay,[106] and prejudice to the accused.[107]

(i) The Length of the Delay

This factor requires an examination of the period from charge to the end of the trial. 'Charge' in this context means the date on which an information is sworn or an indictment is preferred.

(ii) Waiver of Time Periods

Waiver by an accused of her section 11(*b*) rights must be clear and unequivocal, and may be explicit or implicit. It is not waiver 'if the mind of

---

[101] (1992) 71 CCC (3d) 1. See S. G. Coughlan, 'Trial within a Reasonable Time: Does the Right Still Exist?' (1992) 12 *Criminal Reports* (4th) 34.

[102] With La Forest, Stevenson, and Iacobucci JJ concurring.

[103] (1992) 71 CCC (3d) 1, 12–13.   [104] Ibid. 14–15.   [105] Ibid. 15–16.

[106] Ibid. 16–23.   [107] Ibid. 23–5.

the accused or his or her counsel is not turned to the issue of waiver and is not aware of what his or her conduct signifies'.[108]

(iii) The Reasons for the Delay

It is necessary to consider all reasons for the delay, including (1) inherent time requirements; (2) actions of the accused; (3) actions of the Crown; and (4) limits on institutional resources. In relation to (4), it was accepted by Sopinka J. that there is a period of time beyond which delay based on the plea of inadequate resources should no longer be tolerated, and that this period may serve as a guide-line. Sopinka J. was careful to emphasize, however, that such a guide-line is not to be treated as an inflexible limitation period or a fixed ceiling on delay.[109]

(iv) Prejudice to the Accused

Such prejudice may be inferred from the length of the delay. But apart from inferred prejudice, both parties are at liberty to adduce evidence either to demonstrate prejudice or to dispel such a finding. An accused may wish, for example, to adduce evidence tending to show prejudice to her liberty interest as a result of pre-trial incarceration or restrictive bail conditions. Conversely, the prosecution may adduce evidence that the accused does not want an early trial and that the delay benefited rather than prejudiced the accused.

(c) Post-Charge Delay Only

The above discussion of the approach of the Canadian Supreme Court to the interpretation of section 11(b) demonstrates that the considerations taken into account by the Court are broadly similar to those taken into account in the United States in relation to the speedy-trial right. Furthermore, just as the Sixth Amendment speedy-trial right in the United States is regarded as applicable to postaccusation delay only, so the operation of section 11(b) of the Canadian Charter is considered by the Canadian Supreme Court to be confined to post-charge delay. It has been held, however, that pre-charge delay may be relevant under sections 7 and 11(d) of the Charter.[110] Section 7 provides that 'everyone has the right to life, liberty and security of the person and the right not to be deprived thereof except in accordance with the principles of fundamental justice', while section 11(d) affords any person charged with an offence the right 'to be presumed innocent until proven guilty according to law in a fair and public hearing by an independent and impartial tribunal'. In *R. v. L. (WK)*[111] the accused was charged in January 1987 with seventeen counts of sexual

---

[108] Ibid. 15.   [109] Ibid. 19.
[110] See generally the judgment of Lamer J. in *Mills* v. *R.* (1986) 52 CR (3d) 1.
[111] (1991) 6 CR (4th) 1.

assault, gross indecency, and assault relating to his stepdaughter and two daughters. The first incident was alleged to have taken place in 1957 and the last in 1985. The charges were laid after two of the alleged victims complained to the police in 1986, this being the first time that either of them had reported any incidents to the police. The accused applied for a stay of the proceedings under section 24(1) of the Canadian Charter of Rights and Freedoms[112] on the basis that some thirty years had elapsed since the first alleged incident.

On appeal to the Canadian Supreme Court, it was held that this was not a case in which a stay should have been granted. An accused, the Court held, could not rely solely on the passage of time apparent on the face of the indictment as establishing a violation of section 7 or section 11(d). To stay proceedings merely on the basis of the passage of time, when there was no evidence of 'ulterior purpose' on the part of the prosecution, would be tantamount to 'imposing a judicially created limitation period for a criminal offence'.[113] The Court also regarded the nature of the offences charged as significant:

For victims of sexual abuse to complain would take courage and emotional strength in revealing those personal secrets, in opening old wounds. If proceedings were to be stayed based solely on the passage of time between the abuse and the charge, victims would be required to report incidents before they were psychologically prepared for the consequences of that reporting.[114]

What is required now is clarification by the Court of precisely what must be shown, over and above mere pre-charge delay, before a stay of the proceedings will be ordered.

SOME OBSERVATIONS

The fact that there does not exist in England a written Constitutional right to a speedy trial or to a trial within a reasonable time means that English courts can face the relevant issues squarely instead of becoming immersed in the interpretation of Constitutional provisions. Of course, examination of the analyses undertaken in the United States and in Canada has the advantage of bringing out, more clearly than an examination of the English cases is capable of doing, the different considerations implicit in the issue of delay in bringing persons to trial. In the light of the above discussions,[115]

---

[112] S. 24(1) provides: 'Anyone whose rights or freedoms, as guaranteed by this Charter, have been infringed or denied may apply to a court of competent jurisdiction to obtain such remedy as the court considers appropriate and just in the circumstances.'
[113] (1991) 6 CR (4th) 1, 9.   [114] Ibid. 10.
[115] Also worthy of note is the position in Australia, where, as in England, but in contrast to the position in the two other jurisdictions which we have considered, there does not exist a written Constitutional right to a speedy trial or to a trial within a reasonable time. However,

therefore, it is now timely to offer some recommendations as to the way in which an application for a stay of proceedings on the ground of pre-trial delay by the executive should be approached.

PRELIMINARY ISSUES

The first step is to determine whether the delay in question can be regarded as improper. In many cases there will be nothing improper about bringing a person to trial after a substantial period has elapsed either since the commission of the offence or since she was first 'accused' of the offence.[116] To determine whether a delay in bringing a person to trial can be considered improper, it is necessary to consider the explanation or reason given by the executive for the delay.[117] Any of the following reasons, for example, will weigh in favour of a conclusion that the delay was not improper:

the issue of delay in criminal litigation has been recently brought to prominence in Australia by a decision of the High Court of Australia (*Jago* v. *District Court (NSW)* (1989) 168 CLR 23; for criticisms see A. S. Hodge, 'The Process of Abuse' (1990) 20 *Hong Kong Law Journal* 195, 225) and by a number of decisions of the New South Wales Court of Appeal: see *Herron* v. *McGregor* (1986) 6 NSWLR 246; *Watson* v. *A–G (NSW)* (1987) 8 NSWLR 685; *A–G (NSW)* v. *Kintominas* (1987) 28 A. Crim. R. 371; *Carver* v. *A–G (NSW)* (1987) 29 A. Crim. R. 24; *Young* v. *Torrington*, unreported, 22 Sept. 1987; *Aboud* v. *A–G (NSW)* (1987) 10 NSWLR 671; *Gorman* v. *Fitzpatrick* (1987) 32 A. Crim. R. 330; *R.* v. *Sams* (1988) 36 A. Crim. R. 245; *Jago* v. *District Court (NSW)* (1988) 12 NSWLR 558; *Cooke* v. *Purcell* (1988) 14 NSWLR 51; *R.* v. *Grassby* (1988) 15 NSWLR 109; *R.* v. *Hakim* (1989) 41 A. Crim. R. 372; *Adler* v. *District Court (NSW)* (1990) 19 NSWLR 317; *Gill* v. *Walton* (1991) 25 NSWLR 190.

Other Australian cases include *R.* v. *Helmhout* (1981) 5 A. Crim. R. 42; *R.* v. *Hill* (1982) 7 A. Crim. R. 161; *Tebbutt* v. *Muggleton* (1985) 6 NSWLR 583; *R.* v. *McConnell* (1985) 2 NSWLR 269; *R.* v. *Climo and Bentley* (1986) 7 NSWLR 579; *Whitbread* v. *Cooke (No. 2)* (1986) 5 ACLC 305; *R.* v. *Clarkson* [1987] VR 962; *Joel* v. *Mealey* (1987) 27 A. Crim. R. 280; *Clayton* v. *Ralphs and Manos* (1987) 26 A. Crim. R. 43; *R.* v. *Cawley and Clayton* (1987) 30 A. Crim. R. 324; *Higgins* v. *Tobin*, unreported, 5 Nov. 1987; *Newby* v. *Moodie* (1987) 88 ATC 4072; *Murphy* v. *Tavernstock* (1988) 93 FLR 14; *R.* v. *Gonis and Farinola* (1988) 48 SASR 228; *Boehm* v. *DPP* [1990] VR 475; *Wilson* v. *DPP (Vic.)*, unreported, 22 Aug. 1989.

For New Zealand, see generally J. Kovacevich, 'The Inherent Power of the District Court: Abuse of Process, Delay and the Right to a Speedy Trial' [1989] *New Zealand Law Journal* 184.

[116] 'There is a vast difference between a case in which an accused who has successfully concealed his crime for twenty years is brought to trial expeditiously after the crime is discovered and a case in which the prosecutor fails to bring a person to trial within, for instance, five years when there were eyewitnesses to the incident and all the facts were known within days of the commission of the alleged crime' (*Cooke* v. *Purcell* (1988) 14 NSWLR 51, 79 per Clarke JA). See also *Doggett* v. *US* 112 S. Ct. 2686, 2693 (1992): 'Our speedy trial standards recognize that pretrial delay is often both inevitable and wholly justifiable. The government may need time to collect witnesses against the accused, oppose his pretrial motions, or, if he goes into hiding, track him down.'

[117] Cf. *R.* v. *Cawley and Clayton* (1987) 30 A. Crim. R. 324, 330: 'In the circumstances of this case I am satisfied that the delay, notwithstanding its duration, has been explained and has been justified. Two Crown witnesses have admitted to lying at the coronial inquest and a third Crown witness (Hansberry) has come forth at a very late stage: the prosecuting authorities having no prior knowledge of his evidential worth. Notwithstanding that two of these three people were police officers at the relevant time, I do not consider that that is the responsibility of the prosecuting authorities.'

1. Search for a missing prosecution witness.
2. Genuine difficulties in preparing for trial owing to the complexity of the case. As we have seen, the US Supreme Court has acknowledged that a delay which would be presumptively improper in the case of a street crime might not be so in the case of a serious complex crime.
3. Efforts by the police to identify persons in addition to the defendant who may have participated in the offence in question.[118] (Failure by the police to do so may result in multiple trials involving the same set of facts.)
4. Deliberate slowness to act by the police in the hope that the defendant would lead them to 'bigger fish'.[119]

In contrast to these factors, which, as mentioned, would tend in favour of a conclusion that there was no impropriety on the part of the executive, a delay which was motivated by a desire to gain tactical advantage over or to harass the defendant must, of course, be regarded as having been improper.

In determining the propriety of the actions of the State in permitting the lapse of a substantial period of time before bringing a person to trial, it is also relevant to have regard, as was pointed out by the Privy Council in *Bell* v. *DPP*[120] and *Mungroo* v. *R.*,[121] to the prevailing system of legal administration and the prevailing economic and other conditions. For instance, longer delays in bringing persons to trial can obviously be expected in 'bad times', when overcrowded courts are commonplace, than in 'good times'. And, as acknowledged by Lamer J. of the Canadian Supreme Court in *Mills* v. *R.*, statutes laying down specific time periods may provide some guidance as to what should constitute proper time periods.[122] Similarly, evidence of the normal length of time that people are kept awaiting trial in similar cases can usefully be taken into account in determining the propriety of the conduct of the executive in the case at hand.[123]

Another preliminary issue which must be addressed concerns situations in which it is found that the lapse of time in question is attributable in part to

---

[118] Cf. *Lovasco*; see the text accompanying n. 80 above.

[119] Cf. *R.* v. *Canterbury and St Augustine JJ, ex p. Turner* (1983) 147 JPR 193. The offence in question was alleged to have been committed between 1 Sept. 1980 and 15 Oct. 1980, but the applicant was not interviewed and charged until 23 Dec. 1982. The detective inspector in evidence refuted the suggestion that there had been some impropriety in the failure to interview the applicant earlier, pointing out that the interview had been delayed in the hope that it might be possible for the applicant to lead the police to 'bigger fish'. This explanation was accepted by the court.   [120] [1985] AC 937.   [121] [1991] 1 WLR 1351.

[122] (1986) 52 CR (3d) 1, 77–83.

[123] Note, however, that the average length of time which people are kept awaiting trial can be expected to increase over time. See *Aboud* v. *A–G (NSW)* (1987) 10 NSWLR 671, 695 per McHugh JA: 'Considerations applicable in an age when cases depended upon the oral evidence of a few witnesses are not comparable with cases where great masses of documents and other exhibits must be analysed and put together. The laborious preparation of this class of case stands outside the experience of earlier times.'

delay by the executive and in part to delay by the defendant.[124] In such a situation, the court should make an estimate of what proportion of the delay is attributable to the conduct of the executive.[125] Only the delay attributable to the executive is relevant to the consideration of the defendant's application for a stay of proceedings.

Further, any delay which has been caused by the executive but waived by the defendant is no longer, of course, attributable to the executive. In determining whether a period of delay can be regarded as having been waived by the defendant, the observations of Sopinka J. in *Morin*, discussed above,[126] should be adopted.

PROTECTION OF JUDICIAL LEGITIMACY

As we have seen, the principle of judicial legitimacy suggests that a judicial stay of the proceedings in a particular case should be premised on the public need (1) to protect the innocent from wrongful conviction and/or (2) to protect the moral integrity of the criminal justice system. Either basis will be sufficient to lead to a stay. The public interest in bringing offenders to conviction must also be borne in mind at the same time.

(a) Protection of the Innocent from Wrongful Conviction

The first basis on which improper pre-trial executive delay may require a stay of the proceedings relates to the notion that the executive cannot justifiably bring a person to trial after leaving her without a fair opportunity to defend herself as a result of its improper conduct. With the passage of time, 'memories fade'; 'recollection is replaced by reconstruction which is in turn transformed into recollection.'[127] 'Relevant evidence becomes lost.'[128] Accordingly, pre-trial police or prosecutorial delay may well leave the

[124] It may even be the case that the delay attributable to the defendant was caused by a deliberate attempt on her part to delay matters. The US Supreme Court noted in *Barker* v. *Wingo* 407 US 514 (1972) that deprivation of an accused's right to a speedy trial may work to her advantage and that, accordingly, 'delay is not an uncommon defense tactic' (ibid. 521).

[125] Cf. *R.* v. *West London Stipendiary Magistrate, ex p. Anderson* (1984) 148 JPR 683, in which the Divisional Court considered the problem of delay which 'can be attributed in part to, for example, inefficiency on the part of the prosecution, and in part to the conduct of the defendant'. It was said that it is necessary in such circumstances to 'consider, taking into account the conduct of the defendant, to what extent the delay which has occurred is attributable to the inefficiency of the prosecution'; if it is considered 'that there has been *substantial delay* resulting from the inefficiency of the prosecution and that the defendant has been or must have been prejudiced by such delay', the proceedings may be stayed (ibid. 687 (emphasis added)). [126] See the text accompanying n. 108 above.

[127] *Cooke* v. *Purcell* (1988) 14 NSWLR 51, 87 per Clarke JA. In *Gill* v. *Walton* (1991) 25 NSWLR 190, Gleeson CJ said (ibid. 198): 'In the very nature of the adversarial process ... a person's capacity to wage a forensic contest in defence of conduct which occurred some fifteen or more years earlier may reasonably be expected to be diminished by the lapse of time. That is a matter of common experience and commonsense.'

[128] *Herron* v. *McGregor* (1986) 6 NSWLR 246, 254.

defendant without a fair opportunity to defend herself. This could lead to the defendant being convicted even if innocent.

It is, of course, impossible to determine definitively whether the delay in question has *actually* deprived the defendant of a fair opportunity to defend herself. I would therefore suggest that a substantial risk that the delay has left the defendant without a fair opportunity to defend herself should be sufficient to lead to a stay of proceedings.[129] The gravity of the offence charged is irrelevant here; defendants are entitled to a fair opportunity to defend themselves, regardless of whether they are accused of a minor offence or a serious one.[130]

In determining whether a stay of proceedings should be ordered on this basis, the court must consider and weigh up all factors which it regards as relevant to the inquiry. It will be relevant, for example, to consider the length of the delay since the time of the alleged offence. Obviously, the longer the delay, the more likely that the defendant will be prejudiced in the preparation and conduct of her defence. In cases of very great delay, the length of the delay may of itself suffice to lead to a stay of proceedings. Speaking of delay in civil procedure, a New South Wales judge, Cross J., observed in an unreported case[131] that 'there probably comes a time when the delay has been so great that the best and most honest recollections would begin to play substantial tricks, so that the trial of the action would be valid only as to form but, other than in an unreal sense, not as to substance.'[132]

Schneider[133] has pointed out that a delay in the prosecution of a crime proven primarily by testimonial evidence creates a greater possibility of prejudice to the defence than does delay in the prosecution of a crime proven primarily by documentary evidence. As was said in *Tynan* v. *US*: 'The transactions involving individual witnesses are generally unique in

[129] See *Doyle* v. *Leroux* [1981] RTR 438, in which the Divisional Court said (ibid. 443) that proceedings may be stayed as an abuse of process where 'something had been done, deliberately or by accident, by the prosecution which has *seriously prejudiced the possibility of the accused defending himself successfully*' (emphasis added). Cf. *Zurich Australian Insurance Ltd.* v. *Cannata, The Australian*, 4 Jan. 1988, in which the Full Court of the Supreme Court of Victoria held that a fire insurance claim should be dismissed for want of prosecution because the delay since the fire meant that there was a substantial risk that a fair trial of the issues could not take place.

[130] 'The interest of an accused in the availability and reliability of substantiating evidence will exist irrespective of the nature of the offence with which that person is charged' (*R.* v. *CIP Inc.* (1992) 12 CR (4th) 237, 254).

[131] *Calvert* v. *Stoliznow*, unreported, 1980. This decision was affirmed by the NSW Court of Appeal (*Stoliznow* v. *Calvert* [1980] 2 NSWLR 749), which described the judgment of Cross J. as 'most valuable' (ibid. 750). An extract from the judgment of Cross J. is to be found in M. I. Aronson, J. B. Hunter, and M. S. Weinberg, *Litigation: Evidence and Procedure* (4th edn., 1988), 120–2.

[132] For further discussion of delay in civil procedure see R. Cranston, P. Haynes, J. Pullen, and I. R. Scott, *Delays and Efficiency in Civil Litigation* (1985).

[133] Schneider, 'The Right to a Speedy Trial', 499.

their experience, and where documentary evidence is accepted, it, by its very nature, retains its reliability.'[134] This point would appear to have been appreciated in a number of English cases. In *R. v. Telford JJ, ex p. Badhan*, for example, it was said that an accused 'may find his task [of obtaining a stay of the proceedings] more difficult in a case wholly dependent on contemporary and available documents than he would in a case such as is the present which is dependent wholly upon a late complaint and oral testimony'.[135] Additionally, the factual circumstances common to a class of cases may also be relevant. For example, the possibility of prejudice to the defence is relatively great when a narcotics addict is being prosecuted for the possession or sales of narcotics, since addicts have difficulty remembering events even over very short periods of time.[136]

Another relevant factor for consideration relates to whether the delay occurred before or after the defendant had been alerted to the prospect of litigation against her. In *R. v. Norwich Crown Court, ex p. Belsham* the court regarded as significant the fact that

the applicant has been aware of the allegations made against him for some considerable time. They were ventilated at the extradition proceedings in New Zealand for one thing and for another he was interviewed at length upon his return to this country and has had since then every opportunity to prepare himself for the very straightforward allegations which are made . . .[137]

As has been noted earlier in the chapter, a person who has been 'accused' of a specific offence is able at least to take steps to preserve her memory, or the memories of witnesses, of relevant details relating to the alleged occurrences.[138] But a person unaware that criminal charges will eventually be brought against her will have no reason to do so.

---

[134] 376 F. 2d 761, 763 (DC Cir. 1967).

[135] [1991] 2 WLR 866, 876–7. Cf. *R. v. Buzalek and Schiffer* [1991] Crim. LR 115, where the Court of Appeal said that, since the instant case turned largely on documents, it would be possible for the memories of witnesses to be charged by referring to these. It was important to distinguish between a case where what was going to be in issue at the trial was the recollection of witnesses about some event unsupported by documents, and a case which largely turned upon documents. If, after a period of six and a half years, a case was going to have to turn on what witnesses had seen in an affray, in the course of an assault, or in a road accident, the passage of time was going to be much more prejudicial than if there was relevant documentary evidence. See also *R. v. Norwich Crown Court, ex p. Belsham* [1992] 1 WLR 54, 69; *R. v. Bow Street Metropolitan Stipendiary Magistrate, ex p. DPP* (1992) 95 Cr. App. R. 9, 16–17.

[136] Schneider, 'The Right to a Speedy Trial', 499.

[137] [1992] 1 WLR 54, 69. See also *R. v. Bow Street Magistrates' Court, ex p. Watts* [1991] COD 87 and *R. v. Cheltenham JJ, ex p. Millin* [1992] COD 108. Cf. *R. v. Bow Street Stipendiary Magistrate, ex p. DPP and Cherry* (1989) 91 Cr. App. R. 283, 300: 'The mere fact that more than a thousand police officers know that their conduct is under investigation can, it seems to us, in no sense diminish the prejudice suffered by a particular officer against whom there was a prima facie case of the commission of a criminal offence at a very early stage of the investigation.'

[138] Cf. *Calvert* v. *Stoliznow*, unreported, 1980: 'If [the defendant] is served with a statement of claim promptly after the incidents giving rise to the litigation, he has the opportunity of

The death or disappearance, during the delay, of a person who would otherwise have been a vital witness (either for the defence or for the prosecution) may be a relevant factor. In the case of a potential defence witness the defence will have lost the opportunity of calling her as a witness, and in the case of a potential prosecution witness the opportunity of cross-examining her.

Finally, the prior attitude of the defendant to the delay is also a relevant factor. The fact that the defendant has acquiesced silently in the delay will make it difficult for her to assert that, as a result of the delay, there is a substantial risk that she has been left without a fair opportunity to defend herself. On the other hand, any efforts which she has made to secure a trial without further delay[139] will weigh in her favour. The stronger her efforts, the stronger the case for a stay of proceedings.

(b) Protection of Moral Integrity

Even where there is no danger of wrongful conviction, judicial legitimacy may none the less be compromised if improperly delayed proceedings were allowed to continue in certain circumstances. What is relevant here is what Wilson J. of the Canadian Supreme Court termed in *Mills* v. *R.* the 'psychological' and 'sociological' effects rather than the 'legal' effect of the delay.[140] We have adverted throughout this chapter to the possible effects of pre-trial executive delay on a person who has been 'accused' of a crime and is awaiting trial. Whether in jail or on bail, she is likely to suffer restraints on her liberty, stigmatization, loss of privacy, and considerable stress and anxiety.[141] Such considerations are by no means confined solely to postaccusation delay. Indeed, certain consequences of preaccusation delay may be more serious than those of postaccusation delay. It is possible, for example, that greater anxiety and concern may be felt by an individual who has not been formally indicted or arrested, 'for, to him, exoneration by a jury of his peers may be only a vague possibility lurking in the distant future'.[142]

---

consulting legal advisers, preparing his defence, marshalling his witnesses, obtaining statements from them, inspecting the scene (if such is relevant), etc.—all when time has not affected the observable, physical phenomena or the location and memories of his witnesses.'

[139] e.g. by attempting to obtain a court order requiring the police or prosecution (as the case may be) to act with greater expedition.

[140] (1986) 52 CR (3d) 1, 91–2.

[141] See *R.* v. *Guildhall JJ and DPP, ex p. Carson-Selman* (1983) 148 JPR 392, 396: 'It needs hardly [to] be said that where a prosecution is delayed (as this was and undoubtedly is) for a substantial period of time . . . [t]here is . . . acute embarrassment and not a little hardship. Each of these three applicants has had to change his form of employment, or become unemployed as the case may be. Each one of them is restricted in his movements. Carson-Selman, who has . . . his home in the United States, has had his movements restricted to a very significant extent.'

[142] *US* v. *Marion* 404 US 307, 330–1 (1971).

Thus the issue of whether, and to what extent, the defendant has suffered oppression (prior to trial) as a result of the delay should be considered in determining whether the proceedings ought to be stayed. In appropriate circumstances it may be considered that, in spite of the public interest in bringing the offender to conviction, the delay has, by causing the defendant to suffer oppression, anxiety, or concern, compromised the moral integrity of the criminal process to such an extent that the public interest still requires a stay of the proceedings.[143]

In considering this second limb of the principle of judicial legitimacy, it is to be noted that, in contrast to the position in relation to the first limb, the gravity of the offence charged is a relevant consideration. Thus the oppression, anxiety, or concern suffered by a defendant as a result of delay may be more readily tolerated if the offence charged is a serious rather than a minor one. However, this is not to suggest that prosecutions for certain types of offences can *never* be stayed on account of delay. It was suggested in one English case that, where the offence charged is a sexual one involving a young victim, it may be inappropriate, as a rule, for the proceedings to be stayed on account of delay:

It is difficult to envisage any circumstances in which it would be right for the court to conclude, in advance of hearing the complainant's evidence at trial, that a trial based on a delayed—even a very long-delayed—complaint by an alleged victim of sexual abuse within the home would amount to an abuse of the Court's process. In my judgment, applications to stay proceedings for abuse of process in cases such as this one are misconceived.[144]

This view has not, however, proved popular and has not been followed in subsequent cases.[145] The Divisional Court said recently that separate rules did not apply to cases of sexual offences; any suggestion that a particular category of prosecution could not constitute an abuse of process even where

---

[143] Contra the case of *Daventry District Council* v. *Olins* (1990) 154 JPR 478, where the Court apparently took the (in my submission incorrect) view that delayed proceedings can be stayed only on account of prejudice to the preparation of the defence; the anxiety, uncertainty, and distress suffered by a defendant as a result of delay is relevant only to the exercise of the sentencing discretion of the judge: 'The other factor referred to by the justices, namely that the respondent had suffered anxiety, uncertainty and distress because of the delay, is not one which, in my judgment, they could properly take into account in arriving at their decision. If guilt is proved, distress caused by needless delay may no doubt be a factor properly to be taken into account in determining the appropriate sentence, but it does not justify the dismissal of the prosecution case because it is not prejudicial to the preparation of the defence. If this second reason had been the sole or the main reason for the decision of the justices to dismiss the prosecution case, then in my judgment that decision could not stand. As it is, however, they made it plain this was merely an additional factor in their mind and that the reason for their decision was the prejudice to the defence caused by the delay and in particular by the withholding of the identity of the complainant' (ibid. 485).

[144] *R.* v. *LPB* (1990) 91 Cr. App. R. 359, 362 per Judge J. (Central Criminal Court).

[145] *R.* v. *Telford JJ, ex p. Badhan* [1991] 2 WLR 866; *R.* v. *JAK* [1992] Crim. LR 30; *R.* v. *Sheffield Stipendiary Magistrate, ex p. Stephens* (1992) 156 JPR 555.

there had been long delay, or delay causing prejudice and unfairness, had to be wrong. Each case must be decided on its own facts.[146] The Canadian Supreme Court, too, has stressed recently that in appropriate circumstances a stay of the proceedings on account of delay may be warranted notwithstanding that the offence charged is a serious one.[147]

CONCLUSION

The aim here has been to apply the principle of judicial legitimacy to the specific issue of the circumstances in which proceedings should be stayed on account of improper police or prosecutorial delay. Proceedings should be stayed on account of such delay if (1) there is a substantial risk that the delay has left the defendant without a fair opportunity to defend herself; and/or (2) the continuation of the delayed proceedings would compromise the moral integrity of the criminal process to such a degree that a stay should be ordered notwithstanding the public interest in bringing offenders to conviction. In many cases in which a stay is ordered on account of delay, both bases for a stay will be satisfied. It should be emphasized, however, that, even if it is concluded that only one of the two bases is satisfied, a stay must none the less be ordered.

Problems such as delay, as acknowledged earlier in the chapter, often flow from a serious lack of resources, and courts are notoriously unwilling to make decisions which are potentially embarrassing to the executive. It is to be hoped that the discussions in this chapter will have demonstrated that,

---

[146] R. v. *Sheffield Stipendiary Magistrate, ex p. Stephens* (1992) 156 JPR 564.

[147] R. v. *Askov* (1990) 79 CR (3d) 273, 314 per Cory J: 'I am well aware that, as a consequence of this decision, a stay of proceedings must be directed. That is, to say the least, most unfortunate and regrettable. It is obvious that the charges against the appellants are serious. Extortion and threatened armed violence tear at the basic fabric of society. To accede to such conduct would constitute a denial of the rule of law and an acceptance of a rule that unlawful might makes right. The community has good reason to be alarmed by the commission of serious crimes. There can be no doubt that it would be in the best interest of society to proceed with the trial of those who are charged with posing such a serious threat to the community. Yet that trial can be undertaken only if the Charter right to trial within a reasonable time has not been infringed. In this case that right has been grievously infringed and the sad result is that a stay of proceedings must be entered. To conclude otherwise would render meaningless a right enshrined in the Charter as the supreme law of the land.'

[148] See *Jago* v. *District Court (NSW)* (1989) 168 CLR 23, 31–2 per Mason CJ: 'A court may order that a trial be expedited where it sees the delay as warranting such action but not as being of such a kind as to justify staying the proceedings. . . . In deciding whether to make such an order, a court will inevitably give consideration to a range of matters, apart from the mere existence of delay, including whether the conduct of the accused has contributed to the delay, whether the accused has pressed for expedition in a manner consistent with the anxiety and concern he is said to be suffering, whether court resources are available for an expedited trial and whether the displacement of other trials is warranted. . . . It would be unwise to venture upon an abstract consideration, divorced from the concrete facts in specific cases, of the circumstances in which it would be appropriate to order expedition rather than a stay or vice versa.'

in appropriate circumstances, precisely such decisions do need to be made. I am not suggesting that the discretion to stay proceedings represents the only solution to the problem of pre-trial delay. On the contrary, it is of relevance only in situations where delay has occurred, and judicial legitimacy would be compromised *if the proceedings were allowed to continue*. In some circumstances it may be sufficient for the court to take less drastic steps than staying the proceedings, such as making an order that the trial be expedited,[148] releasing the accused on bail, excluding certain evidence, giving appropriate directions to the jury, or taking the delay into account at the sentencing stage.[149] It is only where nothing short of a stay would suffice to prevent judicial legitimacy from being compromised that a stay should be granted.

Furthermore, what is required, as a supplement to the abuse of process discretion and the other powers of the court, is the enactment of specific time limits beyond which a criminal trial cannot commence without leave. 'Setting specific time limits on criminal prosecutions . . . has the advantage of nominating, in advance, a determinate period within which the prosecuting authority must bring the matter to court, rather than having the period assessed as excessive after the event.'[150] To its credit, the English criminal justice system has, as we have seen, made considerable advancements in relation to the setting of time limits. However, statutory provisions of the complexity of the Speedy Trial Act 1974 in the US Federal jurisdiction (discussed above) are as yet unknown in England. Time limits should be set realistically and with due regard to the capacity of the criminal justice system. They should be aimed at ensuring that the criminal justice system functions efficiently at full capacity, rather than at forcing the system to achieve standards of which it is incapable.[151]

---

[149] See *R. v. Derby Crown Court, ex p. Brooks* (1984) 80 Cr. App. R. 164, 169: 'We are however well aware that in other respects the applicant has suffered considerable hardship as a result of the delay which has taken place in this case . . . The fact is however that this can and should form part of an effective plea in mitigation of sentence when the time comes. These proceedings have been hanging over Mr Brooks's head for a very long time. No doubt his sentence for the value added tax offences which, had the prosecution been in a position to proceed with the main charges, would have been made concurrent with his sentence on those charges, will be taken into account, together with the fact that he would by now probably have served the greater part, if not all, of his sentence.' See also R. Pattenden, 'The Power of the Courts to Stay a Criminal Prosecution' [1985] *Criminal Law Review* 175, 186.

[150] R. G. Fox, 'Criminal Delay as Abuse of Process' (1990) 16 *Monash University Law Review* 64, 66–7.

[151] Hodge, 'The Process of Abuse', 230, suggests that statutory time limits should be accompanied by provision for their extension on a number of grounds: 'Statutory time limits should be imposed to govern a period between charge and committal, and committal and trial. Obviously there should be provision for these periods to be extended by a trial judge ex parte, if the accused has escaped, by consent inter-parties, or in the interests of justice on the application of either party.'

4

Police Impropriety at the Investigatory Stage

The issue of police misconduct in the course of criminal investigation is one which has received much attention in recent times. One question which has not generally been addressed, however, is the extent to which a prosecution may be stayed as an abuse of process on account of police impropriety at the investigatory stage. In England, circumvention by the police of proper extradition procedures in securing the presence of the defendant from outside the jurisdiction has been essentially the only kind of malpractice to have raised the issue. There are, of course, certain traditional avenues of redress available to victims of police misconduct in the shape of civil[1] and criminal actions against the police, and complaints procedures.[2] Further, where the impropriety has led to the obtaining of evidence and the suspect is subsequently prosecuted, she may in certain circumstances be able to seek the exclusion of the evidence from the trial. It will be argued, however, that a stay of proceedings should also be recognized as an entirely appropriate part of the weaponry available to a court for dealing with pre-trial investigatory misconduct by the police. A discretion to stay proceedings on account of such misconduct will be shown to be an obvious corollary of a discretion to exclude improperly obtained evidence. Accordingly, extensive reference will be made in this chapter to the latter discretion.

The 'Illegal Extradition' Cases

As a preliminary to discussion of the English cases on illegal extradition,[3] it

---

[1] The most common tort actions are likely to be for assault, false imprisonment, malicious prosecution, trespass to land, and seizure of goods, the elements of which have been adequately discussed by a number of commentators. See in particular D. Feldman, *The Law Relating to Entry, Search and Seizure* (1986), ch. 15; J. Harrison and S. Cragg, *Police Misconduct: Legal Remedies* (2nd edn., 1991), ch. 5; L. Lustgarten, *The Governance of Police* (1986), 132–8.

[2] PACE, Pt. IX.

[3] For further discussion of the English cases, see generally P. O'Higgins, 'Unlawful Seizure and Irregular Extradition' (1960) 36 *British Yearbook of International Law* 279; J. K. Bentil, 'When Extradition Masquerades as Deportation' (1983) 127 *Solicitors' Journal* 604; A. N. Khan, 'Trial without Extradition—Abuse of Court's Process' [1986] *New Zealand Law*

is convenient to look at the decision of the New Zealand Court of Appeal in *R. v. Hartley.*[4] Proper extradition procedures were not followed in securing the presence in New Zealand of one of the co-defendants, Bennett, who was arrested in Australia by the Melbourne police and placed on the next flight to New Zealand. The New Zealand police had not obtained a warrant for Bennett's extradition, but had simply telephoned the Melbourne police to ask them to place Bennett on the next flight to New Zealand. The Court of Appeal held, applying *R. v. O/C Depot Battalion, RASC, Colchester, ex p. Elliott,*[5] that these circumstances did not rob the trial court of jurisdiction to try Bennett: 'although Bennett was brought here unlawfully, he was eventually lawfully arrested within the country and then by due process of law he was brought before the Court.'[6] However, the Court of Appeal considered that the trial judge would probably have been justified, had the appropriate application been made, to exercise his discretion, either under section 347(3) of the Crimes Act 1961 (NZ) or pursuant to the 'abuse of process' power recognized in *Connelly,* to direct that the accused be discharged:

In our opinion there can be no possible question here of the Court turning a blind eye to action of the New Zealand police which has deliberately ignored those imperative requirements of the statute. Some may say that in the present case a New Zealand citizen attempted to avoid a criminal responsibility by leaving the country: that his subsequent conviction has demonstrated the utility of the short cut adopted by the police to have him brought back. But this must never become an area where it will be sufficient to consider that the end has justified the means. The issues raised by this affair are basic to the whole concept of freedom in society.[7]

In other words, the nature of the illegality meant that the proceedings should be stayed notwithstanding the public interest in bringing the offender to conviction. To allow the prosecution to proceed would involve the court in turning a blind eye to the flagrant illegality. *Hartley* thus provides a recognition of the utility of the abuse of process discretion as an instrument for dealing with executive misconduct which occurred at the investigatory stage.[8]

Journal 123; A. N. Khan, 'Extradition in the Guise of Deportation' (1986) 130 *Solicitors' Journal* 657; A. L.-T. Choo, 'The Consequences of Illegal Extradition' [1992] *Criminal Law Review* 490.
 For the position in South Africa, see M. G. Cowling, 'Unmasking "Disguised" Extradition— Some Glimmer of Hope' (1992) 109 *South African Law Journal* 241.

[4] [1978] 2 NZLR 199.   [5] [1949] 1 All ER 373.
[6] [1978] 2 NZLR 199, 215.   [7] Ibid. 216–17.
[8] But see *Moevao v. Department of Labour* [1980] 1 NZLR 464, in which Richmond P., who had been one of the members of the Court of Appeal in *Hartley,* said (ibid. 470): 'I am now inclined to the view that Bennett's case could not have been properly disposed of on the basis that the prosecution was an abuse of process. That is because I now see difficulty in using the oppressive conduct of the police towards Bennett to support an argument that the process

A similar issue arose in England in *R. v. Bow Street Magistrates, ex p. Mackeson*.[9] The applicant, a British citizen, was in Zimbabwe–Rhodesia when allegations of fraud were made against him in the United Kingdom. The Metropolitan Police did not request the authorities in Zimbabwe–Rhodesia to extradite him, because at the time the *de facto* government of Rhodesia was in rebellion against the Crown and considered illegal. Instead, the Metropolitan Police informed the authorities in Zimbabwe–Rhodesia that the applicant was wanted in England in connection with fraud charges. The applicant was arrested in Zimbabwe–Rhodesia and a deportation order made against him. He was accordingly returned to the United Kingdom. On his application to the Divisional Court for an order of prohibition to prevent the hearing of committal proceedings against him in the Magistrates' Court, it was held, on the basis of *Hartley*, that the circumstances of the applicant's return had amounted to an 'extradition by the back door',[10] and that his application should accordingly be granted. This was despite the fact that the Metropolitan Police had 'no doubt' acted 'due to an excess of enthusiasm, certainly not due to any conscious intent to do wrong'.[11]

The following year, *Mackeson* was distinguished in *R. v. Guildford Magistrates' Court, ex p. Healy*[12] on the basis that there had been no attempt in *Healy* to circumvent the provisions of the relevant extradition treaty. There was, the Divisional Court found, no ground for supposing that the police had tried to persuade the US authorities to deport the applicant so that they could arrest him in this country.[13]

The authority of *Mackeson* and *Healy* has been, however, thrown into doubt by the decision of the Divisional Court in *R. v. Plymouth Magistrates' Court, ex p. Driver*.[14] This is particularly surprising in the light of the fact that one of the judges in *Mackeson* had remarked that 'in my view the principles to be applied in a case of this nature are now well established'.[15] Driver, who was wanted for questioning in the United Kingdom about a murder, had travelled to Turkey, with which the United Kingdom had no extradition treaty. The UK police informed the Turkish authorities that, if it was within their power, the deportation of Driver to the United Kingdom would be helpful. The Turkish authorities held Driver in custody for four days, and then informed him that he was to be released as the UK police were no longer interested in him. He was told to leave Turkey and placed on a flight to London. On his arrival in London, he was arrested and charged

---

of the Supreme Court was itself being abused.' He, however, added: 'The question whether illegal or "unfair" conduct by the police in the course of investigating a crime can so taint a subsequent prosecution as to render it an abuse of process must remain for determination in a suitable case.' Note that in the same case Woodhouse J., who also had been a member of the Court of Appeal in *Hartley*, stood by the opinion of the Court in *Hartley* (ibid. 476).

⁹ (1981) 75 Cr. App. R. 24.   ¹⁰ Ibid. 30.   ¹¹ Ibid. 33.
¹² [1983] 1 WLR 108.   ¹³ Ibid. 112.   ¹⁴ [1985] 2 All ER 681.
¹⁵ (1981) 75 Cr. App. R. 24, 34 per Michael Davies J.

with murder. He applied to the Divisional Court for an order of certiorari to quash the murder charge, and for an order of prohibition to prevent the hearing of the committal proceedings.

It was concluded that *Mackeson* and *Healy* had been decided per incuriam,[16] and that a court had in fact no power to inquire into the circumstances in which a person was found in the jurisdiction, for the purpose of refusing to try her.[17] This conclusion of the Divisional Court was reached by a questionable application of the doctrine of stare decisis, and without any consideration of issues of principle. The reasoning of the Court,[18] essentially, was that the New Zealand Court of Appeal in *Hartley* had been wrong to treat the decision in *R. v. O/C Depot Battalion, RASC, Colchester, ex p. Elliott*[19] as authority *only* for the proposition that a court had jurisdiction to try a prisoner found within its territory. In actual fact, the Court pointed out, Lord Goddard CJ in *Elliott* had dealt with other points including an allegation of unreasonable delay. This meant, the Court in *Driver* thought, that Lord Goddard must have had in mind the questions both of 'jurisdiction' and of 'discretion'. Thus, in the view of the Court in *Driver*, *Elliott* stood not only for the proposition that impropriety in bringing a prisoner into the country did not deprive a court of jurisdiction, but also for the proposition that such impropriety could not lead to a stay of proceedings in the exercise of discretion.

There are two problems with the reasoning of the Court in *Driver*. First, even if Lord Goddard CJ had indeed had in mind the question of 'discretion' in addition to the question of 'jurisdiction', it does not follow that the way in which he exercised this 'discretion' should not be reconsidered. For example, Lord Goddard CJ said in relation to the allegation of unreasonable delay that

if a man is kept an unreasonable time awaiting trial to such an extent that this court thinks it is oppressive, they can interfere and admit him to bail . . . the condition of the bail being that he shall surrender at the court martial when he receives notice that that court is to proceed. That is the utmost extent to which this court could go.[20]

In recent times, however, it has become clear that to admit a defendant to bail is not the utmost extent to which a court can go in dealing with oppressive delay; as we have seen in the preceding chapter, such delay can now lead to a stay of proceedings. By the same token, the fact that illegal extradition may have been incapable of leading to a stay of proceedings in Lord Goddard's day is no reason why it should still be incapable of doing so today.

The other problem with the reasoning of the Court in *Driver* is that discussion of issues of principle was completely eschewed. No attempt was

---

[16] [1985] 2 All ER 681, 698. [17] Ibid. 697. [18] Ibid. 695.
[19] [1949] 1 All ER 373. [20] Ibid. 379.

made to justify, in principle, the holding that a court should not inquire into the circumstances in which an accused person was brought into the jurisdiction.

It should be noted that, even though the reasoning in *Driver* can be challenged, the result itself may be justifiable. In particular, two points may be said to distinguish *Driver* from *Mackeson*. First, it will be recalled that, in *Mackeson*, there had been a deliberate attempt by the English authorities to circumvent proper extradition procedures because at the time the *de facto* government of Rhodesia was in rebellion against the Crown and considered illegal. In *Driver*, however, there was no evidence of improper dealing on the part of the English authorities leading to the illegal extradition of the applicant from Turkey. 'All that the Devon and Cornwall police did was, first, to inquire of the whereabouts of the suspected person and, second, to invite the Turkish authorities *acting within their powers* to make such arrangements as would enable the Devon and Cornwall police to interview the fugitive.'[21] Secondly, what was being investigated in *Driver* was a murder. Accordingly it is arguable that, in view of the seriousness of the offence charged, the public interest required that the proceedings should be allowed to continue.[22] Thus, even though the reasoning in *Driver* is flawed, the result itself may be justifiable.

The principle in *Driver* would appear to have been endorsed recently by the Divisional Court in *R. v. Horseferry Road Magistrates' Court, ex p. Bennett*.[23] In this case it was accepted that a court had no power to inquire into the circumstances whereby a criminal defendant had been brought within the jurisdiction. The appropriate remedy for being brought into the jurisdiction by unlawful means was, the Court thought, to be obtained by invoking rights under international law or pursuing a civil remedy.

In the light of this uncertainty in the state of the law, one would have been grateful for a consideration of the issue by the Court of Appeal or House of Lords. Sadly, such consideration has not been forthcoming. In *R. v. Bateman and Cooper*,[24] the Court of Appeal expressly declined to resolve the *Mackeson/Driver* conflict. The applicants were each convicted upon two

---

[21] [1985] 2 All ER 681, 690 (emphasis in original).

[22] It is interesting to note that a number of cases involving illegal extradition have come to public attention not so much because of the circumstances of the illegal extraditions, as because of the gravity of the offences charged. See e.g., the case of Adolf Eichmann: *A-G of the Government of Israel v. Eichmann* (1961) 36 ILR 5 (affirmed by the Supreme Court of Israel in (1962) 36 ILR 277); J. E. S. Fawcett, 'The *Eichmann* Case' (1962) 38 *British Yearbook of International Law* 181. For further discussion of issues associated with illegal extradition, see C. V. Cole, 'Extradition Treaties Abound but Unlawful Seizures Continue' (1975) 9 *Law Society Gazette* 177; D. Lanham, 'Informal Extradition in Australian Law' (1987) 11 *Criminal Law Journal* 3; C. E. Lewis, 'Unlawful Arrest: A Bar to the Jurisdiction of the Court, or Mala Captus Bene Detentus? Sidney Jaffe: A Case in Point' (1986) 28 *Criminal Law Quarterly* 341; S. A. Williams, 'Comment' (1975) 53 *Canadian Bar Review* 404.

[23] *The Times*, 1 Sept. 1992.

[24] [1989] Crim. LR 590 (transcript available on LEXIS).

counts of conspiracy to handle stolen goods and upon two counts of conspiracy to obtain property by deception. One of the twenty-eight grounds on which they sought leave to appeal was that their deportation from New Zealand had been unlawful because it had been a disguised extradition. Accordingly, it was argued, the trial court should have stayed the proceedings. The Court of Appeal considered that it was unnecessary to resolve the *Mackeson/Driver* conflict in the present case because there was no evidence to support the proposition that the deportation had been a disguised extradition: the applicants had simply been deported by the New Zealand authorities. Further, the issue had not been raised at trial.

More recently, the Court of Appeal was faced in *R. v. Gilmore*[25] with a similar problem. Gilmore sold to an innocent buyer a car which he had obtained on hire-purchase. He went to live in Northern Ireland, and the English police obtained a warrant for his arrest there under section 38(3) of the Criminal Law Act 1977. An arrangement was made whereby he would be arrested and taken by the Royal Ulster Constabulary police to Belfast airport to await the arrival of English police officers. As it turned out, however, the warrant of arrest was executed by English officers, rather than by RUC officers as required under the 1977 Act. Gilmore's application for a stay of the proceedings was rejected by the trial judge, and he pleaded guilty to the charge of obtaining property by deception. He then applied for leave to appeal against conviction.

The Court of Appeal refused the application on the basis that, as any breach of the 1977 Act in this case was purely technical, the trial judge had not erred in allowing the proceedings to continue. The Court of Appeal commented that, although the case had been argued on the *assumption* that there was a judicial discretion to stay proceedings on account of illegal extradition, it was in fact still an open question whether this discretion existed. In other words, the Court accepted that there was a conflict between *Mackeson* on the one hand and *Driver* on the other.

The English position in relation to whether proceedings may be stayed as an abuse of process on account of illegal extradition is, therefore, not as yet completely settled. For the moment, however, it may be assumed that the *Driver* principle has prevailed over the *Mackeson* principle. Of interest, from a comparative perspective, is the US position on the consequences of illegal extradition.[26] In *Ker v. Illinois*[27] the Supreme Court accepted the proposition that

[25] [1992] Crim. LR 67.
[26] See generally Y. G. Grassie, 'Federally Sponsored International Kidnapping: An Acceptable Alternative to Extradition?' (1986) 64 *Washington University Law Quarterly* 1205; R. L. King, 'The International Silver Platter and the "Shocks the Conscience" Test: US Law Enforcement Overseas' (1989) 67 *Washington University Law Quarterly* 489; Note, 'The Extraterritorial Applicability of the Fourth Amendment' (1989) 102 *Harvard Law Review* 1672; S. A. Saltzburg, 'The Reach of the Bill of Rights Beyond the *Terra Firma* of the United

forcible seizure in another country, and transfer by violence, force or fraud to this country . . . is no sufficient reason why the party should not answer when brought within the jurisdiction of the court which has the right to try him for such an offense, and presents no valid objection to his trial in such court.[28]

This was reaffirmed by the Court in 1952, in the case of *Frisbie* v. *Collins*,[29] and in the recent case of *US* v. *Alvarez-Machain*.[30] In *Alvarez-Machain* the Supreme Court expressly answered the question of 'whether a criminal defendant, abducted to the United States from a nation with which it has an extradition treaty, thereby acquires a defense to the jurisdiction of this country's courts'[31] in the negative. This is, of course, no different from the English position, as was seen earlier.

However, in the United States, a qualification to the principle would appear to have been articulated by the Court of Appeals in *US* v. *Toscanino*.[32] In doing so the Court relied largely upon due-process principles.[33] A classic illustration of the application of due-process principles in a case involving pre-trial police illegality is to be found in the decision of the Supreme Court in *Rochin* v. *California*.[34] After police officers, having information that the defendant was selling narcotics, illegally entered his dwelling, he swallowed two capsules containing morphine. He was taken to a hospital where, at the direction of one of the officers, and against his will, a doctor forced an emetic solution through a tube into his stomach. The defendant was convicted of illegal possession of morphine. The Supreme Court held that this conviction should be reversed because the methods by which it had been obtained offended due process. In a remarkable passage, the Court stated: 'we are compelled to conclude that the proceedings by which this conviction was obtained do more than offend some fastidious squeamishness or private sentimentalism about combatting crime too energetically. This is conduct that shocks the conscience.'[35]

The facts in *Toscanino* were as follows. The defendant had been allegedly kidnapped from his home in Montevideo, Uruguay, by US agents, detained for three weeks of interrogation accompanied by physical torture in Brazil, and then brought to the United States. It was acknowledged by the Court of

States', in R. B. Lillich (ed.), *International Aspects of Criminal Law: Enforcing United States Law in the World Community (Fourth Sokol Colloquium)* (1981); S. H. Theisen, 'Evidence Seized in Foreign Searches: When Does the Fourth Amendment Exclusionary Rule Apply?' (1983) 25 *William and Mary Law Review* 161.

[27] 119 US 436 (1886). For criticism of the decision, see E. D. Dickinson, 'Jurisdiction Following Seizure or Arrest in Violation of International Law' (1934) 28 *American Journal of International Law* 231.   [28] 119 US 436, 444 (1886).

[29] 342 US 519 (1952). See also *Gerstein* v. *Pugh* 420 US 103, 119 (1975).

[30] 112 S. Ct. 2188 (1992).   [31] Ibid. 2190.

[32] 500 F. 2d 267 (2nd Cir. 1974).

[33] See Ch. 3 n. 74, where the due-process clauses of the Fifth and Fourteenth Amendments are quoted.   [34] 342 US 165 (1952).   [35] Ibid. 172.

Appeals that, if proved, these actions would have violated two international treaties obliging the US Government to respect the territorial sovereignty of Uruguay. The Court considered that due process required a court to divest itself of jurisdiction over a defendant whose presence had been secured as the result of the government's deliberate, unnecessary, and unreasonable invasion of her constitutional rights. Accordingly, Toscanino should be entitled to some relief if his allegations were true.[36] The case was remanded to the district court for further proceedings not inconsistent with this opinion.[37]

In subsequent cases, however, courts have striven to confine the *Toscanino* decision within strict boundaries. *US ex rel. Lujan* v. *Gengler*[38] is illustrative. Lujan contended that his abduction in Bolivia by Bolivian police acting as paid agents of the United States, and subsequent placement on a flight bound for the United States, violated due process. At no time had a request for extradition been made by the United States, nor had he been formally charged by the Bolivian police. The Court distinguished *Toscanino* on the ground that 'the cruel, inhuman and outrageous treatment allegedly suffered by Toscanino [at the hands of US agents] brought his case within the *Rochin* principle'.[39] In the present case, however, there was no allegation of governmental conduct sufficient to convert a simply illegal abduction into one which violated due process. Indeed, Lujan suffered no greater deprivation than he would have endured through lawful extradition.[40] Thus the position would appear to be that, where illegal extradition is accompanied by torture, brutality, or similar physical abuse *by US agents*, due process is violated; otherwise, the holdings of the Supreme Court in *Ker* and *Frisbie* apply.[41] This position has been reiterated by courts in a number of subsequent cases.[42] For example, it was held in *US* v. *Lira* that due process had not been violated where, on the request of the US Government for the arrest and expulsion of the defendant from Chile, the defendant was arrested and tortured by the Chilean police before being expelled:

Unlike *Toscanino*, where the defendant was kidnapped from Uruguay in defiance of the laws of the country, here the Government merely asked the Chilean Government to arrest and expel Mellafe [Lira's true name] in accord with its own procedures. This action can hardly be faulted. Agencies such as the DEA presumably must cooperate with many foreign governments in seeking transfer to the United States of violators of United States law. The DEA can hardly be expected to monitor the conduct of representatives of each foreign government to assure that a request for

[36] 500 F. 2d 267, 275–6 (2nd Cir. 1974). [37] Ibid. 281.
[38] 510 F. 2d 62 (2nd Cir. 1975). [39] Ibid. 65–6. [40] Ibid. 66.
[41] Ibid. 69.
[42] See *US* v. *Lira* 515 F. 2d 68 (2nd Cir. 1975); *US* v. *Valot* 625 F. 2d 308 (9th Cir. 1980); *Weddell* v. *Meierhenry* 636 F. 2d 211 (8th Cir. 1980); *US* v. *Reed* 639 F. 2d 896 (2nd Cir. 1981); *US* v. *Cordero* 668 F. 2d 32, 36 (1st Cir. 1981).

extradition or expulsion is carried out in accordance with American constitutional standards.[43]

Thus it would seem highly unlikely that the *Toscanino* principle would often be given practical application. What is significant, however, is that US law, unlike its English counterpart, has acknowledged that proof of illegal extradition *can* bar a trial in appropriate circumstances.

Cases of illegal extradition provide an illustration of situations in which the entire prosecution has been commenced in consequence of police impropriety at the investigatory stage. The impropriety does not, therefore, relate merely to a specific item of prosecution evidence, but to the proceedings as a whole. To put it more simply, the entire prosecution, and not just a particular item of evidence, represents the 'fruit' of the impropriety. It is in this respect that the exclusion of evidence which has been improperly obtained, and a stay of proceedings which have been made possible by an illegal extradition, share the same foundation. Both measures effectively deprive the prosecution of whatever 'fruit' its impropriety happens to have produced—evidence in one case, the entire prosecution in the other.[44] It might be expected, therefore, that the judicial attitude to the exclusion of improperly obtained evidence would shed useful light upon the illegal extradition issue.

There are, essentially, three possible solutions to the problem of whether proceedings should be stayed on account of illegal extradition. The first solution is to insist that proceedings should never be stayed on account of illegal extradition, whatever the circumstances.[45] Such an approach is consistent with a policy of mandatory inclusion of improperly obtained evidence—that is, the admission of all relevant and reliable evidence regardless of the manner in which it was obtained.[46] Advocates of such an approach would argue that the impropriety 'is by no means condoned' but 'is merely ignored',[47] as 'it is irrelevant at this stage. It is properly a matter for separate inquiry or a subsequent action.'[48] To conduct collateral inquiries into improprieties which occurred during criminal investigation offends the administration of justice 'by interrupting, delaying, and confusing the investigation in hand, for the sake of a matter which is not a

---

[43] 515 F. 2d 68, 71 (2nd Cir. 1975).

[44] See also J. Hunter, ' "Tainted" Proceedings: Censuring Police Illegalities' (1985) 59 *Australian Law Journal* 709; D. M. Paciocco, 'The Stay of Proceedings as a Remedy in Criminal Cases: Abusing the Abuse of Process Concept' (1991) 15 *Criminal Law Journal* 315.

[45] This solution can be seen as reflecting the 'crime control' model of the criminal process: see generally H. L. Packer, *The Limits of the Criminal Sanction* (1969), 158–63.

[46] Ashworth has called this the 'reliability principle' (see A. J. Ashworth, 'Excluding Evidence as Protecting Rights' [1977] *Criminal Law Review* 723, 723–4).

[47] J. H. Wigmore, 'Using Evidence Obtained by Illegal Search and Seizure' (1922) 8 *American Bar Association Journal* 479, 479.

[48] J. A. Andrews, 'Involuntary Confessions and Illegally Obtained Evidence in Criminal Cases—I' [1963] *Criminal Law Review* 15, 17.

part of it'.[49] 'Criminal courts exist for the protection of society, and they fail this purpose, this duty, if they release a prisoner in the face of evidence of his guilt because another has failed the same duty.'[50] The concern of a trial judge is with the guilt or innocence of the particular accused. The judge

does not hold court in a street-car to do summary justice upon a fellow-passenger who fraudulently evades payment of his fare; and, upon the same principle, he does not attempt, in the course of a specific litigation, to investigate and punish all offences which incidentally cross the path of that litigation. Such a practice might be consistent with the primitive system of justice under an Arabian sheikh; but it does not comport with our own system of law.[51]

The second possible solution is to adopt the other 'extreme' position: proceedings commenced in consequence of an illegal extradition must automatically be stayed.[52] Like the first solution, such a rule has the advantage of being relatively easy to apply. Once it is determined that the proceedings have been commenced in consequence of an illegal extradition, they must be stayed regardless of the circumstances.

The third solution is essentially a 'compromise' one, and treats the problem as one to be resolved in the circumstances of the particular case. Thus, proceedings should be stayed on account of illegal extradition in some cases but not in others.

As a background to determining which of the three possible solutions should be adopted, it is instructive to examine the problem of improperly obtained evidence in some detail. We shall see that the major Anglo-American legal systems have all abandoned rules of mandatory inclusion and mandatory exclusion of improperly obtained evidence in favour of more flexible positions whereby such evidence is to be admitted in some circumstances but excluded in others. This suggests that rules of mandatory inclusion and mandatory exclusion have been perceived to be undesirable. Why this is so will be explored, as analogous reasons would account for why it would be inappropriate to adopt an inflexible rule that proceedings which represent the fruit of investigatory misconduct should either automatically be allowed to continue, or automatically be stayed. The identification of an underlying principle which is capable of accommodating the fact that such proceedings are to be allowed to continue in some circumstances, but stayed in others, is clearly required. It will be argued that this principle is the principle of judicial legitimacy—the same principle that should be applied in determining the admissibility of improperly obtained evidence.

[49] J. H. Wigmore, 'Using Evidence Obtained by Illegal Search and Seizure', 479.
[50] W. T. Plumb, jun., 'Illegal Enforcement of the Law' (1939) 24 *Cornell Law Quarterly* 337, 378.   [51] Wigmore, 'Using Evidence Obtained by Illegal Search and Seizure', 479.
[52] This solution can be seen as reflecting the 'due process' model of the criminal process: see generally Packer, *The Limits of the Criminal Sanction*, 163–73.

THE EXCLUSION OF IMPROPERLY OBTAINED EVIDENCE

A RETREAT FROM EXTREME POSITIONS

(a) Mandatory Inclusion

Early English cases on improperly obtained evidence[53] simply emphasized that such evidence had to be admitted, and made no mention of the existence of any exclusionary discretion.[54] However, the Privy Council had acknowledged by the 1950s that improperly obtained evidence could be excluded in the discretion of the trial judge if its admission would be unfair to the accused.[55] Now, section 78 of PACE provides evidence of legislative recognition that improperly obtained evidence should not be admitted whatever the circumstances.[56]

It is, however, in Canada that the retreat from mandatory inclusion has occurred particularly strikingly. Prior to the enactment of the Canadian Charter of Rights and Freedoms in 1982, the Canadian approach to the problem of improperly obtained evidence had been embodied in the decision of the Supreme Court in *R. v. Wray*.[57] The majority in *Wray* adopted, in effect, a rule of mandatory inclusion. However, section 24(2) of the Charter now requires improperly obtained evidence to be excluded if its admission 'would bring the administration of justice into disrepute'.[58]

A brief examination of the attitude in Germany[59] to the problem of improperly obtained evidence shows that even the criminal courts in an inquisitorial system have found it necessary to evolve an exclusionary

---

[53] See A. L.-T. Choo, 'Improperly Obtained Evidence: A Reconsideration' (1989) 9 *Legal Studies* 261, which is based on my earlier views on the issues.

[54] See generally *R. v. Warickshall* (1783) 1 Leach 263; *R. v. Griffin* (1809) Russ. & Ry. 151; *R. v. Gould* (1840) 9 Car. & P. 364; *R. v. Berriman* (1854) 6 Cox CC 388; *R. v. Leatham* (1861) 8 Cox CC 498.   [55] *Kuruma* v. R. [1955] AC 197.

[56] S. 78 will be discussed in greater detail later.   [57] (1970) 11 DLR (3d) 673.

[58] S. 24(2) will be discussed in greater detail later.

[59] Some of the problems associated with comparative study are noted by M. Damaška, 'Evidentiary Barriers to Conviction and Two Models of Criminal Procedure: A Comparative Study' (1973) 121 *University of Pennsylvania Law Review* 506, 509: 'Within each of the two general legal systems, that of common law and that of civil law, proof processes change as we move from jurisdiction to jurisdiction. It is therefore only on a rather general level that styles of factfinding exhibit certain common characteristics. Nor are evidentiary rules applied with equal rigor in all types of criminal cases, even within a single jurisdiction. An additional difficulty resides in the fact that, at least at first blush, there is so much highly complex law on the common law side and so little law on the civil law side. Also, there is in the law of evidence a very pronounced disparity between the law on the books and actual practice. Everywhere so many tendencies seem to be at work, often operating in opposite directions, that one is tempted to suspect that a kind of self-canceling Brownian motion may be the end-result. Finally, conceptual tools and systematic arrangements in the civil and common law differ so widely in the evidentiary field, that one finds oneself groping for common denominators in order to make issues comparable.'

doctrine.[60] As Professor Arenella has pointed out, the traditional view of a criminal trial in an inquisitorial system is that its main objective is 'truth discovery', with the role of the judge being to 'discover the truth by examining all sources of relevant information, including the defendant'.[61] There is much about the German prosecution system which reflects this philosophy.[62] The principle of *Legalitätsprinzip*, or compulsory prosecution, requires that the public prosecutor pursue every significant crime.[63] Section 244(II) of the German Code of Criminal Procedure provides: 'In order to explore *the truth* the court shall on its own motion extend the reception of the evidence to *all facts* and to *all means of proof which are important for the decision*.'[64] Further evidence that 'the basic purpose of a

[60] As my purpose here is not to provide a detailed description of the German position in relation to improperly obtained evidence, only secondary sources have been relied upon for the material presented here. The following have been consulted: P. Arenella, 'Rethinking the Functions of Criminal Procedure: The Warren and Burger Courts' Competing Ideologies' (1983) 72 *Georgetown Law Journal* 185; C. M. Bradley, 'The Exclusionary Rule in Germany' (1983) 96 *Harvard Law Review* 1032; J. H. Langbein, 'Controlling Prosecutorial Discretion in Germany' (1974) 41 *University of Chicago Law Review* 439; Y.-M. Morissette, 'The Exclusion of Evidence under the *Canadian Charter of Rights and Freedoms*: What to Do and What Not to Do' (1984) 29 *McGill Law Journal* 521; W. Pakter, 'Exclusionary Rules in France, Germany, and Italy' (1985) 9 *Hastings International and Comparative Law Review* 1; B. F. Shanks, 'Comparative Analysis of the Exclusionary Rule and its Alternatives' (1983) 57 *Tulane Law Review* 648; J. H. Langbein, *Comparative Criminal Procedure: Germany* (1977); L. H. Leigh and L. Zedner, *The Royal Commission on Criminal Justice: A Report on the Administration of Criminal Justice in the Pre-Trial Phase in France and Germany* (1992); *The German Code of Criminal Procedure*, trans. H. Niebler (1965).
See also Damaška, 'Evidentiary Barriers to Conviction'.
[61] Arenella, 'Rethinking the Functions of Criminal Procedure', 206. See also M. R. Damaška, *The Faces of Justice and State Authority: A Comparative Approach to the Legal Process* (1986), 68: 'Continental judges are ideally still expected to anchor their decisions in a network of outcome-determinative rules; they are reluctant to "politicize" or "moralize" matters that come before them. . . . By contrast . . . [t]he American professional judiciary is notoriously politicized and expected to consider "the equities" of cases so that the door remains open to the consideration of various extralegal factors. Even in England, where professional judges are much more technically oriented than in America, Continental lawyers register their surprise at the apparent flexibility of the judiciary to respond to contours of individual cases in commonsensical ways.'
[62] Cf. the prosecution systems of Denmark, Sweden, and the Netherlands: see generally L. H. Leigh and J. E. Hall Williams, *The Management of the Prosecution Process in Denmark, Sweden and the Netherlands* (1981).
[63] S. 152(II) of the German Code of Criminal Procedure provides: 'Except as otherwise provided by law, [the prosecution] is obliged to take action in case of all acts which are punishable by a court and capable of prosecution, so far as there is a sufficient factual basis.' Pakter, 'Exclusionary Rules in France, Germany, and Italy', 39, points out: 'The "rule of compulsory prosecution" was itself a reflection of the "theory of absolute punishment" embodied in Kant's famous dictum requiring execution of the last murderer in prison as a duty of a society before that society disbands.' See also L. H. Leigh and L. Zedner, *The Royal Commission on Criminal Justice: A Report on the Administration of Criminal Justice in the Pre-Trial Phase in France and Germany* (1992), 57. The precise scope of the compulsory prosecution rule is considered by Langbein, 'Controlling Prosecutorial Discretion in Germany', who also examines the means adopted to enforce the rule.
[64] Emphasis added.

German criminal trial is to investigate thoroughly all the facts to arrive at the objective truth' is provided by the principle of 'unfettered evaluation of evidence *(freie Bewerswurdigung)*'.[65]

Not surprisingly, German law has been traditionally hostile to the exclusion of reliable evidence simply on the ground that it was improperly obtained. In recent times, however, there has emerged an exclusionary doctrine based on two constitutional principles, the *Rechtsstaatsprinzip* and the *Verhältnismässigkeit*. Under the *Rechtsstaatsprinzip* (principle of a state governed by the rule of law), police brutality or deceit in the seizure of evidence would lead automatically to the exclusion of the evidence. The purpose of exclusion is 'to preserve the purity of the judicial process *(Reinheit des Verefahrens)*'.[66] Considerations such as the probative value of the evidence and the seriousness of the offence charged are irrelevant. Where the evidence is not excluded under the *Rechtsstaatsprinzip*, the court must then consider the *Verhältnismässigkeit* (principle of proportionality). This requires the court to balance, on a case-by-case basis, such factors as the defendant's interests in privacy and whether less intrusive measures will have sufficed against the importance of the evidence and the seriousness of the offence charged.[67] 'One should not shoot sparrows with a cannon.'[68] The Federal Constitutional Court has developed a three-tiered analysis *(Dreistufentheorie)* to determine the admissibility of evidence under the *Verhältnismässigkeit*. First, evidence which would violate the most basic rights of an individual *(Kernbereich)* must be excluded irrespective of the seriousness of the offence charged. The second 'private' sphere *(Privatbereich)* can be intruded upon only in the event of an overriding public interest. Thirdly, evidence which would not violate the defendant's privacy rights—for example, a tape recording of a business meeting—cannot be excluded.[69]

A 1977 decision of the Federal Constitutional Court[70] is instructive. The case concerned the admissibility of medical records seized at a drug rehabilitation centre. It was held that, because the evidence had not been seized by means of brutality or deceit, the seizure did not violate the *Rechtsstaatsprinzip*. On considering the *Verhältnismässigkeit*, the Court held that the evidence fell into the second category of the *Dreistufentheorie*, the *Privatbereich*. Thus, the defendant's privacy could have been intruded upon only in the event of an overriding public interest. It was concluded that there had been no such interest, since the public itself had a strong interest in

---

[65] Shanks, 'Comparative Analysis of the Exclusionary Rule and its Alternatives', 667.
[66] Bradley, 'The Exclusionary Rule in Germany', 1042.   [67] Ibid. 1034, 1041.
[68] Morissette, 'The Exclusion of Evidence under the *Canadian Charter of Rights and Freedoms*', 530.
[69] See generally Bradley, 'The Exclusionary Rule in Germany', 1044 ff.
[70] See ibid. 1046–7.

encouraging people to seek treatment for drug addiction and other health problems.

The German position outlined above is only one example of the evolution of an exclusionary doctrine on the Continent; it should be noted that similar trends have been apparent in other jurisdictions such as France and Italy.[71]

But why has mandatory inclusion been generally abandoned in favour of the exclusion of improperly obtained evidence in certain circumstances? This abandonment clearly stems from a recognition that it is entirely inappropriate to regard a criminal trial as being concerned solely with determination of the 'truth'. The criminal trial is an integral part of the entire criminal justice system:

the governmental action for which a criminal court incurs responsibility is not merely the trial but the whole course of conduct called the prosecution. The trial is a part of the whole prosecution, just as the court is a part of the whole government that is investigating, charging, judging, and sentencing the individual.[72]

Hence the presentation of evidence in court may be viewed as the natural conclusion of a criminal investigation.[73] The mandatory inclusion of all relevant and reliable evidence, regardless of how it was obtained, may be crucial in the pursuit of the 'truth', but 'truth, like all other good things, may be loved unwisely—may be pursued too keenly—may cost too much'.[74] If the importance of determining the issue of improperly obtained evidence is accepted, then surely it is immaterial that this determination inevitably involves a collateral inquiry.[75]

(b) Mandatory Exclusion

That firm adherence to a rule of mandatory exclusion may be impossible to maintain can be demonstrated with reference to the background and development in the United States of what is generally known as the Fourth Amendment exclusionary rule. In 1914 the US Supreme Court held in *Weeks* v. *US*[76] that evidence obtained in contravention of the Fourth

---

[71] See generally Pakter, 'Exclusionary Rules in France, Germany, and Italy'.

[72] T. S. Schrock and R. C. Welsh, 'Up from Calandra: The Exclusionary Rule as a Constitutional Requirement' (1974) 59 *Minnesota Law Review* 251, 258.

[73] Ashworth, 'Excluding Evidence as Protecting Rights', 725.

[74] *Pearse* v. *Pearse* (1846) 1 De G. & Sm. 12, 28–9; quoted in *Bunning* v. *Cross* (1978) 141 CLR 54, 72 per Stephen and Aickin JJ.

[75] A judge of the Irish Supreme Court has stated that 'there are many kinds of evidence which require a collateral inquiry before their admissibility can be decided. I instance but one— the question whether a statement, which would otherwise transgress the hearsay rule, was made by a deceased man in the course of his duty. I do not think that the necessity of a collateral inquiry is an adequate reason for establishing a general rule that all relevant evidence is admissible notwithstanding the illegality of the means used to prove it'. (*The People (AG)* v. *O'Brien* [1965] IR 142, 162 per Kingsmill Moore J.)   [76] 232 US 383 (1914).

Amendment[77] would be automatically inadmissible in Federal proceedings. The Court in 1961 extended this rule to cover State courts: *Mapp* v. *Ohio*.[78] By the 1970s, however, the Court had begun to recognize the undesirability of a rule of mandatory exclusion, and become aware of 'the strains imposed by reality, in terms of the costs to society and the bizarre miscarriages of justice that have been experienced because of the exclusion of reliable evidence when the "constable blunders" '.[79] Accordingly, it was decided that tainted evidence should be excluded only where such exclusion would have the effect of deterring future violations. On this basis the impeachment exception to the exclusionary rule was recognized: this exception permits the prosecution to introduce illegally obtained evidence to impeach the defendant's own testimony.[80] It has been held, too, that the exclusionary rule should not be extended to grand jury proceedings.[81] Further, 'a state prisoner may not be granted federal habeas corpus relief on the ground that evidence obtained in an unconstitutional search or seizure was introduced at his trial'.[82] Most recently, the Court has created a 'good faith exception' to the exclusionary rule, whereby evidence obtained in 'good faith' violation of the Fourth Amendment is not to be excluded from criminal trials.[83]

Objections to mandatory exclusion which are of a rather practical nature have been put forward by some commentators.[84] In particular, it is argued that frustration with a rule of mandatory exclusion could result in the courts being extremely reluctant to hold that an item of evidence has been obtained improperly, and could also encourage police perjury. Police officers may be encouraged either (1) to lie in court about the way in which improperly obtained evidence was obtained, or (2) to use the improperly obtained evidence as a lead to other evidence and then to lie in court about the connection between them.[85] Indeed it is likely that 'a substantial percentage of policemen [would] take the view that two wrongs make a right and that

---

[77] The Fourth Amendment provides: 'The right of the people to be secure in their persons, houses, papers, and effects, against unreasonable searches and seizures, shall not be violated, and no Warrants shall issue, but upon probable cause, supported by Oath or affirmation, and particularly describing the place to be searched, and the persons or things to be seized.'

[78] 367 US 643 (1961).

[79] *Stone* v. *Powell* 428 US 465, 496 (1976) per Burger CJ.

[80] See *Harris* v. *New York* 401 US 222 (1971) and *James* v. *Illinois* 110 S. Ct. 648 (1990).

[81] *US* v. *Calandra* 414 US 338 (1974).

[82] *Stone* v. *Powell* 428 US 465, 494–5 (1976).

[83] *US* v. *Leon* 104 S. Ct. 3405 (1984); *Massachusetts* v. *Sheppard* 104 S. Ct. 3424 (1984); *Illinois* v. *Krull* 107 S. Ct. 1160 (1987).

[84] See generally J. Kaplan, 'The Limits of the Exclusionary Rule' (1974) 26 *Stanford Law Review* 1027, 1036; Australian Law Reform Commission, *Criminal Investigation* (1975) para. 295.

[85] See generally J. D. Heydon, 'Illegally Obtained Evidence (2)' [1973] *Criminal Law Review* 690, 694; Kaplan, 'The Limits of the Exclusionary Rule', 1032; Australian Law Reform Commission, *Criminal Investigation*, paras. 295, 297; Australian Law Reform Commission, *Evidence*, i (Report No. 26: Interim) (1985), para. 961.

perjury is a permissible method'[86] of avoiding the effect of mandatory exclusion.

The possibility of (increased) perjury seems to be supported by empirical research conducted in the United States.[87] However, whilst it may indeed be the case that a rule of mandatory exclusion could encourage police perjury, it is clearly inappropriate to treat this as a valid objection to mandatory exclusion. Such a line of argument is reminiscent of the specious pre-nineteenth century justification for forbidding accused persons from testifying in court—that is, that they would perjure themselves if given the opportunity to testify. If the police commit such a serious criminal offence as perjury as a result of frustration with a rule of mandatory exclusion, then surely there is a public interest in dealing with that perversion of justice (through dismissal of the offender from the police force and, possibly, a prosecution for perjury). Similar objections apply to the argument that a rule of mandatory exclusion could encourage judges to hold that items of evidence which they regard as improperly obtained have not been, in fact, obtained improperly.[88] Surely it is the duty of judges to decide such issues dispassionately and in accordance with the law.

These difficulties with the 'practical' objections to mandatory exclusion do not, however, invalidate an independent point: that a rule of mandatory exclusion is undesirable *in principle* because it flies in the face of the duty of the law to bring criminal offenders to conviction. Mandatory exclusion fails to take account of the circumstances of the individual case. It could result in a dangerous offender going free even where the executive impropriety in question was a trivial one.[89] Thus, a rule of mandatory exclusion may give the law an appearance of regarding 'the over-zealous officer of the law as a greater danger to the community than the unpunished murderer or embezzler or panderer'.[90] Such an appearance can hardly enhance public respect for the administration of justice. The public, after all, expects the criminal law to fulfil the role of bringing to conviction those who commit serious crimes. As Kaplan points out:

The disparity in particular cases between the error committed by the police officer and the windfall given by the rule to the criminal is an affront to popular ideas of justice. . . . Proportionality is a major element of our sense of justice. The lack of

[86] Kaplan, 'The Limits of the Exclusionary Rule', 1038.
[87] See e.g., 'Effect of *Mapp* v. *Ohio* on Police Search-and-Seizure Practices in Narcotics Cases' (1968) 4 *Columbia Journal of Law and Social Problems* 87, 94–5. For other empirical evidence of police perjury in this context, see M. W. Orfield, jun., 'Deterrence, Perjury, and the Heater Factor: An Exclusionary Rule in the Chicago Criminal Courts' (1992) 63 *University of Colorado Law Review* 75. See also *People* v. *McMurty* 314 NYS 2d 194, 196 (1970).
[88] For empirical evidence of this type of judicial manipulation, see Orfield, 'Deterrence, Perjury, and the Heater Factor'.
[89] See *People* v. *Defore* 150 NE 585, 587 (1926) per Cardozo J: 'The criminal is to go free because the constable has blundered.'
[90] Wigmore, 'Using Evidence Obtained by Illegal Search and Seizure', 482.

proportionality between the crime and the punishment was shocking when Jean Valjean received what amounted to a life sentence for stealing a loaf of bread, and a similar sense of injustice arises from the disparity between the police officer's error and the failure because of it to punish one who has committed a serious crime.[91]

Thus, to adopt a rule of mandatory exclusion would be to fly in the face of the duty of the law to apprehend and bring to conviction those who commit criminal offences. The US experience clearly suggests that a rule of mandatory exclusion is difficult to maintain. Recognition of the right of society 'to expect rationally graded responses from judges in place of the universal "capital punishment" we inflict on all evidence when police error is shown in its acquisition'[92] has led to the abandonment of mandatory exclusion of all evidence obtained in contravention of the Fourth Amendment.

(c) The Search for a Rationale

It has been seen that the problem of improperly obtained evidence cannot be dealt with either by mandatory inclusion or by mandatory exclusion. Accordingly, it is necessary to identify a rationale for exclusion which properly explains the need to exclude improperly obtained evidence in some circumstances but not in others. I shall first embark upon an analysis of two rationales for exclusion which are commonly advanced—the compensatory and deterrent rationales—before moving on to defend the argument that the principle of judicial legitimacy represents the most appropriate rationale for the exclusion of improperly obtained evidence.

(i) Compensation

The compensatory rationale for the exclusion of improperly obtained evidence[93] takes the following form. A suspect's rights are infringed if she is subjected to improper treatment by the police in the course of their investigations. And where it is established that the rights of a defendant have been infringed in this manner, it is the responsibility of the court to protect her from any disadvantage flowing from the infringement. Thus, any evidence obtained as a result of the infringement should be excluded from the trial.[94] It is said that exclusion is especially appropriate, since it puts the individual in the position in which she would have been had the infringement not occurred.[95] 'Only an exclusionary sanction places the person in no greater risk of criminal conviction than he would have been in had the violation of protected interests not occurred.'[96]

---

[91] Kaplan, 'The Limits of the Exclusionary Rule', 1036.

[92] *Bivens* v. *Six Unknown Named Agents of Federal Bureau of Narcotics* 403 US 388, 419 (1971).

[93] Ashworth has called this the 'protective principle' (Ashworth, 'Excluding Evidence as Protecting Rights').   [94] See generally ibid.

[95] See Australian Law Reform Commission, *Evidence*, i, para. 959; E. W. Cleary (ed.), *McCormick on Evidence* (3rd edn., 1984), 462–3.   [96] Ibid. 463.

There are, however, difficulties with the view that compensation for the infringement of rights of accused persons is the justification for exclusion. Consider the issue of evidence which has been obtained as a result of the infringement of the rights, not of the accused, but of a third party. Under the compensatory rationale such evidence can never be excluded.[97] Even the fact that the evidence had been obtained by means of torturing the third party would be irrelevant. It is evident from this illustration that the compensatory rationale for exclusion is unduly narrow. This rationale assumes that, where the executive has obtained evidence by violating individual rights and seeks on the basis of this evidence to bring a person to conviction, the only relevant harm has been that done to the person whose rights were violated, and thus the duty of the law is merely to restore her to the position in which she had been prior to the violation. If this cannot be achieved by exclusion, then there can be no exclusion. Yet this completely ignores the fact that, in a case involving improperly obtained evidence, the infringement of rights in the obtaining of the evidence does not represent the only relevant harm. There is also the harm which could be done to the administration of justice as a whole if the evidence were admitted. Thus, not only must the law seek to compensate for the infringement of individual rights which has already occurred, but it must also avert any possible injury to the criminal justice system as a whole. The compensatory rationale is directed to the former but not to the latter.

A further problem with the compensatory rationale is that it fails to explain adequately the need for improperly obtained evidence to be admitted in some circumstances but excluded in others. Under the compensatory rationale, it would have to be said that the law is sometimes justified in not compensating for the infringement of individual rights, in the interest of a greater public interest in the conviction of the guilty. The difficulties with such a formulation are obvious. A judge, in deciding whether to admit or to exclude an item of improperly obtained evidence, would be attempting to weigh incommensurables: she would be seeking to weigh a private interest against a public interest to determine which should prevail in the particular case—individual rights on the one hand, or the public interest in the conviction of the guilty on the other.[98] Further, the very notion that it is possible for an individual right to be meaningfully sacrificed to a social goal in this way is a problematic one. Dworkin has contended that to take rights seriously is to regard them as 'trumps' which prevail over social goals.[99] As Dennis points out, the law does not allow a

---

[97] Note, however, that the US Supreme Court has decided that the deterrent rationale, too, does not require the exclusion of evidence obtained as a result of the infringement of the rights of a third party: *Alderman* v. *US* 394 US 165 (1969).

[98] I. H. Dennis, 'Reconstructing the Law of Criminal Evidence' (1989) 42 *Current Legal Problems* 21, 30–1.

[99] See R. Dworkin, *Taking Rights Seriously* (1977), ch. 4.

well-founded claim for damages for breach of contract to be defeated on the basis that the payment of the damages would be contrary to the public interest.[100]

(ii) Deterrence

A second justification for the exclusion of improperly obtained evidence is the deterrent rationale. It is said that, being an integral part of the criminal justice system, the courts have a responsibility, inasmuch as it lies within their power to do so, to deter the police from the commission of future improprieties. The disciplining of police officers is not a matter which is solely the concern of the executive. By the 1970s the US Supreme Court had begun to adopt the view that the exclusionary rule 'is a judicially created remedy designed to safeguard Fourth Amendment rights generally through its deterrent effect . . .'.[101] It is to be noted that, while adopting the view that the sole aim of exclusion was to deter, the US Supreme Court did not overlook the absence of conclusive empirical evidence supporting the deterrent effect of exclusion. In *US* v. *Janis* the Court observed that 'no empirical researcher, proponent or opponent of the rule, has yet been able to establish with any assurance whether the rule has a deterrent effect even in the situations in which it is now applied'.[102] And in *Stone* v. *Powell* it was said that, 'despite the absence of supportive empirical evidence, we have assumed that the immediate effect of exclusion will be to discourage law enforcement officials from violating the Fourth Amendment by removing the incentive to disregard it'.[103]

There are two bases on which it might be suggested that the exclusion of improperly obtained evidence could deter future improprieties.[104] The first concerns the police officer responsible for the impropriety. It is said that such an officer would be likely to feel aggrieved if her efforts were thwarted by exclusion and that exclusion would accordingly induce her to take greater care in the future. Secondly, it is said that exclusion would also deter police misconduct in a broader sense: the dissemination of the significance of individual rulings on the admissibility of improperly obtained evidence would be relatively manageable in a bureaucratic framework such as that in which the police and prosecution function, and thus a judicial policy of excluding improperly obtained evidence from criminal trials would be likely

---

[100] Dennis, 'Reconstructing the Law of Criminal Evidence', 30.

[101] *US* v. *Calandra* 414 US 338, 348 (1974). See also e.g., *Stone* v. *Powell* 428 US 465, 486 (1976): 'The primary justification for the exclusionary rule . . . is the deterrence of police conduct that violates Fourth Amendment rights.'

[102] 428 US 433, 450 n. 22 (1976).   [103] 428 US 465, 492 (1976).

[104] See generally D. H. Oaks, 'Studying the Exclusionary Rule in Search and Seizure' (1970) 37 *University of Chicago Law Review* 665; W. C. Heffernan and R. W. Lovely, 'Evaluating the Fourth Amendment Exclusionary Rule: The Problem of Police Compliance with the Law' (1991) 24 *University of Michigan Journal of Law Reform* 311, 321.

to result, *inter alia*, in the formulation of education programmes and administrative directives for the police, leading, in the long term, to some improvement in police practices.[105]

The deterrent rationale for the exclusion of improperly obtained evidence raises two important issues. First, it is to be noted that the rationale reflects an instrumentalist approach to criminal justice: the criminal process may legitimately be used as a tool for achieving good results in the future. Thus, on this view, the goal of deterrence of future police misconduct justifies the impairment of the public interest in bringing offenders to conviction. In an article written in defence of the deterrent rationale for punishment, Rawls has emphasized the importance of distinguishing between the justification of a rule, practice, or institution and the justification of a particular action falling under it. 'Where a form of action is specified by a practice there is no justification possible of the particular action of a particular person save by reference to the practice. In such cases the action is what it is in virtue of the practice and to explain it is to refer to the practice.'[106] Acceptance of this view would suggest that, where an item of improperly obtained evidence is excluded for deterrent reasons, it is inappropriate to attempt to justify the particular action except by reference to the deterrent rationale for the exclusion of improperly obtained evidence.

The second issue relates to the extent to which exclusion actually deters. Whilst the exclusion of improperly obtained evidence would be likely to have *some* deterrent effect, the extent of this effect is inherently incapable of proper measurement. However, in spite of the obvious methodological difficulties associated with any empirical research conducted for the purpose of evaluating the deterrent effect of exclusion, several such research projects have been undertaken in the United States and given rise to an important body of literature.[107] An examination of this literature reveals that there is little consensus as to the actual extent to which exclusion deters. It should be remembered, of course, that it is possible to attach too much significance to the absence of conclusive empirical evidence supporting the deterrent effect of exclusion: there is, for example, a similar lack of conclusive empirical evidence to support the deterrent theory of punishment. What is more important—accepting that exclusion will deter to some

[105] It is possible that, in the US, hearings held to determine admissibility may also act as a deterrent: Orfield, 'Deterrence, Perjury, and the Heater Factor', 90.

[106] J. Rawls, 'Two Concepts of Rules' (1955) 64 *Philosophical Review* 3, 32.

[107] Oaks, 'Studying the Exclusionary Rule in Search and Seizure'; J. E. Spiotto, 'Search and Seizure: An Empirical Study of the Exclusionary Rule and its Alternatives' (1973) 2 *Journal of Legal Studies* 243; B. C. Canon, 'Is the Exclusionary Rule in Failing Health? Some New Data and a Plea against a Precipitous Conclusion' (1974) 62 *Kentucky Law Journal* 681; M. W. Orfield, jun., 'The Exclusionary Rule and Deterrence: An Empirical Study of Chicago Narcotics Officers' (1987) 54 *University of Chicago Law Review* 1016; Heffernan and Lovely, 'Evaluating the Fourth Amendment Exclusionary Rule'; Orfield, 'Deterrence, Perjury, and the Heater Factor'.

extent—is the courts' assumption as to *when* it would do so. The US Supreme Court has made the assumption that exclusion would be likely to contribute adequately to the deterrence of future improprieties unless the evidence was obtained in 'good faith' violation of the Fourth Amendment.

In sum, the adoption of deterrence as the rationale for the exclusion of improperly obtained evidence would not be without considerable difficulties. It is arguable that the public interest in the conviction of the guilty should not be compromised on such a speculative basis. The deterrent rationale requires assumptions to be made as to when exclusion would contribute sufficiently to deterrence, and when it would not. To determine admissibility on the basis of such assumptions is, in my view, unsatisfactory. Further, adoption of the deterrent rationale might well have the undesirable effect of providing an excuse for not improving the traditional police disciplinary procedures. The preferable approach to the problem of police discipline would not be to rely upon the law of evidence and procedure, but to overhaul completely the present disciplinary procedures. The new procedures introduced in Part IX of PACE are a step in the right direction, but they are insufficient.[108] What is required now in England is the establishment of a completely independent police disciplinary court which is under judicial supervision.

(iii) Towards a Principle of Judicial Legitimacy

We have seen that it has been recognized in a number of jurisdictions that to deal with the problem of improperly obtained evidence either by mandatory inclusion or by mandatory exclusion is inappropriate. To be able to be taken seriously, therefore, any possible rationale for exclusion must be capable of accommodating properly the need for improperly obtained evidence to be excluded in some circumstances but not in others. In other words, the public interest in the conviction of the guilty must be able to be weighed meaningfully against the rationale in question: if it is concluded that in the circumstances the public interest in the conviction of the guilty is weightier and should prevail, then the evidence should be admitted regardless of the impropriety. Both the compensatory and deterrent rationales discussed above do not satisfy this requirement of 'weighability' comfortably. The compensatory rationale would require that the public interest in the conviction of the guilty be weighed against individual rights, while the deterrent rationale would require the same public interest to be

---

[108] See generally S. Cragg, 'Putting the Police on Trial' (1992) 89(20) *Law Society's Guardian Gazette* 17; A. Hall, 'Time for a Change?' [Aug. 1990] *Legal Action* 7; A. Hall, 'Still Time for a Change?' [June 1991] *Legal Action* 9; R. Smith, 'Is Anybody Listening?' (1992) 142 *New Law Journal* 816; M. Tregilgas-Davey, 'The Police and Accountability: Part 1' (1990) 140 *New Law Journal* 697; M. Tregilgas-Davey, 'The Police and Accountability: Part 2' (1990) 140 *New Law Journal* 738; L. H. Leigh, *Police Powers in England and Wales* (2nd edn., 1985), 286.

weighed against the speculative future benefits of exclusion. The difficulties involved in these weighing exercises have already been demonstrated.

A preferable approach to the problem of improperly obtained evidence would be to attempt to deal with it in the context of the functions of criminal justice and the duties and responsibilities of the judge in a criminal trial. It is suggested, therefore, that the principle of judicial legitimacy should be applied in determining whether an item of improperly obtained evidence is to be admitted or excluded. One accepted function of criminal justice is, of course, to secure the conviction of the guilty and the acquittal of the innocent. This suggests that a trial judge should attempt to secure the admission of relevant and reliable evidence, and the exclusion of any evidence which may be irrelevant or unreliable. But this is subject to the need to take account of the public interest in the moral integrity of the criminal process.

The idea that a court may assist in protecting the moral integrity of the criminal process by excluding improperly obtained evidence has received considerable attention in the United States, where it is referred to as the imperative of judicial integrity.[109] Several US cases contain statements on why the public interest in the moral integrity of the criminal process weighs in favour of the exclusion of improperly obtained evidence. 'By admitting unlawfully seized evidence,' it has been observed, 'the judiciary becomes a part of what is in fact a single governmental action.'[110] The judiciary becomes, in a sense, an accomplice to the improper governmental action. This is not appropriate, since 'a court sworn to uphold and promote observance of the law cannot adequately perform its function if it ignores illegality in the enforcement of the law'.[111] 'Courts which sit under our Constitution cannot and will not be made party to lawless invasions of the constitutional rights of citizens by permitting unhindered governmental use of the fruits of such invasions.'[112] The admission of illegally obtained evidence 'has the necessary effect of legitimizing the conduct which produced the evidence, while an application of the exclusionary rule withholds the constitutional imprimatur'.[113]

Thus, by refusing to turn a blind eye to executive misconduct which occurred at the investigatory stage, a trial court is safeguarding the moral

---

[109] The use of this phrase has been criticized by P. Arenella, 'Rethinking the Functions of Criminal Procedure: The Warren and Burger Courts' Competing Ideologies' (1983) 72 *Georgetown Law Journal* 185, 203: 'Indeed, the "judicial integrity" label is misleading because the issue is not whether the courts are "condoning" improper executive action or whether they are "vicariously responsible" for the executive's misconduct. The issue is not the court's integrity but the criminal process' integrity as a self-regulating legal order.'

[110] *US* v. *Leon* 104 S. Ct. 3430, 3432 (1984).

[111] H. Schwartz, 'Retroactivity, Reliability, and Due Process: A Reply to Professor Mishkin' (1966) 33 *University of Chicago Law Review* 719, 752.

[112] *Terry* v. *Ohio* 392 US 1, 13 (1968). See also *Elkins* v. *US* 364 US 206, 223 (1960).

[113] *Terry* v. *Ohio* 392 US 1, 13 (1968).

integrity of the trial process. And, as the trial process is a part of the entire criminal justice process, the moral integrity of the administration of justice as a whole is also protected. The moral integrity of the administration of justice will, it is true, have been compromised already (at the investigatory stage) by the executive impropriety in question. The impropriety is a historical fact; it has already occurred and the court cannot prevent it from compromising the moral integrity of the administration of justice. However, the important consideration is that, by safeguarding the moral integrity of the trial process, the court would be preventing the moral integrity of the administration of justice as a whole from being *further* compromised.

In short, then, the public interest in the moral integrity of the criminal process requires that a court disassociate itself from executive impropriety which occurred at the investigatory stage, and refrain from bringing such impropriety to fruition; this may be achieved by the exclusion of any evidence obtained as a result of the impropriety.

While the public interest in the moral integrity of the criminal justice system favours the exclusion of relevant and reliable evidence which happens to have been obtained improperly, the public interest in the conviction of the guilty favours its admission. Thus, the issue of whether an item of improperly obtained evidence should be included or excluded effectively involves a determination of whether the public interest would be better served by inclusion or exclusion. If in the circumstances it is concluded that the public interest in the conviction of the guilty outweighs the public interest in the moral integrity of the criminal process, then the evidence should be admitted regardless of the impropriety.

The principle of judicial legitimacy, or something approaching it, has been expressly adopted in a number of jurisdictions in the context of improperly obtained evidence. In both Ireland and Australia the admissibility of improperly obtained evidence is determined by weighing the public interest in the conviction of the guilty against the public interest in the moral integrity of the criminal process. The Irish Supreme Court, for instance, has acknowledged that

a choice has to be made between desirable ends which may be incompatible. It is desirable in the public interest that crime should be detected and punished. It is desirable that individuals should not be subjected to illegal or inquisitorial methods of investigation and that the State should not attempt to advance its ends by utilising the fruits of such methods. It appears . . . that in every case a determination has to be made by the trial judge as to whether the public interest is best served by the admission or by the exclusion of evidence of facts ascertained as a result of, and by means of, illegal actions, and that the answer to the question depends on a consideration of all the circumstances.[114]

This approach to the problem of improperly obtained evidence is also

[114] *The People (AG) v. O'Brien* [1965] IR 142, 160 per Kingsmill Moore J.

taken in Australia. Reservations about the previously prevailing approach had been expressed in the High Court of Australia as early as 1963,[115] but it was not until its 1970 decision in *R. v. Ireland*[116] that the Court expressly formulated a new approach. This approach was explained and refined by the High Court in the later case of *Bunning* v. *Cross*,[117] but it is in the decision of the New South Wales Court of Criminal Appeal in *R. v. Dugan* that the best summation of the approach is to be found:

The court is required to make a relative, balanced assessment of the interests of the community in facilitating the apprehension of offenders and bringing them to conviction, on the one hand, and, on the other hand, repudiating conduct and subterfuge in the processes of criminal investigation that are unfair or unlawful in the sense of bearing so gross a character as to offend relevant concepts of democratic decency.[118]

Also relevant is the Canadian position subsequent to the enactment in 1982 of the Canadian Charter of Rights and Freedoms. Section 24(2) of the Charter provides:

Where . . . a court concludes that evidence was obtained in a manner that infringed or denied any rights or freedoms guaranteed by this Charter, the evidence *shall* be excluded if it is established that, having regard to all the circumstances, the admission of it in the proceedings would *bring the administration of justice into disrepute.*[119]

The interpretation of this provision was the subject of comment by the Canadian Supreme Court in *R. v. Collins.*[120] It was pointed out that[121] police misconduct in the investigatory process would often have some effect on the repute of the administration of justice and that, accordingly, the purpose of section 24(2) is really to prevent the administration of justice from being brought into *further* disrepute by the admission of the evidence. This further disrepute could result 'from judicial condonation of unacceptable conduct by the investigatory and prosecutorial agencies'. The Supreme Court pointed out that it would be necessary, on the other hand, to consider any disrepute which might result from the *exclusion* of the evidence. What the Court clearly had in mind was the disrepute which could result from the failure of the criminal justice system to bring a guilty person to conviction. 'It would be inconsistent with the purpose of s. 24(2) to exclude evidence if its exclusion would bring the administration of justice into greater disrepute than would its admission.'

---

[115] See *Wendo* v. *R.* (1963) 109 CLR 559, 562 per Dixon CJ: 'It is . . . unnecessary to deal with the controversial question whether evidence which is relevant should be rejected on the ground that it is come by unlawfully or otherwise improperly. I do not think that in this or any other jurisdiction the question has been put at rest by [*Kuruma* v. *R.* [1955] AC 197]'.

[116] (1970) 126 CLR 321.   [117] (1978) 141 CLR 54.
[118] [1984] 2 NSWLR 554, 558.   [119] Emphasis added.
[120] (1987) 56 CR (3d) 193.   [121] Ibid. 208.

But what exactly does 'disrepute' mean? The clue to this lies in the treatment by the Canadian Supreme Court of the question of whether the results of public opinion polls can usefully be taken into account in determining admissibility. The idea that such polls may be so used was rejected by the Court.[122] The Court emphasized that the issue of disrepute should be determined by applying a 'reasonable person' test. Thus the relevant question is whether the admission of the impugned evidence would bring the administration of justice into disrepute in the eyes of a reasonable person, dispassionate and fully apprized of the circumstances of the case. 'The reasonable person is usually the average person in the community, but only when that community's current mood is reasonable.'[123] A decision should not be rendered 'that would be unacceptable to the community when that community is not being wrought with passion or otherwise under passing stress due to current events'.[124] It is, therefore, to be noted that the Canadian Supreme Court has refused to interpret section 24(2) of the Charter in a literal manner. A literal interpretation of the provision would require courts to pander to public mood—for instance, public clamour for the conviction of a person who has committed a serious offence may mean that all illegality should be excused in order to secure her conviction. Rather, the concern of the Supreme Court is with what may be termed 'objective disrepute', and it is for this reason that the results of public opinion polls are regarded as irrelevant.

That the Canadian Supreme Court has not interpreted section 24(2) literally has been noted succinctly by one commentator:

As a matter of construction, s. 24(2) decidedly focuses on . . . the maintenance of popular trust in the judicial branch of government. The phrase states that the concern is with whether the admission of the evidence would bring the administration of justice into *disrepute*. Disrepute has to do with reputation and reputation has to do with what others think of you, not with what standards you would like to emulate. . . . Despite this, the Supreme Court of Canada has fashioned what has proved, in at least a wide spectrum of cases, to be an extremely aggressive exclusionary remedy. It set the stage for doing so by leaving the partially implicit but unmistakable message that s. 24(2) should be understood as though it was intended to preserve judicial integrity, regardless of the impact of exclusion on the reputation of the judicial branch.[125]

Clearly, then, despite the wording of section 24(2), the approach required by this provision may in effect be identical to that required by the principle of judicial legitimacy which I am defending. The Canadian Supreme Court

---

[122] *R. v. Collins* (1987) 56 CR (3d) 193, 209. See also *R. v. Therens* (1985) 18 DLR (4th) 655, 687–8 per Le Dain J.   [123] *R. v. Collins* (1987) 56 CR (3d) 193, 209.
[124] Ibid. 210.
[125] D. M. Paciocco, 'The Judicial Repeal of S. 24(2) and the Development of the Canadian Exclusionary Rule' (1990) 32 *Criminal Law Quarterly* 326, 341–2 (emphasis in original).

has made it clear that what is required is a moral calculation rather than a factual one. It may be expected that the circumstances in which judicial legitimacy would be compromised would equate with those in which the administration of justice would be brought into disrepute in the eyes of a 'reasonable person'.[126]

THE ENGLISH POSITION

As a preliminary to discussion of the exercise of the abuse of process discretion in the context of police impropriety at the investigatory stage, it is instructive to consider briefly the English position on the exclusion of improperly obtained evidence. We shall see that the English courts have begun to take a more liberal approach to the issue, and may indeed be coming close to adoption of the principle of judicial legitimacy.

The key judicial pronouncements on improperly obtained evidence prior to the coming into force of PACE were the 1955 Privy Council decision in *Kuruma* v. *R.*[127] and the 1979 House of Lords case of *R.* v. *Sang.*[128] More important now, however, are the provisions of PACE. Part VIII of the Act is headed 'Evidence in Criminal Proceedings—General'.[129] The relevant provision for our purposes is the famous section 78(1), which has been judicially described as a provision which 'is by now known almost by heart by most people who have anything to do with the law'.[130] Section 78(1) provides:

In any proceedings the court may refuse to allow evidence on which the prosecution proposes to rely to be given if it appears to the court that, having regard to all the circumstances, including the circumstances in which the evidence was obtained, the admission of the evidence would have such an adverse effect on the fairness of the proceedings that the court ought not to admit it.

The interpretation of section 78 has yet to be considered by the House of Lords, but there are several decisions of the Court of Appeal and other courts in which the issue has been addressed. The Court of Appeal has generally shied away, however, from providing any general guidance as to the way in which the section 78 discretion should be exercised. The following comment is typical: 'It is undesirable to attempt any general guidance as to the way in which a judge's discretion under section 78 or his

---

[126] For an interesting discussion of empirical research conducted in Canada on public attitudes to the exclusion of improperly obtained evidence, see A. W. Bryant, M. Gold, H. M. Stevenson, and D. Northrup, 'Public Attitudes toward the Exclusion of Evidence: Section 24(2) of the Canadian Charter of Rights and Freedoms' (1990) 69 *Canadian Bar Review* 1.
[127] [1955] AC 197.   [128] [1980] AC 402.
[129] It should be noted that s. 82(3) provides: 'Nothing in this Part of this Act shall prejudice any power of a court to exclude evidence (whether by preventing questions from being put or otherwise) at its discretion.'   [130] *Hudson* v. *DPP* [1992] RTR 27, 34 per Hodgson J.

inherent powers should be exercised. Circumstances vary infinitely.'[131] It has been stressed, however, that the discretion may not be used to discipline the police,[132] and that 'the mere fact that there has been a breach of the Codes of Practice does not of itself mean that evidence has to be rejected'.[133] However, 'significant and substantial' breaches will weigh heavily in favour of exclusion,[134] even if the police did not act in bad faith.[135] As was summed up by the Court in *R. v. Walsh*:

> To our minds it follows that if there are significant and substantial breaches of section 58 [of PACE] or the provisions of the Code, then prima facie at least the standards of fairness set by Parliament have not been met. So far as a defendant is concerned, it seems to us also to follow that to admit evidence against him which has been obtained in circumstances where these standards have not been met, cannot but have an adverse effect on the fairness of the proceedings. This does not mean, of course, that in every case of a significant or substantial breach of section 58 or the Code of Practice the evidence concerned will automatically be excluded. Section 78 does not so provide. The task of the court is not merely to consider whether there would be an adverse effect on the fairness of the proceedings, but such an adverse effect that justice requires the evidence to be excluded. . . . although bad faith may make substantial or significant that which might not otherwise be so, the contrary does not follow. Breaches which are in themselves significant and substantial are not rendered otherwise by the good faith of the officers concerned.[136]

A similar approach would appear to have been taken in decisions of the Divisional Court. In *Thomas* v. *DPP*[137] the Court seemed to suggest that proof of mala fides (bad faith) was a prerequisite to the exclusion of evidence under section 78, but this has been doubted in two subsequent decisions of the Court, *DPP* v. *McGladrigan*[138] and *DPP* v. *Godwin*.[139] In *McGladrigan* it was expressly acknowledged that the section 78 discretion was a 'new discretion' and not merely a restatement of the common law.[140] Referring to *Thomas*, the Court thought that, had the Court of Appeal decision in *R. v. Samuel*[141] been cited to the Court in *Thomas*, the Court in *Thomas* would not have suggested that there had to be a finding of mala fides before evidence could be excluded under section 78.[142]

---

[131] *R. v. Samuel* [1988] 2 WLR 920, 934. See also *R. v. O'Leary* (1988) 87 Cr. App. R. 387.

[132] *R. v. Mason* [1987] 3 All ER 481, 484; *R. v. Delaney* (1988) 88 Cr. App. R. 338, 341; *R. v. Keenan* [1989] 3 All ER 598, 609.

[133] *R. v. Delaney* (1988) 88 Cr. App. R. 338, 341. See also *R. v. Parris* (1988) 89 Cr. App. R. 68, 72; *R. v. Keenan* [1989] 3 All ER 598, 609; *R. v. M (A Juvenile)* (1989) 153 JP 691; *R. v. Maguire* (1989) 90 Cr. App. R. 115, 120; *R. v. Quinn, The Times*, 31 Mar. 1990; *R. v. Gillard and Barrett* (1990) 92 Cr. App. R. 61.

[134] *R. v. Keenan* [1989] 3 All ER 598, 609. Cf. *R. v. Beycan* [1990] Crim. LR 185 (breach of a 'fundamental' right led to exclusion) and *R. v. Canale* [1990] 2 All ER 187 (breaches described as 'flagrant', 'deliberate', and 'cynical' also resulted in exclusion). See also *R. v. Sanusi* [1992] Crim. LR 43.

[135] *R. v. Quinn, The Times*, 31 Mar. 1990.   [136] (1989) 91 Cr. App. R. 161, 163.

[137] [1991] RTR 292.   [138] [1991] RTR 297.   [139] [1991] RTR 303.

[140] [1991] RTR 297, 301.   [141] [1988] 2 WLR 920.   [142] [1991] RTR 297, 302.

In *Godwin*, it was expressly acknowledged that

it is not necessary for justices to be satisfied that the police or the prosecuting authorities have acted in bad faith or oppressively for the discretion under section 78 to be exercised. . . . It is enough to say that the discretion in section 78 is phrased in general terms, that section 78 has been so construed in what is now a series of cases and that the need to show mala fides was emphatically rejected in the well known case of *R. v. Samuel* . . .[143]

More recently still, the Divisional Court appears in *Daniels* v. *DPP* to have expressly endorsed the *McGladrigan* view in preference to the *Thomas* one; the presence or otherwise of *mala fides*, it was said, was only *one factor* for consideration in deciding whether to exclude evidence under section 78.[144] It seems likely, therefore, that this more liberal view will come to represent the prevailing approach.

Significantly, a recent Divisional Court decision, *R. v. Governor of Pentonville Prison, ex p. Chinoy*,[145] suggests that evidence obtained illegally outside the jurisdiction is capable of being excluded under section 78. The applicant was arrested in England on the basis of evidence provided by two US undercover agents. This evidence included transcripts of unauthorized tape recordings of conversations which took place in France between the applicant and the agents. The applicant was committed to prison to await his return to the United States to face charges, and applied for a writ of habeas corpus on the basis that the committal was unlawful. He argued, *inter alia*, that the magistrate should have excluded the evidence of the tape-recorded conversations under section 78.

The Divisional Court held[146] that, in deciding whether to exclude evidence under section 78, a court could take into account any breach of foreign or international law arising from the manner in which the evidence had been obtained. But the Divisional Court thought that, in the present case, the means employed by the US agents were legitimate by reference to English law, regardless of whether they involved breaches of French law and of the European Convention on Human Rights: 'Our law has always acknowledged the fact, unpalatable as it may be, that the detection and proof of certain types of criminal activity may necessitate the employment of underhand and even unlawful means.'[147] Thus the Court concluded that the magistrate had not erred in not excluding the evidence under section 78.

In spite of the actual conclusion reached, the real significance of *Chinoy* lies in its recognition that the section 78 discretion *can* be exercised to exclude evidence obtained outside the jurisdiction in breach of foreign or international law. It is to be noted that the Appeal Committee of the House of Lords[148] refused leave to appeal in *Chinoy*.

[143] [1991] RTR 303, 308.   [144] (1991) 156 JPR 543, 548–50.
[145] [1992] 1 All ER 317.   [146] Ibid. 331–3.   [147] Ibid. 333.
[148] Lord Keith of Kinkel, Lord Oliver of Aylmerton, and Lord Lowry.

In sum, that the courts are willing to interpret section 78 as not merely restating the common law would seem clear. What is still lacking, however, is an authoritative judicial statement from the Court of Appeal or House of Lords on the precise principles on which the section 78 discretion is to be exercised. However, some relevant clues appear to have surfaced from the cases. It would seem that a fundamental (or 'significant and substantial') breach of the law, or of some other standard of propriety, would weigh heavily in favour of exclusion. Proof of mala fides is an important consideration, but it is not the only one. Such proof may convert an otherwise relatively minor breach into a significant and substantial one, but a breach may be significant and substantial even in the absence of proof of mala fides.

It is possible to find, in the case law on section 78, strong judicial statements which appear to suggest that, even though the acquittal of a technically guilty person may result from the use of the provision, this consideration should not influence the willingness of courts to use the provision. In *Powell* v. *DPP* the Divisional Court remarked:

The appeal must be allowed with the appropriate acquittal. This may mean that a guilty man goes free and this is certainly not an event to be welcomed. However all police officers, and for that matter all prosecution authorities, should realise that a defendant who is charged by the state needs protection and a man in custody is in a very vulnerable position. Society recognises the Codes of Practice as an attempt by Parliament to provide protection. Failure to follow those Codes is at the least suspicious and at worst, as here, it can be expensive and lead to an unsatisfactory but nevertheless inevitable result.[149]

In fact it is arguable that, in its decisions on section 78, the English Court of Appeal has already moved towards an implicit adoption of the judicial legitimacy principle. As has been mentioned, the Court has acknowledged that *either* proof of mala fides, *or* the fact that a fundamental right of the defendant was violated, will suffice as a ground for exclusion. Now, if the Court of Appeal is adopting the compensatory rationale for exclusion, then the issue of whether the impropriety was committed in good or bad faith is irrelevant; the question is whether the defendant should be compensated via the exclusion of evidence for the infringement of her rights. If, however, it is the deterrent rationale which is being adopted, then the issue of whether the breach was deliberate (or at least negligent) is crucial, while it is immaterial whether the breach violated fundamental rights of the defendant. In any event the Court of Appeal has expressly disassociated itself from the idea of exclusion for deterrent purposes. However, as will be demonstrated below, under the judicial legitimacy principle the culpability of the person(s) responsible for the impropriety, and the importance of the right(s) infringed,

---

[149] [1992] RTR 270, 276.

are *both* relevant considerations. It may therefore be the case that the Court of Appeal is in fact coming close to the adoption of the principle of judicial legitimacy. If this is so, then it would be preferable if such adoption could be explicit rather than implicit.[150]

PROPOSALS FOR REFORM

THE ABUSE OF PROCESS DISCRETION AND THE PRINCIPLE OF JUDICIAL LEGITIMACY

The conservative approach taken by the English courts to the issue of whether proceedings can be stayed on account of illegal extradition is beginning to appear anomalous when viewed against the increasing willingness of the courts to exclude improperly obtained evidence. Both the exclusion of improperly obtained evidence, and a stay of proceedings on account of police impropriety at the investigatory stage, share the same foundation. The difference is merely one of degree, being dependent upon the extent of the *effect* of the impropriety. Has the effect of the impropriety been to taint a specific item or items of evidence, or has the impropriety effectively tainted the proceedings as a whole? In the former situation, the issue arises as to whether the item or items of evidence should be excluded, and in the latter situation whether the proceedings should be stayed. Cases where proceedings have been commenced in consequence of the illegal extradition of the defendant from abroad represent a paradigm of the latter situation.

A discretion to stay such proceedings is, therefore, an obvious corollary of a discretion to exclude improperly obtained evidence. It would be anomalous if the law were to recognize the latter discretion but not the former. The view of the court in *Driver* that there is no discretion to stay proceedings on account of illegal extradition is, perhaps, unsurprising when seen against the traditional reluctance of English courts to exclude reliable evidence on the ground that it was improperly obtained. Times, however, have changed, and we have seen that section 78 of PACE has prompted a far greater judicial willingness to exclude improperly obtained, but reliable, evidence. Indeed, it has been recognized in the case of *Chinoy* that evidence

[150] A number of other interpretations of s. 78 have been advanced by commentators. See generally C. J. W. Allen, 'Discretion and Security: Excluding Evidence under Section 78(1) of the Police and Criminal Evidence Act 1984' [1990] *Cambridge Law Journal* 80; D. Feldman, 'Regulating Treatment of Suspects in Police Stations: Judicial Interpretation of Detention Provisions in the Police and Criminal Evidence Act 1984' [1990] *Criminal Law Review* 452; M. A. Gelowitz, 'Section 78 of the Police and Criminal Evidence Act 1984: Middle Ground or No Man's Land?' (1990) 106 *Law Quarterly Review* 327; B. Robertson, 'The Looking-Glass World of Section 78' (1989) 139 *New Law Journal* 1223. Gelowitz and Robertson favour restrictive interpretations of the concept of 'fairness' under s. 78, though Gelowitz does so with regret.

obtained abroad, in breach of foreign or international law, can be excluded under section 78 in appropriate circumstances. Consistency requires, therefore, that the *Mackeson/Driver* conflict be firmly resolved in favour of the *Mackeson* view that there exists a judicial discretion to stay proceedings which have been made possible by an illegal extradition.

Acceptance that the abuse of process discretion should be exercisable in cases where the proceedings as a whole have been tainted by investigatory misconduct raises the question, then, of how it is to be determined whether a stay should be ordered on this basis. It was argued earlier that application of the principle of judicial legitimacy represents the most appropriate solution to the problem of the admissibility of improperly obtained evidence. It is suggested now that the same principle should be applied in determining whether proceedings commenced in consequence of misconduct by the police at the investigatory stage should be stayed. The continuation of 'tainted' proceedings would compromise the moral integrity of the criminal justice system in the same way as would the admission of improperly obtained evidence. Thus, the principle of judicial legitimacy requires that, in determining whether a prosecution should be stayed on account of investigatory impropriety, the public interest in bringing offenders to conviction must be weighed against the public interest in the moral integrity of the criminal process. The other possible rationales for a stay—compensation and deterrence—suffer from the same problems as they do in relation to improperly obtained evidence. If the stay of 'tainted' proceedings is seen as a mechanism for compensating the defendant for the violation of her rights, we are confronted with the problem of having to weigh incommensurables against each other (the defendant's private interest in compensation on the one hand, and the public interest in bringing offenders to conviction on the other). The problem with the deterrent rationale is that it is unclear whether the public interest in the conviction of the guilty should be compromised on a basis as speculative as that of the deterrent effect of a stay. Of course, it is likely that a stay could have a greater deterrent effect than exclusion. However, there still arises the fundamental problem of the necessity of making assumptions as to when a stay would contribute adequately to deterrence, and when it would not. Further, it is not generally accepted in England that deterrence of police or prosecutorial misconduct should be a legitimate concern of a criminal court.[151] Of course, it is arguable that it should be, and this, indeed, is the attitude taken by the US Supreme Court. However, it is not proposed to pursue this argument here. All that is suggested in this book is that, as a corollary of the traditional concern of the English criminal law with moral

---

[151] 'It should . . . be borne in mind that a stay on the basis of abuse of process must never be seen to be used simply as a form of disciplinary disapproval of the CPS' (*R. v. Norwich Crown Court, ex p. Belsham* [1992] 1 WLR 54, 69).

integrity (as illustrated in Chapter 1), the principle of judicial legitimacy should be recognized even on concepts of criminal justice as presently accepted in England. If the doctrine of mens rea is entrenched in the English criminal law as a moral principle, so too should be the principle of judicial legitimacy.

There is a basic difference between application of the principle of judicial legitimacy in the context of double jeopardy and delay, on the one hand, and application of the principle in the context of investigatory impropriety on the other. We have seen that, in the case of double jeopardy and delay, the aspects *both* of protection of the innocent from wrongful conviction, and of protection of moral integrity, are relevant. In the case of investigatory impropriety, however, only the latter is normally relevant: there is typically no issue of whether the misconduct might in some way cause the defendant to be convicted even if innocent. For example, a defendant applying for a stay of the proceedings on account of illegal extradition is not challenging the veracity or reliability of the proceedings in terms of their ability to determine her guilt or innocence accurately. The sole issue is whether the continuation of the proceedings would compromise the moral integrity of the criminal process to such an extent that a stay should be ordered notwithstanding the public interest in bringing offenders to conviction. The analogy with the admissibility of improperly obtained, but reliable, evidence is therefore immediately apparent.

OTHER JURISDICTIONS

In Australia, the High Court recognizes the ability of a court to stay proceedings which are an abuse of the process of the court[152] but has not yet had the opportunity to acknowledge that this discretion extends, as an obvious corollary of the discretion to exclude improperly obtained evidence recognized in *Ireland* and *Bunning* v. *Cross*, to the staying of proceedings on grounds such as illegal extradition. However, the New South Wales Court of Appeal, the highest court in the State of New South Wales, stated unequivocally in *Levinge* v. *Director of Custodial Services*[153] that a stay of proceedings should be available in 'illegal extradition' cases in appropriate circumstances.[154] *Hartley*, *Mackeson*, and *Healy* were adopted in preference to *Driver*. *Levinge* has been subsequently followed in *R.* v. *Fan*,[155] a decision by a single judge of the Supreme Court of New South Wales. In both *Levinge* and *Fan*, however, it was held that a stay of the proceedings was not warranted in the circumstances of the case at hand.

---

[152] *Barton* v. R. (1980) 147 CLR 75. See also the discussions in the recent case of *Williams* v. *Spautz* (1992) 66 ALJR 585.   [153] (1987) 9 NSWLR 546.

[154] It is to be noted, however, that one of the three judges expressly reserved his opinion on the issue.   [155] (1989) 98 FLR 119.

The Irish Supreme Court, too, has acknowledged that it would be anomalous to recognize, as a procedural measure for dealing with pre-trial executive misconduct, a discretion to exclude evidence but not a discretion to stay proceedings. The case of *The State (Trimbole)* v. *The Governor of Mountjoy Prison*[156] is illuminating. At approximately 2 p.m. on 25 October 1984 Trimbole, an Australian citizen, was arrested in purported pursuance of section 30 of the Offences Against the State Act 1939, and detained in Dublin. He made an application to the Irish High Court the following day to have the legality of his detention ascertained. An inquiry held at 7 p.m. found that his arrest and hence his detention were illegal, and he was accordingly released. In the meantime, extradition arrangements between Ireland and Australia (previously non-existent) had been brought into existence at approximately 1.15 p.m. Immediately after his release Trimbole was arrested again, pursuant to a provisional warrant authorizing his arrest and detention on a number of charges relating to offences alleged to have been committed in Australia. An application was made by Trimbole to the Irish High Court for an inquiry into the legality of his detention. It was held by Egan J. that 'the only rational explanation' for the section 30 arrest on 25 October 1984 was to ensure that Trimbole would be available for arrest and detention when extradition arrangements between Ireland and Australia came into effect. Trimbole's present detention in extradition proceedings was 'the ultimate result of a conscious and deliberate violation of constitutional rights' and he should, accordingly, be released.[157]

This decision was affirmed by the Irish Supreme Court. McCarthy J., in particular, made strong statements about the need to refrain from turning a blind eye to executive improprieties:

If . . . the Executive itself abuses the process of law as in this case by the wrongful use of s. 30 . . . and, for what it is worth, persists in that abuse by giving false evidence in the course of the constitutional enquiry, are the courts to turn aside and, apart from administering severe strictures to those concerned, appear to sanction the procedure that has been adopted to secure the extradition of an individual to the requesting State?[158]

It was emphasized that this refusal to turn a blind eye to the executive misconduct should not be affected by the fact that Trimbole was an Australian citizen on a temporary visit to Ireland.[159] McCarthy J. then proceeded to acknowledge that, whilst there was a strong public interest in the continuation of the extradition proceedings, a far greater principle was at stake:

The release upon what may appear to have been a technical ground of an individual 'wanted' on serious charges may seem, at first sight, undesirable and, indeed,

---

[156] [1985] IR 550.   [157] Ibid. 566–7.   [158] Ibid. 581.
[159] Ibid. 581–2.

contrary to public policy; it may seem highly contrary to public policy that elaborate arrangements for extradition should be set at nought by what may be termed an excess of zeal. In my judgment, however, a far greater principle is at stake: that part of the Executive represented by the Garda authorities and those others responsible for what I have termed the plan to extradite the prosecutor must not be permitted to think that conduct of this kind will at worst result in a judicial rebuke, however severe.[160]

RELEVANT CRITERIA, CONCEPTS, ISSUES, AND FACTORS

It is proposed to embark now upon an examination of a number of criteria, concepts, issues, and factors which may be relevant in applying the judicial legitimacy principle to determine whether proceedings made possible by police misconduct at the investigatory stage should be stayed. Since, as emphasized above, the discretion to stay 'tainted' proceedings is simply the complement of the discretion to exclude improperly obtained evidence, discussions undertaken in judicial decisions on improperly obtained evidence are highly relevant. In *O'Brien*, the Irish Supreme Court set out a number of factors which it thought might be taken into account in determining whether or not an item of improperly obtained evidence should be excluded.[161] The High Court of Australia did the same thing in *Bunning* v. *Cross*,[162] as did the Supreme Court of Canada in *R. v. Collins*.[163] Law-reform bodies and academic commentators, too, have contributed significantly in this area.

(a) Was a Serious Infringement of Rights Involved?

An important factor to be considered is whether the investigatory impropriety in question involved a serious infringement of the rights of the accused. Such an infringement would obviously weigh more heavily in favour of a stay of the proceedings than would a less serious infringement. The more serious the infringement, the greater the likelihood that the moral integrity of the criminal justice system, and hence judicial legitimacy, would be compromised by the continuation of the proceedings. The Supreme Court of Canada has acknowledged that 'a violation of the sanctity of a person's body is much more serious than that of his office or even of his home'.[164]

---

[160] Ibid. 585.

[161] [1965] IR 142, 160–1. It was emphasized, however, that 'it would not be in accordance with our system of jurisprudence for this Court to attempt to lay down rules to govern future hypothetical cases' (ibid. 161). [162] (1978) 141 CLR 54.

[163] (1987) 56 CR (3d) 193.

[164] *R. v. Pohoretsky* (1987) 58 CR (3d) 113, 116. See also *R. v. Wise* (1992) 11 CR (4th) 253, in which it is suggested that an invasion of privacy of a motor vehicle is less serious than that of a home or office.

Clearly, the infringement of what the law regards as a fundamental right of the accused would easily tip the scales in favour of a stay. It is possible to conceive of situations where rights of the accused which are of such fundamental importance are violated that the presumption will be that a stay of the proceedings is called for. Suppose, for example, that the illegal extradition of the accused was accompanied by the torture of the accused by the UK authorities—a clear infringement of the basic right to freedom from physical abuse. In such a situation it is difficult to imagine a trial judge declaring that judicial legitimacy would not be compromised by the continuation of the proceedings. Indeed, there is a lot to be said for the adoption of a *rule* that any proceedings which are 'tainted' by very serious infringements of rights by UK authorities—for example, torture—must be automatically stayed. Some conduct is so egregious that it should never be excused, factors such as the seriousness of the crime charged notwithstanding. Indeed, there has been legislative recognition of this in England in the context of the admissibility of confessions: section 76(2)(*a*) of PACE renders any confession obtained by oppression automatically inadmissible.

Situations may arise where a serious infringement occurred of the rights not of the accused, but of a third party. Judicial legitimacy is obviously less likely to be compromised where a court excuses a serious violation of the rights of a third party than where it excuses a similar violation of the rights of the defendant. A third party is not exposed to the possibility of conviction and punishment (and the attendant social stigma). However, there would still be a strong case for a stay of the proceedings where, for example, torture of the third party was involved.

(*b*) Did the Police Act in Good Faith?

Whether the police knowingly exceeded the bounds of legality is another factor which ought to be taken into account in applying the judicial legitimacy principle. Turning a blind eye to an executive impropriety would have a higher tendency to compromise judicial legitimacy if the police deliberately flouted the law than if they were, for example, simply mistaken about the scope of their powers.[165]

---

[165] See R. v. *Duarte* (1990) 65 DLR (4th) 240, 262: 'What strikes one here is that the breach was in no way deliberate, wilful or flagrant. The police officers acted entirely in good faith. They were acting in accordance with what they had good reason to believe was the law—as it had been for many years before the advent of the Charter. The reasonableness of their action is underscored by the seriousness of the offence. They had reasonable and probable cause to believe the offence had been committed, and had they properly understood the law, they could have obtained an authorization under the *Code* to intercept the communication. Indeed, they could have proceeded without resorting to electronic surveillance and relied solely on the evidence of the undercover officer or the informer. In short, the Charter breach stemmed from an entirely reasonable misunderstanding of the law by the police officers who would otherwise have obtained the necessary evidence to convict the accused in any event. Under these circumstances, I hold that the appellant has not established that the admission of the evidence

(c) Were there Circumstances of Urgency, Emergency, or Necessity?

The presence of circumstances of urgency, emergency, or necessity would tend in favour of excusing an executive impropriety which occurred at the investigatory stage. It is frequently pointed out in the context of improperly obtained evidence, for example, that it may happen that an item of evidence will almost certainly be destroyed if it is not seized immediately. Again, 'much may be forgiven a police officer in pursuit of a homicidal maniac, or of a robber about to flee the jurisdiction, or of a sexual offender against children who is likely to repeat his crime.'[166]

In the absence of circumstances of urgency, emergency, or necessity, however, what is the relevance of the fact that the police resorted to underhand methods of investigation because proper methods were unavailable? The Canadian case of *R. v. Kokesch*,[167] although pertaining to illegally obtained evidence, is instructive. The police resorted to an illegal search because they did not have the requisite grounds to obtain either a search warrant or an authorization to intercept private communications. Should the fact that the police did not have the requisite grounds go any way towards excusing the impropriety? The Canadian Supreme Court correctly thought not: 'the unavailability of other, constitutionally permissible, investigative techniques is neither an excuse nor a justification for constitutionally impermissible investigative techniques.'[168] In other words, if the police cannot proceed legally, they should not (in the absence of circumstances of urgency, emergency, or necessity) proceed at all; it is not for them to charge ahead and then try to justify their actions later by asserting that they acted illegally because they could not act legally. The circularity of such a line of reasoning is obvious.

(d) How Serious was the Offence Charged?

The Irish Supreme Court,[169] High Court of Australia,[170] and Supreme

---

would bring the administration of justice into disrepute.' See also *R. v. DeBot* (1989) 73 CR (3d) 129, 157 per Wilson J.; *R. v. Wong* (1990) 1 CR (4th) 1, 19 per La Forest J.; S. G. Coughlan, 'Good Faith and Exclusion of Evidence under the *Charter*' (1992) 11 *Criminal Reports* (4th) 304.

[166] New South Wales Law Reform Commission, *Working Paper on Illegally and Improperly Obtained Evidence* (1979) para. 3.12. In a similar vein the Canadian Supreme Court has acknowledged (*R. v. Genest* (1989) 45 CCC (3d) 385, 407) that 'whether the circumstances of the case show a real threat of violent behaviour, whether directed at the police or third parties', is a relevant consideration. 'Obviously, the police will use a different approach when the suspect is known to be armed and dangerous than they will in arresting someone for outstanding traffic tickets.' See also *R. v. Wise* (1992) 11 CR (4th) 253, 270: 'there was a real threat of urgency flowing from the two most recent homicides in the community coupled with the telephone threat of further murders which motivated police action.'

[167] (1990) 1 CR (4th) 62.   [168] Ibid. 67.

[169] *The People (AG) v. O'Brien* [1965] IR 142, 160–1.

[170] *Bunning v. Cross* (1978) 141 CLR 54, 80. The Australian Law Reform Commission

Court of Canada[171] have all acknowledged that the gravity of the offence charged is an important factor to be considered in applying the judicial legitimacy principle. Obviously the more serious the offence charged, the greater the public interest in bringing the perpetrator to conviction, and hence the lower the likelihood of judicial legitimacy being compromised should the impropriety be excused by the court. Thus in *Bunning* v. *Cross* the Australian High Court stated that 'some examination of the comparative seriousness of the offence and of the unlawful conduct of the law enforcement authority'[172] is called for. In *O'Brien*, a decision on illegally obtained evidence, Kingsmill Moore J. of the Irish Supreme Court referred to two US decisions[173] involving gambling offences, in which evidence of conversations overheard by means of microphones illegally concealed on private property was excluded. He added: 'I can, however, conceive that if a discretionary rule were applicable a judge might take a different view if the conversation revealed a conspiracy to murder or the activities of a narcotic organisation.'[174]

The concept of offence seriousness is one which plays an important role in sentencing. For example, section 2(2)(*a*) of the Criminal Justice Act 1991 provides that a custodial sentence, other than one fixed by law, is to be for a term which in the opinion of the court is 'commensurate with the seriousness of the offence, or the combination of the offence and other offences associated with it'. It is suggested, therefore, that useful guidance on the relative seriousness with which various offences should be regarded may be obtained from judicial decisions on sentencing.[175]

---

takes the same view (Australian Law Reform Commission, *Evidence*, i, para. 964): 'There is, for example, a greater public interest that a murderer be convicted and dealt with under the law than someone guilty of a victimless crime.'

[171] *R.* v. *Collins* (1987) 56 CR (3d) 193, 212.

[172] (1978) 141 CLR 54, 80.

[173] *People* v. *Cahan* 282 P. 2d 905 (1955); *Silverman* v. *US* 365 US 505 (1961).

[174] [1965] IR 142, 161. It is to be noted that a suggested modification to the US exclusionary rule, proposed by Professor Kaplan in 1974, was that the rule should be inapplicable 'in the most serious cases—treason, espionage, murder, armed robbery, and kidnaping by organized groups'. See generally Kaplan, 'The Limits of the Exclusionary Rule', 1027. For criticism of this proposal, see W. R. LaFave, *Search and Seizure: A Treatise on the Fourth Amendment*, i (2nd edn., 1987) 43–4 and associated section in *1992 Pocket Part*. See also Y. Kamisar, ' "Comparative Reprehensibility" and the Fourth Amendment Exclusionary Rule' (1987) 86 *Michigan Law Review* 1.

[175] The word 'serious' is not defined in the Act. A. Samuels, 'Serious: What is a Serious Offence?' (1992) 156 *Justice of the Peace* 59, 59 feels that 'matters likely to be relevant will include the degree of knowledge, maturity, wilfulness, premeditation, whether the offence was committed singly or in concert with others, the extent of the injuries or fear or the damage or the loss to the victim. . . . [Further], the aggravating and mitigating circumstances of the offence concerning the particular offender must presumably be brought into play in order to measure the seriousness.' Samuels provides some examples of offences which have been regarded by the Court of Appeal as 'serious' or 'not so serious'. See also S. R. Savage, 'Criminal Justice Act 1991—Sentenced by Seriousness' (1992) 156 *Justice of the Peace* 550; M. D. Dodds, 'The

(e) Was a Direct Sanction Available?

The availability of a direct sanction against the person(s) responsible for the impropriety may also be a relevant factor. Such a view would appear to have been taken by the Australian courts in relation to illegally obtained evidence. In *French* v. *Scarman* the Supreme Court of South Australia said that section 47f of the Road Traffic Act 1961–76 (SA)

imposes no penalty upon a police officer who fails to comply with sub-s. (2). . . . The absence of any sanction other than the exclusion of the evidence of the breath analysis must be an important factor in considering whether to exercise the discretion.[176]

The Australian Law Reform Commission, too, has acknowledged that a relevant factor in applying the judicial legitimacy principle is 'whether any other proceeding (whether or not in a court) has been or is likely to be taken in relation to the impropriety or contravention'.[177]

By contrast, the Supreme Court of Canada has said in relation to illegally obtained evidence that, 'once it has been decided that the administration of justice would be brought into disrepute by the admission of the evidence, the disrepute will not be lessened by the existence of some ancillary remedy'.[178] This is clearly inaccurate as a generality. Turning a blind eye to executive misconduct *could* have a lower tendency to compromise the moral integrity of the criminal justice system, and hence judicial legitimacy, where some other proceeding has been or is likely to be taken in relation to the misconduct, than would otherwise be the case. Obviously, the nature of the ancillary proceeding in question is an important consideration. If the defendant has already received or is entitled to substantial monetary compensation in respect of the impropriety, it may quite legitimately be decided that turning a blind eye to the impropriety would not compromise judicial legitimacy to the extent that turning a blind eye to a totally 'unremedied' or 'unremediable' impropriety would do. On the other hand, the fact that internal disciplinary measures are likely to be taken against the errant police officer would probably be of little relevance.[179]

Restrictions on Custodial Sentences in the Criminal Justice Act 1991—Sentencing Guidelines from the Criminal Justice Act 1982' (1992) 156 *Justice of the Peace* 691, 710, 726; *R.* v. *Coote, The Times*, 7 May 1992. Note that para. 8 of the Code for Crown Prosecutors provides that, 'in assessing the gravity of the offence, it will be necessary to consider whether the victim has suffered significant harm or loss: the meaning of "significant" may be relative to the circumstances of the victim'.

[176] (1979) 20 SASR 333, 340–1.

[177] Australian Law Reform Commission, *Evidence*, ii (Report No. 38) (1987), Draft Evidence Bill, cl. 119(3).

[178] *R.* v. *Collins* (1987) 56 CR (3d) 193, 213.

[179] See also P. Mirfield, 'The Early Jurisprudence of Judicial Disrepute' (1988) 30 *Criminal Law Quarterly* 434, 463–4.

(*f*) Issues of 'Causation'

A broad approach should be taken to the issue of whether a prosecution is 'tainted' by a pre-trial investigatory impropriety and hence liable to be stayed. It should not be necessary to show that the prosecution would not have been commenced *but for* the impropriety. Rather, the fact that the impropriety made a significant contribution to, or was an important or crucial factor in, the ability to bring the prosecution should suffice. For an item of evidence to be considered 'improperly obtained' and hence liable to be excluded, proof that the evidence would not have been obtained but for the impropriety is unnecessary. Thus there is no reason why a strict causation or 'but for' test should need to be satisfied where the application is for a stay of proceedings rather than for the exclusion of evidence.

Much guidance can be obtained from the approach taken by the Canadian Supreme Court to causation issues pertaining to the exclusion of evidence under section 24(2) of the Canadian Charter of Rights and Freedoms. In *R. v. Strachan*[180] Dickson CJC, with whom the rest of the Court agreed on this point, provided fairly detailed reasoning for his view that a causal connection was unnecessary. He pointed out that the imposition of a causal requirement would give the courts the 'highly artificial task' of speculating whether the evidence would have been discovered had the Charter violation not occurred:

Isolating the events that caused the evidence to be discovered from those that did not is an exercise in sophistry. Events are complex and dynamic. It will never be possible to state with certainty what would have taken place had a Charter violation not occurred. Speculation of this sort is not, in my view, an appropriate inquiry for the courts.[181]

Additionally, to require a causal connection

will tend to distort the analysis of the conduct that led to the discovery of evidence. The inquiry will tend to focus narrowly on the actions most directly responsible for the discovery of evidence rather than on the entire course of events leading to its discovery. This will almost inevitably lead to an intellectual endeavour essentially amounting to 'splitting hairs' between conduct that violated the Charter and that which did not.[182]

Dickson CJC thought that it had to be determined on a case-by-case basis whether evidence obtained following a Charter breach was too remote from the violation to be regarded as having been 'obtained in a manner' which

---

[180] (1988) 56 DLR (4th) 673. Cf. B. Donovan, 'The Role of Causation under S. 24(2) of the *Charter*: Nine Years of Inconclusive Jurisprudence' (1991) 49(2) *University of Toronto Faculty of Law Review* 233, who argues that cases decided by the Canadian Supreme Court subsequent to *Strachan* may not be entirely consistent with *Strachan*.
[181] (1988) 56 DLR (4th) 673, 690.   [182] Ibid.

infringed the Charter: 'there can be no hard and fast rule for determining when evidence obtained following the infringement of a Charter right becomes too remote.'[183]

Finally, Dickson CJC observed that[184] the presence of a causal connection was a factor to be considered in determining whether the admission of the evidence would bring the administration of justice into disrepute—it would weigh in favour of exclusion of the evidence.[185]

For analogous reasons, there is much merit in treating the presence of a causal link as a *factor* to be considered in applying the principle of judicial legitimacy to determine whether proceedings should be stayed on account of police impropriety at the investigatory stage. The stronger the link, the more likely that judicial legitimacy will be compromised by the continuation of the proceedings. It is pointless, therefore, to engage in a separate, preliminary determination of causation issues.

(g) Onus of Proof

An important issue for consideration relates to which party should bear the onus of proof once the relevant impropriety is established. Two possibilities may be suggested. The first is that the accused should bear the onus of satisfying the trial judge that the proceedings should be stayed. Alternatively, it may be suggested that the onus should lie on the prosecution to prove that the proceedings should not be stayed.

One might argue that, if the accused seeks a stay of the proceedings on the ground of executive impropriety which occurred at the investigatory stage, the onus should be on her to justify the stay. I would suggest, however, that it is more appropriate to place the onus on those responsible for the impugned conduct to justify that conduct.[186] In a similar vein, the original

---

[183] Ibid. 693.   [184] Ibid.

[185] See also *R. v. DeBot* (1989) 73 CR (3d) 129, 135: 'Determining the exclusion or admission of evidence obtained as a result of an unreasonable search is quite different from determining the exclusion or admission of evidence obtained as a result of a search which was perfectly valid but which was carried out contemporaneously with a s. 10(*b*) violation. While the violation of s. 8 is directly linked to the obtaining of the evidence, the violation of s. 10 could be very remote; indeed, it could be totally unrelated to the finding of the evidence. For example, in this case the appellant was subjected to a warrantless "frisk" search authorized by s. 37 [now s. 42] of the Food and Drugs Act. The search was carried out contemporaneous with a violation of the appellant's s. 10(*b*) rights under the Charter. But, as Wilson J. notes in her discussion of s. 24(2) in this case, the evidence obtained was real evidence the existence of which, and I hasten to add its seizure, was totally unrelated to the Charter violation. This link, or in this case the lack of it, of course makes a great difference when assessing whether the repute of our system of justice will be harmed by the admission of the evidence.'

[186] See generally Australian Law Reform Commission, *Criminal Investigation*, para. 298; Australian Law Reform Commission, *Evidence*, i, para. 964. It is to be noted that in *R. v. Collins* (1976) 12 SASR 501, 508–9, Bray CJ made the following remarks in relation to the admissibility of a confession: 'I think I must accept these authorities [*R. v. Lee* (1950) 82 CLR

proposal for section 78 of PACE placed upon the prosecution the onus of justifying the inclusion of improperly obtained evidence. An important practical consideration is that it is often the prosecution rather than the defence which will have access to relevant information and witnesses. For example, it was demonstrated earlier in the chapter that a factor which may be taken into account in applying the principle of judicial legitimacy is whether the police acted in good faith. Surely it is more appropriate to place the onus on the prosecution to prove that the police did act in good faith than to place the onus on the accused to prove the reverse. To take another example, for the prosecution to have to prove the existence of circumstances of urgency, emergency, or necessity is surely fairer than for the defence to have to prove the absence of such circumstances.

133; *Wendo* v. R. (1963) 109 CLR 559; *R.* v. *Buckskin* (1974) 10 SASR 1] and therefore hold, the question of voluntariness not being in dispute, that it was for the appellant to establish on the balance of probabilities that the detectives persisted in questioning him after he had declared his unwillingness to answer except in the presence of his solicitor. I may be permitted, with respect, to express some regrets that the law has developed in this way. I agree wholeheartedly that he who asks the court to exercise some discretion in his favour by relaxing the normal operation of the law should show some reason for it. But it might have been thought a sufficient reason to entitle the judge to reject a voluntary confession if he was left in doubt as to whether or not it had been obtained unfairly.'

5

Procedural Issues

In this chapter it is proposed to consider various procedural issues associated with the exercise of the judicial power to stay proceedings as an abuse of process. The fact that the power is a discretionary one does have some significance from the point of view of procedure, and it is therefore necessary at the outset to examine the concept of judicial discretion in some detail. It will be demonstrated that, while the exercise of judicial discretion is indispensable to the attainment of individualized justice, it does have the potential to lead to uncertainty and unpredictability. However, such problems are likely to be minimized if discretion is appropriately confined, structured, and checked. How this might be achieved in relation to the abuse of process discretion will be discussed.

Specific procedural issues associated with the exercise of the abuse of process discretion both in the Crown Court and in the magistrates' courts are also examined in this chapter. In relation to the Crown Court, we examine matters such as the process of the voir dire, pre-trial inquiries, appeals to the Court of Appeal, and whether it is possible to apply to the Divisional Court for judicial review of the exercise by a Crown Court judge of the abuse of process discretion. In relation to magistrates' courts, matters such as the availability of the abuse of process discretion in committal proceedings are discussed.

The Concept of Judicial Discretion

What exactly does it mean to say that a decision to stay proceedings as an abuse of process is one reached in the exercise of judicial discretion rather than one reached as a matter of law, or, to put it another way, pursuant to a rule or principle of law? In other words, what is it that distinguishes a judicial discretion from a rule or principle of law? Two possible interpretations of the concept of judicial discretion may be suggested.[1]

---

[1] See R. Dworkin, *Taking Rights Seriously* (1977) 31 ff., where it is pointed out that the word 'discretion' may be used in both a weak and a strong sense. See also D. Jennex, 'Dworkin and the Doctrine of Judicial Discretion' (1992) 14 *Dalhousie Law Journal* 473. Cf. D. J. Galligan, *Discretionary Powers: A Legal Study of Official Discretion* (1990), 37–46, where

INTERPRETATION 1: TOTALLY UNFETTERED POWER

The first interpretation treats judicial discretion as signifying totally unfettered power on the part of the trial judge. In taking the view that the exclusion of evidence under section 24(2) of the Canadian Charter of Rights and Freedoms did *not* involve the exercise of discretion, Le Dain J. in *R. v. Therens* was obviously subscribing to this interpretation of 'discretion':

> The exclusion of evidence under s. 24(2) does not, as has been suggested by some, involve the exercise of a discretion. Section 24(2) involves the application of a broad test or standard, which necessarily gives a court some latitude, but that is not, strictly speaking, a discretion. A discretion exists where there is a choice to do one thing or another, not merely because what is involved is the application of a flexible standard. Under the terms of s. 24(2), where a judge concludes that the admission of evidence would bring the administration of justice into disrepute, he or she has a duty, not a discretion, to exclude the evidence.[2]

Thus it would seem that, on this interpretation of discretion, a judge is at liberty to reach conclusion *B* even though an application of the relevant test or standard requires that conclusion *A* be reached. In the context of abuse of process, this means that a judge is at liberty to allow proceedings to continue even though she determines that an application of the judicial legitimacy principle requires otherwise. This can hardly be correct. It is difficult to imagine that a judge can, in all conscience *as a judge*, say: 'Taking into account the need to protect the innocent from wrongful conviction, and the need to protect the moral integrity of the criminal justice system, and looking at these against the background of the need to bring offenders to conviction, the proceedings should certainly be stayed, but I am going to exercise my discretion in favour of allowing them to continue.'

INTERPRETATION 2: OPEN-TEXTUREDNESS

The second, and preferable, interpretation of 'discretion' relates to the open-texturedness of the test or standard to be applied in reaching a conclusion. The term 'rule', by contrast, is taken as meaning 'a legal precept attaching a definite detailed legal consequence to a definite detailed state of fact.'[3] It is submitted that it is in this sense that the term 'discretion' is most appropriately used. Hence, 'a discretion necessarily involves a latitude of individual choice according to the particular circumstances, and differs

three aspects of judicial discretion (discretion implied in deciding cases, discretion to change the law, and delegated discretion) are distinguished, and R. Pattenden, *Judicial Discretion and Criminal Litigation* (1990), 1–4, where five usages of the word 'discretion' are broadly distinguished, and the relationship between the usages explained. See also A. Barak, *Judicial Discretion* (1989).

[2] (1985) 18 DLR (4th) 655, 687–8.　　　[3] R. Pound, *Jurisprudence*, ii (1959), 124.

from a case where the decision follows ex debito justitiae once the facts are ascertained.'[4] The principle of judicial legitimacy clearly represents a test or standard which is open-textured in nature. Thus, an application of the principle of judicial legitimacy to determine whether proceedings should be stayed involves judicial discretion in the sense that it

requires a personal assessment of the circumstances. As reasonable men will legitimately differ, except in extreme cases, about [the conclusion reached], it follows that the judge in fact exercises a choice, even if it is an unconscious one.[5]

As will be seen later in the chapter, a corollary of this need for a personal assessment of the circumstances is that an appellate court will overturn an exercise of discretion in limited circumstances only.

The pros and cons of discretion have been actively debated by the judiciary and in the academic literature. On the one hand, it is clear that a measure of discretion is necessary to enable all relevant considerations to be taken into account in the individual case. A rule may have the benefit of predictability and certainty, but 'certainty can be bought at too high a price'.[6] As K. C. Davis has observed: 'Rules without discretion cannot fully take into account the need for tailoring results to unique facts and circumstances of particular cases. The justification for discretion is often the need for individualized justice. This is so in the judicial process as well as in the administrative process.'[7] 'Individualization', Lord Justice James noted extra-judicially, 'cannot be achieved without a discretion being exercised.'[8] And, as Roscoe Pound has put it, very succinctly:

Rules in many matters are needed to guide the weak judge and to save us from his lack of will and lack of judgment. But these same rules may only serve to hamper the

---

[4] *Evans* v. *Bartlam* [1937] AC 473, 489 per Lord Wright.

[5] R. Pattenden, *The Judge, Discretion, and the Criminal Trial* (1982), 4. Cf. Y.-M. Morissette, 'The Exclusion of Evidence under the *Canadian Charter of Rights and Freedoms*: What to Do and What Not to Do' (1984) 29 *McGill Law Journal* 521, 553: 'The range of factors and circumstances which the court can consider under section 24(2) necessarily denotes a discretion. So does the generality of wording of section 24(2) and the lack of any guidance in the *Charter* itself as to the respective weight or significance of these factors and circumstances. The provision manifestly calls for individualized solutions in response to the specific factual features of each case ("having regard to all the circumstances"), something more easily achieved by preserving a good measure of discretion at trial level.' Note also the following comment by Kirby P. in *Gill* v. *Walton* (1991) 25 NSWLR 190, 205: 'The words of the tests to be applied echo detailed legal analysis provided in earlier cases and differing factual circumstances. The later decision-maker will strive faithfully to apply those tests by analogous reasoning to the new circumstances under scrutiny. The answer given to a problem such as the present can be buried in words. But, in the end, it may represent nothing more than an instinctual reaction to the whole of the facts.'

[6] *Firman* v. *Ellis* [1978] QB 886, 911 per Ormrod LJ.

[7] K. C. Davis, *Discretionary Justice: A Preliminary Inquiry* (1971), 17.

[8] Lord Justice James, 'A Judicial Note on the Control of Discretion in the Administration of Criminal Justice', in R. Hood (ed.), *Crime, Criminology and Public Policy: Essays in Honour of Sir Leon Radzinowicz* (1974), 157.

strong judge and to prevent application of the full measure of his sound sense and good judgment to the case in hand. Such a magistrate may know how to take account of some things, which could not be included in a rule, which nevertheless may be more or less controlling in the individual cause.[9]

The judiciary, too, has started to recognize the importance of giving trial judges an appropriate measure of discretion in relation to evidential and procedural matters. Speaking of the issue of directions on corroboration, Roch J. said in *R. v. Chance*:

The aim of any direction to a jury must be to provide realistic, comprehensible and common sense guidance to enable them to avoid pitfalls and to come to a fair and just conclusion as to the guilt or innocence of the defendant. This involves the necessity of the judge tailoring his direction to the facts of the particular case. If he is required to apply rigid rules, there will inevitably be occasions when the direction will be inappropriate to the facts. Juries are quick to spot such anomalies, and will understandably view the anomaly, and often (as a result) the rest of the directions, with suspicion, thus undermining the judge's purpose. Directions on corroboration are particularly subject to this danger . . .[10]

On the other hand, however, there is in some quarters considerable hostility to the idea of judicial discretion. Isaacs wrote of this

aesthetic desire for a complete, rounded system that will take care of every situation almost mechanically. But even if we succeed in getting away from the academic considerations in favor of a law that acts automatically, there is on the human side of the question a desire for a government of laws and not of men, especially in a democratic state, a desire that urges us to minimize, if not to eliminate, the power of the personal judge in the regulation of our affairs.[11]

Those opposed to judicial discretion point to the fact that its inherent flexibility produces considerable uncertainty of application. A rule, on the other hand, would go further in ensuring uniformity of treatment, with 'like' cases being treated alike.[12] Thus it might be argued against adoption of the principle of judicial legitimacy being advocated in this work that whether a particular prosecution should be stayed would be likely in many circumstances to be difficult, or even impossible, to predict. This criticism is clearly unjustifiable. If the flexibility inherent in many of the principles of criminal evidence (such as the similar-facts principle and the principles governing the exclusion of evidence under section 78 of PACE) can be

---

[9] Pound, *Jurisprudence*, ii. 367–8.   [10] [1988] 3 All ER 225, 231.

[11] N. Isaacs, 'The Limits of Judicial Discretion' (1923) 32 *Yale Law Journal* 339, 343. For a strong condemnation of discretion, see American Friends Service Committee, *Struggle for Justice: A Report on Crime and Punishment in America* (1971), ch. 8.

[12] J. Jowell and D. Oliver, *The Changing Constitution* (2nd edn., 1989), 9. See also M. Kelman, *A Guide to Critical Legal Studies* (1987), 44: 'Rules are good because they make the outcome of any possible litigation so certain, so readily ascertainable in advance by both parties, that the administratively expensive process of litigation will rarely be invoked.'

tolerated, it is difficult to see why application of the principle of judicial legitimacy in relation to stays of proceedings should be singled out for criticism. Recognition of the importance of the social need to apply the judicial legitimacy principle in individual cases should offset any worries about the undesirability of unpredictability.[13] Moreover, problems of unpredictability and of uncertainty of application are likely in any event to be minimized with the emergence of a body of decisions, particularly appellate decisions.[14]

In the light of the foregoing discussions, it is now timely to explore some of the theoretical issues associated with discretion in greater detail. There are two important issues underlying the concept of discretion—arbitrariness and fairness—and these will be examined in turn.

(a) Arbitrariness

A common criticism levelled against discretion is that it may result in arbitrary decisions. 'Wherever there is discretion', Dicey wrote, 'there is room for arbitrariness.'[15] An arbitrary decision may be defined as one based upon improper criteria which do not relate in any rational way to the relevant goal. Thus 'the paradigm arbitrary decision', Jowell points out, 'is one based upon particularistic criteria such as friendship, or ascriptive criteria such as race, or upon caprice, whim, or prejudice.'[16] Some illustrations pertaining to arbitrariness in the exercise of police discretion are provided by Jowell. Suppose that, owing to a lack of resources, the police can stop only one of every four motorists found to be speeding. Police discretion moves towards the arbitrary where a police patrolman, instead of randomly selecting one of every four speeding cars, stops only long-haired drivers of speeding blue cars. The decision would certainly be arbitrary if the police officer were to stop black speeders only, or to refrain from

---

[13] Cf. G. J. Postema, *Bentham and the Common Law Tradition* (1986), 347, where he notes Bentham's 'strategy of assigning to the judge, rather than to fixed formal rules, the task of resolving the inevitable conflict amongst the various ends of adjudication. This conflict is to be resolved, upon each occasion, by the judge appealing to the principle of utility. . . . the two conflicting sets of ends which define the proper objectives of procedure simply mark out the most important species of utility and disutility which the judge must weigh in each particular case to determine the appropriate way to proceed. Rules have a place in this scheme, but they never impose absolute requirements on decision or action and the judge is empowered to make decisions which appeal directly to the principle of utility.'

[14] In *O'Brien*, the Irish Supreme Court acknowledged that 'the result of [appellate] decisions, based on the facts of individual cases, may in time give rise to more precise rules' ([1965] IR 142, 161). Morissette, 'The Exclusion of Evidence under the *Canadian Charter of Rights and Freedoms*', 553, has written of s. 24(2) of the Canadian Charter: 'It will be exercised judicially, according to reason and, eventually, precedent; furthermore, appellate courts will continue to supervise closely its use by trial courts.'

[15] A. V. Dicey, *Introduction to the Study of the Law of the Constitution* (10th edn., 1964), 188.

[16] J. L. Jowell, *Law and Bureaucracy: Administrative Discretion and the Limits of Legal Action* (1975), 14.

stopping a speeder who is a friend or relative or who has offered him a bribe. Such criteria for not invoking the criminal process (race, friendship) are not rationally related to the goal of preventing unsafe driving, and are therefore improper. However, the use of improper criteria which may be rationally related to the relevant goal will make a decision nonarbitrary (for instance, if customs officials search only long-haired youths for illicit drugs on the basis that a positive correlation between long-haired youth and drug use has been demonstrated).[17]

Thus arbitrariness is, as Galligan points out, the antithesis of rationality. A rational action is one which the actor believes to be a means to a given end, while an action is arbitrary if she does not have that belief.[18] An action is not arbitrary, however, merely because it is less rational than it might be; it must also fall below or violate a minimum threshold of rationality.[19] Galligan points out that the formulation of some level of general standards would normally serve to enhance the rational basis of decisions and eliminate arbitrariness, but that just how precise and exacting these standards should be depends on a number of factors which relate to the effective realization of the objects of power: the need for guidance, the nature and complexity of the task, the expertise of officials, and the opportunity for participation by individuals and groups.[20]

The rational basis of decisions may be enhanced not only by some level of general standards but also by consistency. The principle of consistency requires that, once a set of reasons has been relied upon in reaching a decision, the same reasons should be followed in future cases, unless further reasons are advanced for not so doing. However, as Galligan points out, consistent treatment does not necessarily imply rational treatment. For instance, a principle of sentencing which required the imprisonment of all first offenders could be applied consistently, but it would be difficult to describe it as rational. Further, it is not necessarily irrational and arbitrary for a judge to depart from, reject, or change a previous ruling in deciding the present case: she might change her mind about its wisdom or justice; she might have been mistaken or have acted on wrong or inadequate information; she might be able to think of better reasons for ruling differently; or the previous ruling might lead in the present case to an unacceptable outcome. In such circumstances it would be rational not only not to apply the previous ruling; it would, in fact, be irrational to do so unless such a course of action could be justified for other kinds of reasons.[21]

---

[17] Jowell, 15.
[18] Galligan, *Discretionary Powers: A Legal Study of Official Discretion*, 143.
[19] Ibid. 144.
[20] See generally ibid. 147–50.
[21] See generally ibid. 150–2.

(*b*) Fairness

The notion of fairness is based upon the risk of unequal treatment: 'treat like cases alike and different cases differently.' Similar cases are treated differently where extraneous matters are taken into account, or where not all relevant matters are considered, or where relevant matters are considered differently in similar cases in areas where important personal interests are at stake. Thus Galligan points out that it may be necessary, at the cost of reducing the degree of individualized attention to the circumstances of the particular case, to specify reasonably clear and objective standards against which decisions may be judged. This would remove any suspicion of unfairness in the sense of unequal treatment. By a similar token, there is also a case for acting consistently by extrapolating standards from precedents. However, in assessing how exacting the standards should be and how rigorously consistency should be maintained, equality of treatment, and hence fairness, should in the final analysis be judged on how well substantive principles of fairness are being achieved. It may be necessary, in order to attain acceptable levels of substantive fairness in particular cases, to maintain open standards and to refrain from applying consistency too strictly.

A further aspect of fairness concerns predictability. However, while some level of predictability may be a requirement of fairness, it may again be necessary to maintain substantial unpredictability in order to facilitate the attainment of substantively fair outcomes.[22]

The above discussions have shown that, whilst the exercise of discretion is indispensable to the attainment of individualized justice, there are a number of difficulties inherent in the notion of discretion. What is clearly necessary, then, is an acceptance of discretion, and a recognition at the same time of principles governing its exercise which are aimed at eliminating these difficulties. As Deane J. pointed out in *Phillips* v. *R.*, the fact that a discretion exists does not mean that the trial judge is free to act arbitrarily in exercising it. Rather, it must be exercised for the purpose for which it was conferred, and 'in the context of relevant legal principle and with due regard being paid to relevant considerations'.[23] It is wrong, it has also been pointed out, 'to equate the process of balancing the relevant factors in the exercise of a judicial discretion to the making of capricious and arbitrary decisions'.[24]

In his seminal work on *Discretionary Justice*, K. C. Davis makes the point that the aim should not be to eliminate discretionary power, but to confine, structure, and check it.[25] It is timely to proceed, therefore, to an

---

[22] See generally ibid. 152–61.
[23] (1985) 60 ALJR 76, 83.
[24] *Jago* v. *District Court (NSW)* (1989) 168 CLR 23, 29 per Mason CJ.
[25] K. C. Davis, *Discretionary Justice: A Preliminary Inquiry* (1971), 26.

examination of how such confining, structuring, and checking may be achieved in relation to the abuse of process discretion.

(*c*) Confining Discretion

To confine discretion is to eliminate and limit discretionary power, or, in other words, to fix the boundaries and keep discretion within them. The ideal would be 'to put all necessary discretionary power within the boundaries, to put all unnecessary such power outside the boundaries, and to draw clean lines'.[26]

A number of ways in which it is possible for the abuse of process discretion to be confined in specific contexts have already been examined in the preceding chapters. In particular, it was seen that double jeopardy represents one area in which it would be highly appropriate to confine discretion. This would be achieved by expanding the scope of the pleas in bar and reviving the doctrine of criminal issue estoppel, all of which represent principles of law, while leaving the abuse of process discretion to be exercised in exceptional cases.

One way of confining discretion has also been suggested in relation to stays of proceedings on the ground of police impropriety at the investigatory stage. This involves the adoption of a rule that any proceedings which are 'tainted' by very serious infringements of rights—for example, torture by UK authorities—must be automatically stayed. Thus discretion would be confined to situations where no such infringement has occurred (which would, presumably, represent the vast majority of cases). Another possible way of confining discretion in this area would be to adopt a rule whereby proceedings cannot be stayed on account of investigatory impropriety by the police where the offence charged is a very serious one. Thus discretion would be confined to situations where other offences are involved. Very serious offences may include offences such as murder, treason, terrorism, and the like. However, I would not propose that such a rule be adopted. While the fact that the offence charged is very serious would tip the scales heavily in favour of the continuation of the proceedings, there may be situations where a stay would still be appropriate. This may be the case, for instance, where the executive misconduct can be regarded as egregious even when viewed against the seriousness of the offence charged.

Thus, putting aside the rule which I have proposed in relation to very serious infringements of rights, I would argue that it is inappropriate to attempt to confine discretion in this field by adopting rules that, where particular conditions are satisfied, mandatory results should follow. The criteria, concepts, issues, and factors which are relevant to the application of the judicial legitimacy principle in cases involving police impropriety at the

---

[26] Davis, 55.

investigatory stage are too various to be subsumed under general rules. It is, indeed, for this very reason that the need for discretion is so crucial in this field.

(d) Structuring Discretion

Structuring discretion is not the same as confining it, although there may be some overlap between the two. The purpose of confining discretion is to keep it within designated boundaries, while the purpose of structuring it is to control the manner of its exercise within these boundaries. To structure discretion is to 'regularize it, organize it, produce order in it, so that . . . decisions affecting individual parties will achieve a higher quality of justice'.[27]

Discretion may be structured through the recognition of guide-lines for its exercise.[28] Guide-lines have the potential to ensure more open and rational decision-making. First, they provide the basis for accountability: public guide-lines can be a yardstick for testing decisions, and thus reduce the scope for reliance upon irrelevant, improper, or arbitrary factors. Secondly, the need to formulate guide-lines may encourage officials to think more carefully and critically about the objects to be attained and the policies to be followed. Thirdly, public guide-lines may advance a sense of procedural fairness by informing the citizen in advance of how she is likely to be treated, and encouraging consistency in treatment.[29]

Guide-lines, however, have a number of disadvantages. In particular, they may by their very nature restrict the factors which will be considered in individual decisions. As guide-lines become more precise and conclusive and therefore more like rules, they may exclude or restrict consideration of other factors. Thus the level of attainment of goals in individual cases may be reduced. Further, guide-lines may tend to ossify once they are formulated, and, instead of being reassessed regularly in the light of experience and purposes, come to be regarded as immutable.[30]

A brief analysis of the present legal position in relation to guide-lines in pre-trial discretionary decision-making is provided by Galligan. First, the policies of guide-lines must be within powers: they cannot be based upon irrelevant considerations, advance improper purposes, or be totally un-reasonable. Secondly, guide-lines must not be applied so strictly that they amount to a fettering of discretion (that is, decision-making on the basis of simply applying the relevant guide-lines). Rather, an attempt must be made

[27] Ibid. 97.
[28] See generally D. J. Galligan, 'Regulating Pre-Trial Decisions', in I. H. Dennis (ed.), *Criminal Law and Justice: Essays from the W. G. Hart Workshop, 1986* (1987), from which I have benefited in this paragraph and in the next two.   [29] Ibid. 184–5.
[30] Ibid. 186–7.

to consider the merits of the individual case, even if this means departing from the guide-lines.[31]

It is clear, therefore, that what is required in relation to guide-lines, as in relation to most matters pertaining to discretion, is the reaching of an appropriate balance or compromise. On the one hand guide-lines must be developed, but on the other hand they must not be applied rigidly to every case. The latter point was emphasized by the Lord Chief Justice in *R.* v. *Nicholas*[32] in the context of the sentencing discretion. Sentencing guide-lines, he stressed, were for assistance only and were not to be used as rules which were never to be departed from. And, as was put by Mason and Deane JJ in *Norbis* v. *Norbis*, in a discussion of the discretionary powers of the Family Court of Australia:

The point of preserving the width of the discretion which Parliament has created is that it maximises the possibility of doing justice in every case. But the need for consistency in judicial adjudication, which is the antithesis of arbitrary and capricious decision-making, provides an important countervailing consideration supporting the giving of guidance by appellate courts, whether in the form of principles or guidelines. ... To avoid the risk of inconsistency and arbitrariness, which is inherent in a system of relief involving a complex of discretionary assessments and judgments, the Full Court, as a specialist appellate court with unique experience in the field of family law in this country, should give guidance as to the manner in which these assessments and judgments are to be made. Yet guidance must be given in a way that preserves, so far as it is possible to do so, the capacity of the Family Court to do justice according to the needs of the individual case, whatever its complications may be. Reconciliation of these goals suggests that in most, if not all, cases the Full Court of the Family Court should give guidance in the form of guidelines rather than binding principles of law. ... The term 'guidelines', though not commonly used in relation to judicial discretions, is familiar enough in the bureaucratic and administrative world, where it denotes rules or standards which are not binding and may be relaxed when it is expedient to do so in order to do justice in the particular case.[33]

Detailed consideration of guide-lines which may be relevant in the exercise of discretion under the judicial legitimacy principle was undertaken in Chapter 3 (in the context of delay) and in Chapter 4 (in the context of investigatory impropriety). For example, it was seen that a determination of whether proceedings should be stayed on account of investigatory impropriety might involve a consideration of factors such as whether a serious infringement of rights was involved; whether the police acted in good faith; the presence or otherwise of circumstances of urgency, emergency, or necessity; the gravity of the offence charged; and the availability or otherwise of a direct sanction against the person(s) responsible for the

---

[31] Galligan, 187–8.   [32] *The Times*, 23 Apr. 1986.
[33] (1986) 60 ALJR 335, 337.

impropriety. From the foregoing discussions it is clear that factors such as these should not be applied rigidly and mechanically in every case. The guide-lines formulated in appellate decisions ought to be applied by lower courts if the possibilities of unfairness by virtue of varying practice are to be obviated. On the other hand, however, it is important that lower courts do not simply defer blindly to the analyses employed in appellate decisions; constant re-evaluation of the factors to be taken into account is required if the judicial legitimacy principle is to reflect its rationale fully. Appellate decisions may be of limited value in as much as decisions taken at first instance are hardly ever reversed (or even seriously reviewed) on appeal, particularly where what is involved is a question of fact.

(e) Checking Discretion

The 'principle of check' implies simply that one officer should check another, as a protection against arbitrariness.[34] For our purposes, checks would be provided primarily by appeals to the Court of Appeal, or applications to the Divisional Court for judicial review, on the basis of incorrect application of the judicial legitimacy principle.[35] The mechanics of such appeals and applications for judicial review will be discussed later in the chapter. It will be argued that the Court of Appeal and Divisional Court must formulate principles which provide sufficient guidance as to how the discretion should be exercised in individual cases, while at the same time leaving the discretion sufficiently unfettered to enable it to be adapted to new factual circumstances. Again, the 'bottom line' is that a careful balance should be reached between flexibility and predictability.

(f) Conclusion

One of the greatest merits of the abuse of process discretion, then, is its flexibility. Occasionally it may be possible and desirable to formulate fixed rules or principles of law, and therefore to confine the discretion (as in the case of the rule against double jeopardy), but most often such confinement would be either impossible or inappropriate. Discretion does not equate with arbitrariness if there exist sufficient guide-lines for the exercise of the discretion, as well as an adequate system of appellate and judicial review. In short, it is difficult to improve upon the following statement by Gaudron J. in *Jago* v. *District Court (NSW)*:

The power to grant a permanent stay of proceedings is a discretionary power. . . . The expression 'discretionary power' generally signifies a power exercisable by

---

[34] Davis, *Discretionary Justice*, 142.

[35] Cf. ibid. where it is suggested that the principle of check may be more effective where it is limited to correction of arbitrariness or illegality than where it includes *de novo* review. This is because a *de novo* review may itself introduce arbitrariness or illegality for the first time and not be checked.

reference to considerations no one of which and no combination of which is necessarily determinative of the result. In other words, it is a power which 'involves a considerable latitude of individual choice of a conclusion' . . . Notwithstanding this latitude, a discretionary power is necessarily confined by general principle. It is also confined by the matters which may be taken into account and by the matters, if any, which must be taken into account in its exercise.[36]

THE CROWN COURT

THE PROCESS OF THE VOIR DIRE

It is usual for applications for the exclusion of prosecution evidence or a stay of the proceedings[37] to be considered on a voir dire,[38] a trial within a trial which is held in the absence of the jury.[39] A voir-dire hearing is generally adversarial rather than inquisitorial in character: it has been remarked in Australia that 'in holding a trial within a trial a judge is not engaged in an inquisitorial procedure'.[40] It is generally thought that the conduct of a voir-dire hearing is a matter best left to be tailored by the trial judge to the circumstances of the individual case. For example, while it has been held on the one hand that an accused is not entitled as of right to give evidence on a voir dire,[41] it has been held on the other that she will be entitled to do so if the justice of the case makes it desirable that this should be done.[42] Mirfield points out that 'it is almost inconceivable that any judge would attempt to prevent the accused giving evidence on such a vital

---

[36] (1989) 168 CLR 23, 75–6.

[37] It would seem that, if the court has any cause to suspect that there is a ground for a stay of the proceedings, it has a duty to consider whether the proceedings should be stayed even in the absence of an application by the defence: *R. v. Liverpool Stipendiary Magistrate, ex p. Ellison* [1990] RTR 220, 227 per Bingham LJ. See also *Gillick v. West Norfolk AHA* [1986] AC 112, 178 per Lord Scarman: 'If there be in the present case an abuse of the process of the court, the House cannot overlook it, even if the parties are prepared to do so . . .'.

[38] 'The title of the procedure comes from the French "vrai dire" and the Latin "veritatem dicere" literally to "tell the truth". "Voir" (sometimes spelt "voire") is the Norman–French for "vrai" and reflects the long lineage of this judicial procedure' (Mr Justice J. H. Phillips, 'The Voir Dire' (1989) 63 *Australian Law Journal* 46, 46).

[39] There was a suggestion in the 1929 decision of the Court of Criminal Appeal in *R. v. Anderson* (1929) 21 Cr. App. R. 178 that an accused is entitled to demand that the jury remain in the courtroom during a voir dire. The correctness of this has, however, been questioned in the decision of the Court of Appeal in *R. v. Hendry, The Times*, 14 June 1988. It was said that, so far as the present day is concerned, and whatever might have been the position at the time of the decision in *Anderson*, it is for the judge to have the final word on whether the jury should remain in court. No doubt the judge would listen to the views of the defence. If this is a departure from *Anderson*—the Court continued—then it is a departure which is necessary in the circumstances of the present day. See also *R. v. Davis* [1990] Crim. LR 860, in which the Court of Appeal endorsed *Hendry*.

[40] *MacPherson v. R.* (1981) 55 ALJR 594, 606 per Brennan J.

[41] *R. v. James* (1963) 107 SJ 516.   [42] *R. v. Cowell* [1940] 2 KB 49.

issue'.[43] Thus, the principle that an accused is not entitled as of right to give evidence on a voir dire is, in practice, doubtful.[44] At a voir-dire hearing conducted to determine the admissibility of a confession, the usual procedure is for the prosecution to call witnesses to testify as to the circumstances in which the confession was obtained, and for the defence to cross-examine these witnesses.[45] The defence may then call any evidence it considers necessary. There is no reason why a similar procedure should not be adopted where the issue for determination is whether the proceedings should be stayed as an abuse of process.

It has been held by the Court of Appeal that a judge cannot try an issue of admissibility of evidence in total isolation on a voir dire; she cannot, and should not, put the whole background of the case out of her mind.[46] Presumably similar principles would apply in relation to an issue of whether the proceedings should be stayed as an abuse of process.

Where the accused testifies on a voir dire, may the prosecution lead evidence in the trial proper regarding this testimony? The common-law position, according to the Privy Council in *Wong Kam-Ming* v. *R*.[47] and the House of Lords in *R*. v. *Brophy*,[48] is that the prosecution may not do so. However, if the voir dire results in the *admission* of the impugned confession, the accused may be cross-examined to expose discrepancies and inconsistencies between her testimonies on the voir dire and in the trial proper. Such cross-examination would, naturally, be directed to testing the credibility of the accused. But it is subject, of course, to the judge's usual 'duty to ensure that the right of the prosecution to cross-examine or rebut is not used in a manner unfair or oppressive to the defendant', and also to ensure that any relevant statutory provisions are strictly complied with.[49] Again, there is no reason why similar principles should not apply in relation to voir-dire hearings held to determine whether the proceedings should be stayed.[50]

The fact that an accused testifies on a voir dire does not affect her right to remain silent in the trial proper.[51]

PRE-TRIAL INQUIRIES

Where a defendant wishes to apply for a stay of the proceedings, the ability

[43] P. Mirfield, *Confessions* (1985), 94.

[44] See also *R*. v. *Clerkenwell Stipendiary Magistrate, ex p. Bell* (1991) 155 JPR 669, discussed below.

[45] The issue cannot be determined on the depositions alone: *R*. v. *Chadwick* (1934) 24 Cr. App. R. 138; *R*. v. *Moore* (1972) 56 Cr. App. R. 373. See also *R*. v. *Little* (1976) 14 SASR 556.

[46] *R*. v. *Tyrer* (1989) 90 Cr. App. R. 446.   [47] [1980] AC 247.

[48] [1982] AC 476.   [49] [1980] AC 247, 259–60.

[50] It should be noted that a possible consequence of s. 76 of PACE is that the common-law prohibition of adduction of an accused's voir-dire testimony in the trial proper may no longer apply: Mirfield, *Confessions*, 98.   [51] *R*. v. *Brophy* [1982] AC 476.

to have the matter determined prior to the commencement of the trial is of special importance. By applying for a stay of proceedings, the defendant is arguing in effect that no trial should take place. It is unnecessary that the determination of whether a trial should take place should wait for the commencement of the trial. Thus, where the defence is aware in advance of the trial of its intention to seek a stay of the prosecution, the ability to obtain a pre-trial inquiry would seem appropriate.[52]

There is certainly evidence in England that some use is being made of pre-trial hearings to determine whether proceedings should be stayed as an abuse of process.[53] Is there, however, a general *duty* on the trial judge to hold such an inquiry where it is justifiably requested by the defence? Unfortunately, the English Court of Appeal refused in *R.* v. *Heston-Francois*[54] to recognize the existence of such a duty. While the appellant was on bail awaiting trial on burglary charges, the police, in the course of investigating another offence, seized from his home privileged documents prepared for use in his defence to the burglary charges. These documents were then perused by police officers involved in the prosecution of the burglary charges. The question before the Court of Appeal was whether a trial judge has a duty, on the application of a defendant before arraignment, to conduct a hearing into allegations of oppressive conduct with view to determining whether the proceedings should be stayed as an abuse of process.

It was held that no such duty existed. In so holding, the Court of Appeal did not doubt the existence, as part of the inherent jurisdiction of a court, of a discretion to stay proceedings. But this discretion, it was thought, did not include an obligation to hold a pre-trial inquiry into allegations of improper conduct said to render the proceedings an abuse of process. The Court considered that the performance of such a duty

would present difficult procedural problems, for example (i) of defining the issues claimed to exist, which may be very complex, (ii) of providing for representation of persons whose conduct is impugned, (iii) of ensuring that the persons affected are sufficiently aware of the case they have to meet. Whilst these problems may be overcome, the issues referred to are best left, we think, to be dealt with during the course of the trial and, if necessary, later by the Court of Appeal.[55]

This reasoning is unconvincing. Problems of defining issues and of protecting the interests of those whose conduct is challenged would arise

---

[52] On pre-trial inquiries, see generally M. Aronson, *Managing Complex Criminal Trials: Reform of the Rules of Evidence and Procedure* (1992), ch. 3.

[53] See e.g., *R.* v. *Manchester Crown Court, ex p. Brokenbrow, The Times*, 31 Oct. 1991.

[54] [1984] 1 All ER 785; see J. Hunter, ' "Tainted" Proceedings: Censuring Police Illegalities' (1985) 59 *Australian Law Journal* 709. Note that the Appeal Committee of the House of Lords dismissed a petition by the appellant for leave to appeal from the decision of the Court of Appeal: [1984] 1 All ER 785, 793.   [55] Ibid. 791–2.

regardless of whether the question of a stay of proceedings was determined at a pre-trial hearing or after the commencement of the trial at a voir-dire hearing.[56] Accordingly it is inappropriate to cite these problems as the reason for refusing to endorse the use of pre-trial hearings for determination of whether proceedings should be stayed.

It is to be noted that pre-trial hearings have recently been formally given a small place in English criminal procedure. The Criminal Justice Act 1987 empowers a Crown Court judge to order that a 'preparatory hearing' be held before the jury is sworn, in cases of fraud which are of 'such seriousness and complexity that substantial benefits are likely to accrue' from such a hearing.[57] At the hearing the judge may determine 'any question as to the admissibility of evidence' and 'any other question of law relating to the case'.[58]

In Australia, the Court of Appeal of the State of New South Wales thought in *Watson* v. *A-G (NSW)*[59] that a trial court in New South Wales had jurisdiction to deal even with matters relating to trials which would take place *if* an indictment was presented. This jurisdiction would be exercisable in respect of existing charges notwithstanding that an indictment might not be presented and a trial might not take place in respect of any particular charge. The jurisdiction would be capable of being exercised to stay further proceedings on any pending charge.[60]

The existence of such a jurisdiction was, however, doubted by Brennan J. in the decision of the High Court of Australia in *Jago* v. *District Court (NSW)*.[61] Brennan J. thought that 'a jurisdiction to intervene in the process of signing and presenting an indictment would be a radical innovation, for it would involve an interference with the function of the Law Officers of the Crown or of the Director of Public Prosecutions under statute to decide whether to proceed with a prosecution.'[62] Brennan J. pointed out, however, that Part 53 Rule 10 of the District Court Rules 1973 (New South Wales), introduced in 1987, did empower the Court to make an order to quash or stay an indictment 'before the day appointed for the hearing of the proceedings'. As this day should be construed as the day on which proceedings on the indictment would be heard, it followed that the District Court did have jurisdiction to hold a pre-trial hearing, after the presentation of the indictment, to determine whether the prosecution should be stayed.[63]

The Australian State of Victoria has enacted an express statutory provision which effectively permits trial courts to hold pre-trial hearings, after the indictment has been presented, to determine, *inter alia*, whether the

---

[56] See generally Hunter, ' "Tainted" Proceedings', 712–13.   [57] S. 7(1).
[58] S. 9(3).   [59] (1987) 8 NSWLR 685.   [60] Ibid. 701.
[61] (1989) 168 CLR 23. But see *R.* v. *Scott* (1992) 59 A. Crim. R. 362, in which the court endorsed *Watson*, without making any mention of *Jago*.
[62] (1989) 168 CLR 23, 38.   [63] Ibid. 37.

proceedings should be stayed. The relevant provision is section 391A of the Crimes Act 1958, which provides:

Where an accused person is arraigned on indictment or presentment before the Supreme Court or the County Court, the Court before which the arraignment takes place, if the Court thinks fit, may before the impanelling of a jury for the trial hear and determine any question with respect to the trial of the accused person which the Court considers necessary to ensure that the trial will be conducted fairly and expeditiously and the hearing and determination of any such question shall be conducted and have the same effect and consequences in all respects as such a hearing and determination would have had before the enactment of this section if the hearing and determination had occurred after the jury had been impanelled.

At present in England there is, as mentioned earlier, no obligation for a pre-trial hearing to be held even where it is justifiably requested by the defence. It is suggested that a similar 'pre-trial hearing' procedure to those available in New South Wales and Victoria could usefully be adopted. There should be no need for defence counsel to have to wait for the trial to commence before indicating her intention to object to the continuation of the proceedings. She should be entitled to indicate such intention prior to trial so that, instead of a voir dire at the commencement of the trial, a pre-trial hearing may be convened if adequate justification for such a hearing has been adduced. The merit of this course of action is that it avoids the need for a jury to be sworn and then excluded almost immediately from the courtroom for an indefinite period. Further, and perhaps more importantly, a pre-trial inquiry would obviate the need for full-scale preparations for a trial which could very well be abandoned at the outset if it is determined on a voir dire that the proceedings should be stayed.[64]

Steps must be taken to ensure that pre-trial inquiries do not generate unwanted publicity which would make a subsequent unbiased trial impossible. For example, an order to suppress publicity can be made by the judge presiding at the pre-trial hearing. It may also be appropriate for Parliament to enact specific legislation to enable courts to control pre-trial publicity arising from pre-trial inquiries.

It is to be noted that a complex and sophisticated scheme of pre-trial hearings is an important feature of US criminal procedure. For example, most US jurisdictions, including the Federal jurisdiction, insist that certain

---

[64] M. Code, 'American Cadillacs or Canadian Compacts: What is the Correct Criminal Procedure for S. 24 Applications under the Charter of Rights?: Part II' (1991) 33 *Criminal Law Quarterly* 407, 440, has written in the Canadian context that, where an inquiry into whether the proceedings should be stayed takes place after the commencement of the trial, 'court room facilities end up being under-utilized as the case collapses and the judge has no work for the remainder of time that had been allotted for the trial. When the same discussions take place well in advance of trial, there is no waste of court facilities and judicial resources as the time required for trial is never set aside in the court's calendar in the first place.'

motions relating to the exclusion of evidence or the dismissal of indictments *must* be made prior to the trial.[65] The position in the Federal jurisdiction is governed by rule 12 of the Federal Rules of Criminal Procedure. Rule 12(*b*) requires that motions to suppress evidence, and certain categories of motions to dismiss indictments, be raised prior to trial. A pre-trial motion must be actually *determined* before the trial, unless the court orders 'for good cause' that it be deferred for determination at a later stage: rule 12(*e*). Rule 12(*f*) provides: 'Failure by a party to raise defenses or objections or to make requests which must be made prior to trial, at the time set by the court pursuant to subdivision (*c*), or prior to any extension thereof made by the court, shall constitute waiver thereof, but the court for cause shown may grant relief from the waiver.'

Thus the effect of rule 12 of the US Federal Rules of Criminal Procedure is that motions to suppress evidence, and certain categories of motions to dismiss indictments, must be raised prior to trial, and that failure to do so will constitute waiver unless relief is granted from the waiver. Such relief may be granted where the defendant was not aware before the trial of the (factual) grounds for the motion. Authority suggests, for example, that ignorance of the legal grounds for having evidence suppressed would not suffice,[66] but that the defendant's ignorance, before the trial, of the *factual* circumstances surrounding the obtaining of the evidence would suffice.[67]

The following question therefore arises for consideration in the English context. Should the defence be regarded as having waived the right to object to the continuation of the proceedings if it did not seek a pre-trial hearing even though it can be proved that it was aware of the relevant ground for a stay? The answer, I would suggest, is no. Where a choice has to be made between promoting trial efficiency and underpinning judicial legitimacy, the latter consideration must prevail. Furthermore, to adopt the US factual grounds/legal grounds distinction would mean that far too much would turn on proof of knowledge of the relevant factual circumstances. Indeed, a rule of waiver would probably have the undesirable effect of encouraging defence counsel to object on slender grounds for fear that she may otherwise lose the right to object altogether. There is, in any event, the issue of whether the defendant should be disadvantaged as a consequence of her

[65] See generally E. W. Cleary (ed.), *McCormick on Evidence* (3rd edn., 1984), 522–3; W. R. LaFave, *Search and Seizure: A Treatise on the Fourth Amendment*, iv (2nd edn., 1987), 188 and associated section in *1992 Pocket Part*.

[66] See *Isaacs* v. *US* 283 F. 2d 587 (10th Cir. 1960).

[67] See *People* v. *Ferguson* 135 NW 2d 357 (1965). It was said (ibid. 359) that 'if the factual circumstances are known to defendant in advance of trial, he is responsible for communicating them to his lawyer immediately and his lawyer, in turn, is responsible for making a proper motion in advance of trial. . . . If, however, factual circumstances are not known sufficiently in advance of trial to permit such a motion then the trial court may exercise its discretion and consider the motion at trial.'

counsel's incompetence: one Canadian commentator has written that the US waiver rule 'discloses an unforgiving attitude towards counsel's lapses, an attitude which is starkly contrasted with the paternal and protective approach taken by Canadian courts.'[68]

SHOULD A HEARING BE CONDUCTED?

There cannot, of course, be a strict set of guide-lines as to the circumstances in which it is appropriate for the trial judge to accede to defence counsel's request for a voir dire or a pre-trial hearing into whether the proceedings should be stayed as an abuse of process. In the South Australian case of *R. v. Williams*[69] Wells J., speaking in the context of confessional evidence, observed that a voir-dire hearing would not normally be allowed simply at the request of counsel. Instead, there must be proper and adequate material before the judge; this material may be constituted by counsel's explicit assurance of her intention to adduce certain evidence, or by some passage or passages in the depositions. It would be wrong for counsel to treat a voir-dire hearing as a fishing expedition[70] (in which she attempts to 'fish' for details of the prosecution case against the defendant).

The issue of voir-dire hearings and the determination of the admissibility of confessions under section 76(2) of PACE was considered in *R. v. Liverpool Juvenile Court, ex p. R.*[71] It was said that a voir dire should take place only if it was *represented* to the court that the confession had been, or might have been, obtained in contravention of section 76(2). 'Representation', it was pointed out, is not synonymous with and does not include cross-examination. A court is not obliged, therefore, to embark upon a voir dire merely because of a suggestion in cross-examination that the alleged confession has been obtained in contravention of section 76(2).[72] It would be sensible to adopt a similar rule in relation to the holding of a voir dire to determine whether proceedings should be stayed as an abuse of process.

APPEALS

(a) The Mechanics

Criminal appeals in England are governed by the Criminal Appeal Act 1968. It should be noted at the outset that this Act does not afford the prosecution the right to appeal to the Court of Appeal. However the Criminal Justice Act 1972 provides that, where a person tried on indictment

---

[68] M. Code, 'American Cadillacs or Canadian Compacts: What is the Correct Criminal Procedure for S. 24 Applications under the Charter of Rights?: Part I' (1991) 33 *Criminal Law Quarterly* 298, 342–3.   [69] (1976) 14 SASR 1.   [70] Ibid. 3.
[71] [1987] 3 WLR 224.   [72] Ibid. 230–1.

has been acquitted, the Attorney-General may refer a point of law which has arisen in the case to the Court of Appeal for its opinion.[73] A further reference may be taken to the House of Lords.[74] But references under the Criminal Justice Act do not affect the trial in relation to which they are made, or any acquittal in that trial.[75]

The Criminal Appeal Act 1968 affords a person convicted of an offence on indictment the right to appeal to the Court of Appeal against her conviction: section 1(1). Subsection (2) provides that such appeal may be on any ground involving 'a question of law alone', or, with the leave of the Court of Appeal, 'on any ground which involves a question of fact alone, or a question of mixed law and fact, or on any other ground which appears to the Court of Appeal to be a sufficient ground of appeal'. An appeal may, however, be taken without the leave of the Court of Appeal if the trial judge grants a certificate that the case is fit for appeal on a ground involving a question of fact, or a question of mixed law and fact. Under section 2(1), the Court of Appeal must allow the appeal if satisfied that the conviction is unsafe or unsatisfactory; or that a wrong decision was reached on a question of law; or that there was a material irregularity in the course of the trial. This is subject, however, to the proviso that 'the Court may, notwithstanding that they are of opinion that the point raised in the appeal might be decided in favour of the appellant, dismiss the appeal if they consider that no miscarriage of justice has actually occurred'.

It was seen above that the Criminal Justice Act 1987 makes provision for preparatory hearings in serious and complex fraud cases. This Act also provides that an order or ruling made at or for the purposes of a preparatory hearing is to have effect during the trial, 'unless it appears to the judge, on application made to him during the trial, that the interests of justice require him to vary or discharge it'.[76] It is possible to appeal to the Court of Appeal from any order or ruling made at a preparatory hearing, but only with the leave of the judge or of the Court of Appeal.[77] A preparatory hearing may be continued notwithstanding that leave to appeal has been granted, but no jury can be sworn until after the appeal has been determined or abandoned.[78] If a general pre-trial hearing mechanism, such as has been advocated earlier, were to be introduced, then it would seem sensible to allow, along similar lines, for the possibility of an appeal to the Court of Appeal *before* the commencement of the trial proper.[79]

---

[73] S. 36(1).   [74] S. 36(3).   [75] S. 36(7).
[76] S. 9(10).   [77] S. 9(11).   [78] S. 9(13).
[79] In NSW, s. 5F of the Criminal Appeal Act 1912 makes provision for an appeal (as of right in the case of the Attorney-General or DPP, but with leave or by certification in the case of the defendant) to the Court of Criminal Appeal from a pre-trial interlocutory judgment or order. Refusal of leave to appeal in this manner does not preclude the bringing of an appeal in the usual manner following conviction. The introduction of this provision in 1987 was apparently prompted by the plethora of interlocutory proceedings which were occurring in NSW: A. S.

(b) Grounds for Overturning the Exercise of a Discretion

Because of the nature of judicial discretion, an appeal on the basis of an allegedly erroneous exercise of discretion is not treated by the Court of Appeal in the same way as an appeal on the basis of an alleged misapplication of a rule or principle of law. Where what is at issue is a conclusion reached pursuant to a rule or principle of law, the appellate court will not hesitate to substitute its own conclusion if it disagrees with that reached by the trial court. It is immaterial that the trial court may have, in reaching its conclusion, taken all relevant factors into account and left irrelevant factors out of consideration.[80] However, where a decision is reached pursuant to judicial discretion and this decision is the subject of an appeal, the appellate court will interfere with the decision only in limited circumstances. In considering the issue of the circumstances in which the Court of Appeal should interfere with a decision reached pursuant to judicial discretion, Lord Denning MR said in *Ward* v. *James*:

The true proposition was stated by Lord Wright in *Charles Osenton & Co.* v. *Johnston*.[81] This court can, and will, interfere if it is satisfied that the judge was wrong. Thus it will interfere if it can see that the judge has given no weight (or no sufficient weight) to those considerations which ought to have weighed with him. ... Conversely it will interfere if it can see that he has been influenced by other considerations which ought not to have weighed with him, or not weighed so much with him ...[82]

And in *R.* v. *Scarrott*, Scarman LJ observed that, so long as a trial judge 'does not err in law, takes into account all relevant matters and excludes consideration of irrelevant matters, his discretion will stand'.[83]

Hodge, 'The Process of Abuse' (1990) 20 *Hong Kong Law Journal* 195, 220. It has been held that the reference to 'interlocutory judgment or order' in s. 5F applies, *inter alia*, to orders made on an application for a stay of proceedings on the ground of abuse of process, but does not apply to rulings, decisions, or advisory opinions of a judge given in advance of the trial on matters affecting the conduct of the trial, such as the admissibility of evidence: *R.* v. *Edelsten* (1989) 18 NSWLR 213. For a discussion of the grounds on which leave to appeal may be granted, see *R.* v. *Matovski* (1989) 15 NSWLR 720.

[80] See *R.* v. *Viola* (1982) 75 Cr. App. R. 125, 130–1.
[81] [1942] AC 130.　　　　　　　　　　　　　　　　[82] [1966] 1 QB 273, 293.
[83] [1978] QB 1016, 1028. 'In my opinion a judge reaches a decision in the exercise of his "discretion" ... where, on the facts found by or agreed before him and on the law correctly stated by him, he is required in the exercise of his judicial function to decide between two or more courses of action without any further rules governing the decision which he should make, other than that he should act judicially. It is just because this is the nature of such a task facing a judge that this court is restricted by the authorities to the extent to which it can interfere. Unless his decision is perverse in the *Wednesbury* sense (see *Associated Provincial Picture Houses Ltd.* v. *Wednesbury Corp.* [1947] 2 All ER 680, [1948] 1 KB 223), it must be one to which a judge, acting judicially, could come' (*Viscount De L'Isle* v. *Times Newspapers* [1987] 3 All ER 499, 504 per May LJ). See also *Hindes* v. *Edwards, The Times*, 9 Oct. 1987; *In re W, The Times*, 22 and 23 Nov. 1990; *R.* v. *Glennon* (1992) 66 ALJR 344, 348 per Mason CJ and

An illustration may be provided by the case of *R. v. Mackie*.[84] In response to an argument that the trial judge should in the exercise of his discretion have excluded certain evidence on the ground that its prejudicial effect outweighed its probative value, the Court of Appeal expressed the view that 'the prejudicial effect of the evidence admitted was enormous and far outweighed its value in proving that the child was frightened of the appellant before April 4'.[85] The Court went on, however, to hold that the judge was entitled to exercise his discretion as he did and to admit the evidence.[86] In other words, even though the Court of Appeal would itself have exercised the discretion differently, it was not prepared to overturn the exercise of the discretion by the trial judge.[87]

On occasion, however, it has been advocated that appellate courts adopt a slightly more interventionist stance when hearing appeals based on the allegedly erroneous exercise of judicial discretion. Such a view was taken by the Irish Supreme Court in *O'Brien*. The Court stated that, if a trial judge decides to admit improperly obtained evidence,

an appeal against his decision should lie to a superior Court which will decide the question according to its own views and will not be bound to affirm the decision of the trial judge if it disagrees with the manner in which the discretion has been exercised, even if it does not appear that such discretion was exercised on wrong principles. *The result of such decisions, based on the facts of individual cases, may in time give rise to more precise rules.*[88]

It is certainly true that it is the duty of appellate courts to formulate guide-lines for the exercise of particular discretions, and that these guide-lines may eventually crystallize into and come to be regarded as 'more precise rules'. However, care must be taken to ensure that these 'more precise rules' do not grow eventually into a rigid body of 'fixed legal principles' which trial judges will in future feel compelled to 'apply' in individual cases. What is required is that appellate courts formulate principles which provide sufficient guidance to trial judges as to how the abuse of process discretion should be exercised in individual cases, while leaving the discretion sufficiently unfettered to enable it to be adapted to new factual circumstances. The very essence of the principle of judicial legitimacy requires that it be capable of taking into account changing public attitudes and public

---

Toohey J. (an exercise of discretion should not be overturned unless the trial judge 'took into account some extraneous consideration, failed to take into account a relevant consideration or mistook the facts . . .').

[84] (1973) 57 Cr. App. R. 453. [85] Ibid. 464. [86] Ibid. 465.

[87] Of course, it is arguable that the Court of Appeal should have held that, because the trial judge was *so* wrong in his conclusion, he must have erred in law. See also *R. v. O'Leary* (1988) 87 Cr. App. R. 387, 391: 'Subject to the question of *Wednesbury* unreasonableness, this is a matter for the discretion of the court below, with which this Court would be loth to interfere.'

[88] [1965] IR 142, 161 (emphasis added).

perceptions of the criminal justice system. In other words, a careful line has to be trod between flexibility and predictability.

JUDICIAL REVIEW

Either the prosecution or the defence may apply to the Divisional Court for judicial review. Applications are typically made for judicial review of magistrates' decisions either to stay the proceedings or to refuse to do so. Is it possible, however, to apply to the Divisional Court for judicial review of the decision of a *trial judge*, either to stay a Crown Court trial as an abuse of process, or to refuse to do so? The clue lies, it seems, in section 29(3) of the Supreme Court Act 1981, which provides:

In relation to the jurisdiction of the Crown Court, *other than its jurisdiction in matters relating to trial on indictment*, the High Court shall have all such jurisdiction to make orders of mandamus, prohibition or certiorari as the High Court possesses in relation to the jurisdiction of an inferior court.[89]

For a long time it was thought that the emphasized words precluded judicial review by the Divisional Court of the decision of a Crown Court judge to grant or refuse a stay of the proceedings.[90] However, two recent decisions of the Divisional Court[91] have exposed this view as incorrect. Essentially, it has been held that an application to stay proceedings does *not* 'relate to trial on indictment'. An application for a stay of proceedings is, in effect, an argument that a trial should not take place at all: 'a decision on an application to stay on grounds of abuse of process does not affect the *conduct* of a trial on indictment, because what is being determined is whether there should ever *be* a trial.'[92] Thus the general principle of section 29(3) applies, and a determination by a Crown Court judge as to whether or not proceedings should be stayed as an abuse of process is amenable to judicial review by the Divisional Court.

   The fact that the prosecution can apply for judicial review of a decision by a Crown Court judge to stay proceedings should go some way to assuaging the concerns of those worried about the inability of the prosecution to appeal to the Court of Appeal against a stay. The Divisional Court has

---

[89] Emphasis added.

[90] See e.g., R. Pattenden, 'Abuse of Process in Criminal Litigation' (1989) 53 *Journal of Criminal Law* 341, 355; R. Pattenden, 'The Power of the Courts to Stay a Criminal Prosecution' [1985] *Criminal Law Review* 175, 187.

[91] *R. v. Central Criminal Court, ex p. Randle and Pottle* (1990) 92 Cr. App. R. 323; *R. v. Norwich Crown Court, ex p. Belsham* [1992] 1 WLR 54. Cf. *R. v. Central Criminal Court, ex p. Director of the Serious Frauds Office*, The Times, 8 Sept. 1992.

[92] *R. v. Central Criminal Court, ex p. Randle and Pottle* (1990) 92 Cr. App. R. 323, 337 (emphasis in original).

emphasized, however, that it will not interfere readily with an exercise of the abuse of process discretion in the Crown Court:

> Only in a case where it can be shown that the trial judge was *clearly and demonstrably wrong* will we interfere with a decision at the Crown Court to stay proceedings on indictment where it has been asserted that to entertain the proceedings would be an abuse of the process of the court. All those who are minded to apply to seek a review, as well as those who have already done so but who have not yet been heard upon an application to review a decision of the Crown Court, should bear that well in mind. To overrule a decision of the Crown Court in this respect will be, in our opinion, to take an unusual, if not exceptional, step.[93]

MAGISTRATES' COURTS

AVAILABILITY OF ABUSE OF PROCESS DISCRETION

In *DPP* v. *Humphrys*, Viscount Dilhorne doubted whether magistrates had a discretion to stay proceedings as an abuse of process, suggesting that, if they did, it would be a power

> fraught with considerable dangers. One bench thinking a prosecution should not have been brought will dismiss it as oppressive and vexatious. Other benches on precisely the same facts may take a completely different view, with the result that there is a lack of uniformity in the administration of justice.[94]

Such concerns notwithstanding, it now seems to be generally accepted that the abuse of process discretion is exercisable in magistrates' courts,[95] in relation to both summary trials[96] and, probably, committal proceedings.[97] The view has been expressed, however, that 'the power to exercise a discretion for a jurisdiction to decline to hear proceedings on the ground of abuse of process is even more limited where the justices are sitting as examining magistrates and not dealing with the case to its final determination'.[98]

---

[93] *R.* v. *Norwich Crown Court, ex p. Belsham* [1992] 1 WLR 54, 69 (emphasis added). *Belsham* has been followed in *R.* v. *Leicester Crown Court, ex p. Russell* [1992] COD 194.

[94] [1977] AC 1, 26. Lord Salmon expressed no concluded view on this point (ibid. 46).

[95] See the useful discussion in *R.* v. *Telford JJ, ex p. Badhan* [1991] 2 WLR 866.

[96] This was firmly established by the cases of *R.* v. *Brentford JJ, ex p. Wong* (1980) 73 Cr. App. R. 67 and *R.* v. *Oxford City JJ, ex p. Smith* [1982] RTR 201.

[97] See *R.* v. *Telford JJ, ex p. Badhan* [1991] 2 WLR 866; *R.* v. *Bow Street Metropolitan Stipendiary Magistrate, ex p. DPP* (1992) 95 Cr. App. R. 9, 16. Cf. *R.* v. *Governor of Pentonville Prison, ex p. Sinclair* [1991] 2 WLR 1028, 1037.

[98] *R.* v. *Canterbury and St Augustine JJ, ex p. Turner* (1983) 147 JPR 193, 199 per McNeill J. It has been held, consistently with this, that 'magistrates sitting as examining justices to decide whether to commit an accused for trial on indictment ought not to exercise their discretion under s. 78 of the Police and Criminal Evidence Act to exclude admissible evidence from their determination save in the clearest case and in exceptional circumstances' (*R.* v.

A recent challenge was made to the availability of the abuse of process discretion in committal proceedings in *R. v. Telford JJ, ex p. Badhan.*[99] The basis of the challenge was that previous judicial observations about the availability of the abuse of process discretion in committal proceedings were erroneous because they had been made in ignorance of the decision of the House of Lords in *Atkinson v. USA Government.* In *Atkinson*, the House of Lords had answered the question of 'whether, *if there is evidence sufficient to justify committal*, the magistrate can refuse to commit on any other ground such as that committal would be oppressive or contrary to natural justice'[100] in the negative. The Divisional Court in *Badhan* thought, however, that *Atkinson* could be distinguished in the following manner. *Atkinson* concerned extradition proceedings, and the House of Lords in that case was addressing only the situation where the magistrates' inquiry had already led to the conclusion that there was sufficient evidence to justify committal for trial (as suggested by the emphasized words in the passage quoted above). Their Lordships were saying that, in this situation, there was no power to stay the proceedings, presumably since in extradition cases the actual decision to return was made by the Secretary of State, who was empowered to consider matters of 'natural justice'. What the House of Lords was not addressing was the question of whether there was a power not to embark upon the inquiry at all. Thus *Atkinson* could not stand for the general proposition that the abuse of process discretion was unavailable in committal proceedings.[101]

In the recent case of *R. v. Governor of Pentonville Prison, ex p. Sinclair*, however, the House of Lords refrained from expressing an opinion on this issue:

Since the decision in *Atkinson's* case, there has been a substantial line of cases to the effect that when exercising their domestic jurisdiction magistrates do have power to stay [committal] proceedings where there has been an abuse of the process of the court. Your Lordships have yet to pronounce upon the validity of those decisions.[102]

King's Lynn Magistrates' Court, ex p. Holland (1992) 156 JPR 825, 829). Thus 'examining justices could exclude the evidence from their consideration only if satisfied that its admission at the trial would be so obviously unfair to the proceedings that no Judge properly directing himself could admit it' (ibid. 828–9). What seems to be required, therefore, is some forecast of what the trial judge would be likely to do if the defendant is in fact committed for trial. *Holland* has been criticized by S. Gilchrist, 'Crime Reporter' (1992) 136 *Solicitors' Journal* 410, 410: 'If committal proceedings are to have any purpose at all and if our rules of evidence are to maintain consistency and integrity then surely the same rules must apply throughout our criminal court system and evidence which should clearly be regarded as inadmissible in one court must also be considered so before another.'

[99] [1991] 2 WLR 866.
[101] [1991] 2 WLR 866, 874–5.
[100] [1971] AC 197, 231 (emphasis added).
[102] [1991] 2 WLR 1028, 1037.

The Law Lords did, however, expressly acknowledge the unavailability of the abuse of process discretion in extradition proceedings. In reaching this conclusion, reliance was placed upon the fact that section 11 of the Extradition Act 1989 had effected a 'radical alteration' of extradition law by giving the High Court, in part at least, the same kind of discretion as to whether to discharge an applicant as the Secretary of State had in deciding whether to order the return of a fugitive criminal to a requesting state. This, the House of Lords thought, represented the 'clearest possible recognition' by the legislature that previously no such discretion had existed in the courts and in particular in the magistrates' courts.[103]

It is to be noted that, in Australia, the High Court has interpreted[104] section 41(6) of the Justices Act 1902 (New South Wales)[105] as leaving no room for a discretion to stay committal proceedings as an abuse of process. 'In committal proceedings a magistrate is performing an administrative or ministerial function which is governed by statute and the terms of the statute afford no basis for the implication of any power to dispose of those proceedings by the imposition of a permanent stay.'[106] On the contrary, the scheme of the section was such as to impose an *obligation* on the magistrate to dispose of the information either by discharging the defendant or by committing her for trial.[107]

The current lack of absolute certainty in English law as to the availability of the abuse of process discretion in committal proceedings raises the possibility that the House of Lords may one day interpret section 6(1) of the Magistrates' Courts Act 1980[108] 41(6) (the English version of section to reach a similar conclusion to that reached by the High Court of Australia. It is to be hoped that this will not occur. Because it is open to the prosecution to seek judicial review of the magistrate's decision, there should be no concern that the discretion may be exercised arbitrarily with the prosecution being left with no recourse. Of course, it is arguable that there is no need to vest the discretion in examining magistrates, since a defendant seeking a

---

[103] Ibid. 1040.   [104] Deane J. dissenting.

[105] 'When all the evidence for the prosecution and any evidence for the defence have been taken, the Justice or Justices shall, after considering all the evidence before the Justice or Justices—(*a*) if of the opinion that, having regard to all the evidence before the Justice or Justices, a jury would not be likely to convict the defendant of an indictable offence—forthwith order the defendant to be discharged as to the information then under inquiry; or (*b*) if not of that opinion—commit the defendant for trial.'

[106] *Grassby* v. *R.* (1989) 168 CLR 1, 19 per Dawson J.

[107] Ibid. 17–18. The same view is taken by the Supreme Court of Canada: *Mills* v. *R.* (1986) 52 CR (3d) 1.

[108] 'If a magistrates' court inquiring into an offence as examining justices is of opinion, on consideration of the evidence and of any statement of the accused, that there is sufficient evidence to put the accused on trial by jury for any indictable offence, the court shall commit him for trial; and, if it is not of that opinion, it shall, if he is in custody for no other cause than the offence under inquiry, discharge him.'

stay of committal proceedings can in any event apply directly to the
Divisional Court for an order of prohibition,[109] or wait and see if she is in
fact committed for trial and, if so, apply to the trial judge for a stay.
However, to deprive the magistrates themselves of the ability to stay in such
a manner introduces an unnecessarily complicated procedure which ignores
the fact that 'a plea of abuse should be open to the accused subject at the
earlier opportunity'.[110]

JUDICIAL REVIEW

(*a*) The Mechanics

An application to the Divisional Court for judicial review may be made
either by the defendant or by the prosecution. In the abuse-of-process
context, the more common orders sought by defendants appear to be those
of prohibition[111] and certiorari.[112] An order of prohibition is effectively an
order staying the proceedings: such an order would prevent the magistrate
from commencing or continuing with the hearing. An order of certiorari, on
the other hand, would quash a decision by the magistrate to allow the
proceedings to continue. Less frequently, an order of mandamus has been
sought to compel the magistrate to exercise the abuse of process
discretion.[113] Defendants have, on occasion, also sought declarations to the
effect that the decision of the magistrate to allow the proceedings to
continue was unlawful.[114] An application for judicial review may be made
without prior application having been made to the magistrate for a

---

[109] This will be explained more fully below.

[110] *R.* v. *Telford JJ, ex p. Badhan* [1991] 2 WLR 866, 875.

[111] See *R.* v. *Manchester City Stipendiary Magistrate, ex p. Snelson* (1977) 66 Cr. App. R.
44; *R.* v. *Brentford JJ, ex p. Wong* (1980) 73 Cr. App. R. 67; *R.* v. *Horsham JJ, ex p. Reeves*
(1980) 75 Cr. App. R. 236; *R.* v. *Oxford City JJ, ex p. Smith* [1982] RTR 201; *R.* v. *Grays JJ,
ex p. Graham* [1982] 3 WLR 596; *R.* v. *Newcastle-upon-Tyne JJ, ex p. Hindle* [1984] 1 All ER
770; *R.* v. *West London Stipendiary Magistrate, ex p. Anderson* (1984) 148 JPR 683; *R.* v.
Derby Crown Court, ex p. Brooks (1984) 80 Cr. App. R. 164; *R.* v. *Willesden JJ, ex p.
Clemmings* (1987) 87 Cr. App. R. 280; *R.* v. *Sunderland Magistrates' Court, ex p. Z* [1989]
Crim. LR 56; *R.* v. *Truro and South Powder JJ, ex p. McCullagh* [1991] RTR 374; *R.* v.
Telford JJ, ex p. Badhan [1991] 2 WLR 866; *R.* v. *Sheffield Stipendiary Magistrate, ex p.
Stephens* (1992) 156 JPR 555; *R.* v. *Newham JJ, ex p. C, The Times*, 26 Aug. 1992.

[112] See *R.* v. *Watford JJ, ex p. Outrim* [1983] RTR 26; *R.* v. *Guildford Magistrates' Court,
ex p. Healy* [1983] 1 WLR 108; *R.* v. *Canterbury and St Augustine JJ, ex p. Turner* (1983) 147
JPR 193; *R.* v. *Liverpool Stipendiary Magistrate, ex p. Ellison* [1990] RTR 220; *R.* v. *Forest of
Dean JJ, ex p. Farley* [1990] RTR 228; *R.* v. *Rotherham JJ, ex p. Brough* [1991] Crim. LR
522; *R.* v. *Redbridge JJ and Fox, ex p. Whitehouse* (1991) 156 JPR 293; *R.* v. *Sheffield
Stipendiary Magistrate, ex p. Stephens* (1992) 156 JPR 555.

[113] See *R.* v. *Newcastle-upon-Tyne JJ, ex p. Hindle* [1984] 1 All ER 770.

[114] See *R.* v. *Liverpool Stipendiary Magistrate, ex p. Ellison* [1990] RTR 220; *R.* v.
Redbridge JJ and Fox, ex p. Whitehouse (1991) 156 JPR 293; *R.* v. *Sheffield Stipendiary
Magistrate, ex p. Stephens* (1992) 156 JPR 555.

stay,[115] or after an application to the magistrate for a stay has failed. The hearing in the magistrates' court will be adjourned pending the outcome of the judicial review.[116]

Where it is the prosecution making application for judicial review, the most common orders sought appear to be mandamus,[117] for the purpose of compelling the magistrate to allow the proceedings to continue, and certiorari,[118] for the purpose of quashing the decision of the magistrate to stay the proceedings.

(b) Grounds for Overturning the Exercise of a Discretion

Not surprisingly, the Divisional Court will interfere with determinations made by magistrates pursuant to the abuse of process discretion in limited circumstances only:

Before this court can properly interfere with a decision of a Bench of Magistrates, which has had to consider an application to say that it is an abuse of the process of the court to continue with criminal proceedings before that court, this court has to be satisfied, either that the Magistrates have not properly directed themselves in law or, alternatively, that on the facts put before them no Bench properly directing themselves could reasonably and properly have come to the conclusion to which the particular Bench did come, in other words, that they acted perversely.[119]

[115] See *R. v. Manchester City Stipendiary Magistrate, ex p. Snelson* (1977) 66 Cr. App. R. 44; *R. v. Grays JJ, ex p. Graham* [1982] 3 WLR 596; *R. v. Guildford Magistrates' Court, ex p. Healy* [1983] 1 WLR 108.

[116] See *R. v. Grays JJ, ex p. Graham* [1982] 3 WLR 596; *R. v. Willesden JJ, ex p. Clemmings* (1987) 87 Cr. App. R. 280; *R. v. Telford JJ, ex p. Badhan* [1991] 2 WLR 866. See also J. Wadham, 'Abuse of Process through Delay in the Criminal Courts' [Feb. 1991] *Legal Action* 15, 16.

[117] See *R. v. Colwyn JJ, ex p. DPP* (1988) 154 JPR 989; *R. v. Bow Street Stipendiary Magistrate, ex p. DPP and Cherry* (1989) 91 Cr. App. R. 283; *R. v. Bow Street Metropolitan Stipendiary Magistrate, ex p. DPP* (1992) 95 Cr. App. R. 9.

[118] See *R. v. Bow Street Stipendiary Magistrate, ex p. DPP and Cherry* (1989) 91 Cr. App. R. 283; *R. v. Bow Street Metropolitan Stipendiary Magistrate, ex p. DPP* (1992) 95 Cr. App. R. 9.

[119] *R. v. Ashton-under-Lyne JJ, ex p. Potts, The Times*, 29 Mar. 1984 (transcript available on LEXIS). See also *R. v. Canterbury and St Augustine JJ, ex p. Turner* (1983) 147 JPR 193, 198 per McNeill J. ('in any case of judicial review, this court is concerned to see whether or not there was material before the Tribunal on which the decision was reached, and this court is also entitled to see whether the decision is one to which no reasonable tribunal, properly applying itself to the material before it, could come'); *R. v. Guildhall JJ and DPP, ex p. Carson-Selman* (1983) 148 JPR 392, 399 ('once an appellate court comes to the conclusion that justices have taken into account relevant matters and have not taken into account irrelevant material, it should not interfere with the exercise of discretion'); *R. v. Willesden JJ, ex p. Clemmings* (1987) 87 Cr. App. R. 280, 286 ('the question is not whether I agree with the decision which they reached (although I do) but whether their decision is so plainly irrational and untenable that no reasonable bench of justices, properly directed, could have reached it'); *R. v. Liverpool Stipendiary Magistrate, ex p. Ellison* [1990] RTR 220, 227 per Leggatt J. ('to succeed in procuring the intervention of this court by certiorari, the applicant would have had to show that the stipendiary magistrate's conclusion was so obviously aberrant that no magistrate properly directing himself could have reached it'); *Sherwood and Hart v. Ross* [1989] Crim. LR 576; *R. v. Redbridge JJ and Fox, ex p. Whitehouse* (1991) 156 JPR 293, 300 ('if the justices

This is consistent with the general approach taken by the Divisional Court to examination of the exercise of discretion by magistrates,[120] and, indeed, as we have seen, with the approach taken by any court to examination of the exercise of discretion by a court lower in the hierarchy.

The Hearing

It would seem that a hearing which is conducted, either by a trial judge or by a magistrate, as the case may be, to determine whether proceedings should be stayed is typically a relatively informal affair. However, the parties should adduce to the hearing all material relevant to their case. In *Mungroo v. R.*, the Privy Council said:

Their Lordships consider that, in any future case in which excessive delay is alleged, the prosecution should place before the court an affidavit which sets out the history of the case and the reasons (if any) for the relevant periods of delay.[121]

It was held recently in *R. v. Manchester Crown Court, ex p. Brokenbrow*[122] that a pre-trial application for a stay of the proceedings as an abuse of process had to be decided by the judge on the material provided by both the prosecution and the defence. The judge was not in a trial situation nor was her role an inquisitorial one, and thus she could not compel any other evidential material to be provided. The witness summons procedure under the Criminal Procedure (Attendance of Witnesses) Act 1965 related to trial on indictment only and was not applicable outside the confines of the trial itself.

That both parties should be entitled to call evidence appears to have been recognized by the Divisional Court in *R. v. Clerkenwell Stipendiary Magistrate, ex p. Bell.*[123] The Court said that, where the issue was whether proceedings should be stayed as an abuse of process on account of delay, it

acting within their jurisdiction exercise their discretion *bona fide* and bring their minds to bear on the question whether they ought to grant a further summons or not, this court is very unlikely to interfere except in an exceptional case where the decision satisfies the strict test of being unreasonable in a *Wednesbury* sense'); *R. v. Bow Street Metropolitan Stipendiary Magistrate, ex p. DPP* (1992) 95 Cr. App. R. 9, 17 (it had to be shown 'that no reasonable magistrate who had directed himself properly on the law and on the facts could have reached this decision. The test is a strict one . . .').

[120] See e.g., *DPP v. Godwin* [1991] RTR 303, 308 on the discretion to exclude evidence under s. 78 of PACE: 'The justices were entitled to exclude the evidence. Some justices and other tribunals might no doubt have made the opposite decision without acting unreasonably. It could well be thought that the defendant in this case was fortunate. None the less this is a discretion invested in the trial court, and so invested in this case in the justices.'

[121] [1991] 1 WLR 1351, 1355.   [122] *The Times*, 31 Oct. 1991.
[123] (1991) 155 JPR 669.

was not sufficient for the prosecution to give an explanation for the delay, as a very relevant matter for consideration was the possible prejudice to the defendant. Thus the refusal of the magistrate to hear evidence from the defendant on this point was a breach of natural justice and the decision to commit for trial should be quashed.

6

Entrapment

When Eve, taxed with having eaten the forbidden fruit, replied 'the serpent beguiled me,' her excuse was, at most, a plea in mitigation and not a complete defence.[1]

This judicial explanation of the events of the Garden of Eden[2] highlights the English courts' attitude to the problem of entrapment.[3] In *R. v. Sang* the issue before the House of Lords was what a trial judge should do 'when he is satisfied that an accused has been deliberately procured, incited or tricked [by an official of the Government] into the commission of a crime which he would not otherwise have committed'.[4] This practice of facilitation or incitement, by an official of the Government, of the commission of a crime which the defendant would not otherwise have committed will be referred to as 'entrapment'. The House of Lords in *Sang* held that entrapment could not be taken into account except in the exercise of the judge's discretion in sentencing. In this chapter I seek to expose the flaws in the reasoning of the House of Lords and to examine a number of alternative approaches.

First, it is necessary to consider briefly the context in which the issue of entrapment may arise.

Generally the police rely on members of the public, typically victims, to report the commission of crimes. In some situations, however, sole reliance on such reporting would prove ineffective. One of these, obviously, is the situation where a potential complainant is unaware that a criminal offence has been committed. Violations of the multiplicity of modern safety laws, for example, could easily go unnoticed by the people they are designed to protect.[5] In order to detect possible breaches, it may be necessary in such cases for the appropriate authorities to offer the opportunity for their

---

[1] *R. v. Sang* [1980] AC 402, 446 per Lord Fraser.

[2] Gen. 3.

[3] See A. Choo, 'A Defence of Entrapment' (1990) 53 *Modern Law Review* 453, on which this chapter is based.

[4] [1980] AC 402, 425.

[5] See also *R. v. Mack* (1988) 67 CR (3d) 1, 13: 'some criminal conduct may go unobserved for a long time if the victims are not immediately aware of the fact that they have been the subject of criminal activity, in the case, for example, of commercial fraud and also bribery of public officials.'

commission. Indeed, in some cases such action may be sanctioned expressly by the statute creating the offence.[6]

Another situation in which pro-active law-enforcement techniques may be employed involves potential complainants who may be aware that an offence has been committed but are unwilling to report it. This unwillingness may be due to any number of reasons. It is well known, for example, that victims of offences do not always report the commission of the offences and that in the case of some common crimes complaints may not be made where it is believed that it would be futile to do so. A further possibility is that the crime involved may be a victimless or consensual offence—generally one constituted by consensual activity involving narcotics, liquor, or sex. Because of the consensual nature of such offences there is no victim to bring a complaint and to provide evidence. Furthermore, independent observers could well be unwilling to come forward, given the widespread acceptance (if not approval) which many of these crimes receive from some sections of the public. Alternatively, the only observers may be those who are either unwilling to incriminate the accused or reluctant to direct police attention to their own illicit affairs.[7] Such considerations suggest that it may be necessary in some circumstances for pro-active law-enforcement techniques to be employed in the detection of victimless offences. Pro-active techniques involve 'modes of investigation in which the reporting, observation and testimony can be done by the officials themselves'.[8] The use of such techniques in the enforcement of narcotics laws is well documented.[9] It is in the context of the use of pro-active law-enforcement techniques that allegations of entrapment typically arise.

In England the issue of entrapment received considerable public attention in 1974 with the murder of Kenneth Lennon, who prior to his death had confessed to having acted as an *agent provocateur* for the Special Branch.[10]

---

[6] e.g. s. 27 of the Trade Descriptions Act 1968 provides: 'A local weights and measures authority shall have power to make, or to authorise any of their officers to make on their behalf, such purchases of goods, and to authorise any of their officers to secure the provision of such services, accommodation or facilities, as may appear expedient for the purpose of determining whether or not the provisions of this Act and any order made thereunder are being complied with.'

[7] J. D. Heydon, 'The Problems of Entrapment' [1973] *Cambridge Law Journal* 268, 269.

[8] G. Dworkin, 'The Serpent Beguiled Me and I Did Eat: Entrapment and the Creation of Crime' (1985) 4 *Law and Philosophy* 17, 18.

[9] Skolnick provides an account of the use of the informer in narcotics control in the US (J. H. Skolnick, *Justice without Trial: Law Enforcement in Democratic Society* (2nd edn., 1975), 120–4). N. L. A. Barlow, 'Recent Developments in New Zealand in the Law Relating to Entrapment: 1' [1976] *New Zealand Law Journal* 304, 309 states: 'Narcotics use being, particularly with soft drugs, a gregarious habit, the objective of the police in this area is the infiltration of the "scene" and the surveillance and detection of its members and those within its wide peripheral fringe.'

[10] See *Report to the Home Secretary from the Commissioner of Police of the Metropolis on the Actions of Police Officers Concerned with the Case of Kenneth Joseph Lennon* (1974); G. Robertson, *Reluctant Judas* (1976).

There has been, in recent years, great public awareness in the United States of the issues associated with entrapment as a result of the John DeLorean and ABSCAM affairs.[11]

It should be noted that an attempt to deal with the problem of entrapment in England is to be found in a circular issued by the Home Office to the police.[12] This circular, the contents of which have received judicial approval,[13] provides *inter alia* that 'no member of a police force, and no police informant, should counsel, incite or procure the commission of a crime'. It was apparently intended that breaches of this should lead to internal disciplinary proceedings,[14] but the extent to which such proceedings are instituted is unknown. Also noteworthy is the fact that the Law Commission recommended in 1977 the creation of an offence of entrapment.[15] However, as the concern in this chapter is not with how the executive should deal with the problem of entrapment but with how the judiciary should do so, it is unnecessary to consider how efficacious such an offence might be in controlling entrapment.[16]

THE ENGLISH APPROACH: SENTENCING CONSIDERATIONS ONLY

R. v. SANG: NON-RECOGNITION OF DEFENCE OF ENTRAPMENT

In *R. v. Sang*,[17] the House of Lords was confronted with the argument that the trial judge should have excluded all prosecution evidence of the commission of certain offences if satisfied that their commission had been

---

[11] See M. F. J. Whelan, 'Lead Us Not into (Unwarranted) Temptation: A Proposal to Replace the Entrapment Defense with a Reasonable-Suspicion Requirement' (1985) 133 *University of Pennsylvania Law Review* 1193, 1197–1200, 1200–3.

[12] Reproduced in Law Commission, *Criminal Law: Report on Defences of General Application* (Law Commission No. 83) (1977), 68.

[13] *R. v. Mealey and Sheridan* (1974) 60 Cr. App. R. 59, 64.

[14] Law Commission, *Criminal Law* (1977), 5.43.   [15] Ibid. 5.48–5.52.

[16] It is likely to be of doubtful efficacy in view of prosecutorial discretion. Indeed it has been expressly acknowledged by the New Zealand Court of Appeal that *agents provocateurs* 'are seldom, if ever, exposed to any danger of prosecution, and . . . in the unlikely event of being prosecuted, would certainly suffer no substantial penalty' (*R. v. Phillips* [1963] NZLR 855, 858). The point has been noted succinctly by two Canadian commentators (J. Shafer and W. J. Sheridan, 'The Defence of Entrapment' (1970) 8 *Osgoode Hall Law Journal* 277, 295): 'One extremely important element, little discussed in the texts, is that the police have a large discretion in the decision whether to arrest or not, including arrests of fellow constables. . . . [I]n charging a policeman or agent with exceeding his authority in law, the broad police discretion is always a first, and perhaps decisive, hurdle.' It is unlikely that administrative law remedies can be used successfully to compel a prosecution: see generally *R. v. Commissioner of Police of the Metropolis, ex p. Blackburn* [1968] 2 QB 118 and *R. v. Commissioner of Police of the Metropolis, ex p. Blackburn (No. 3)* [1973] 1 QB 241. See also *Evans v. Pesce and Atty Gen for Alberta* (1969) 8 CRNS 201; *R. v. Chief Constable of Kent, ex p. GL* (1991) 155 JPR 760.   [17] [1980] AC 402.

incited by an *agent provocateur*. This argument was rejected on two bases. The first was that only evidence obtained *after* the commission of the offence was regarded by the House of Lords as excludable on the ground that it was improperly obtained.[18] That is to say, any evidence obtained improperly *during* the commission of the offence was not considered to be excludable. The rationale of this limitation was not, however, explained by the House of Lords.

Secondly, it was held that entrapment was not a defence known to English law, and that the exclusion of all evidence of the commission of the crimes would have been tantamount to recognition of such a defence.[19] The House of Lords considered that the trial judge's sentencing discretion constituted adequate protection for a defendant who had committed an offence as the result of incitement by an *agent provocateur*. Thus, it was held that the fact of entrapment could be taken into account in mitigation of sentence[20] and that it was even open to a trial judge to grant the defendant 'an absolute or conditional discharge and refuse to make any order for costs against him'.[21]

The House of Lords gave two reasons for the view that entrapment was not a defence in English law, and each of these reasons warrants separate examination.

The first reason outlined by the House of Lords was that neither the actus reus nor the mens rea of the offence would have been negatived by the fact of entrapment.[22] The flaws in this argument are obvious. Quite simply, it is incorrect to suggest that a 'defence' in criminal law must negative the actus reus or the mens rea of the offence in question.[23] Duress and necessity, for example, are considered defences, but it would be extremely artificial to regard them as negativing actus reus or mens rea. Indeed, it was recognized by Lord Hailsham LC in *R. v. Howe* that the defence of duress does not negative mens rea.[24]

---

[18] See ibid. 437.
[19] Ibid. 432 per Lord Diplock; 441 per Viscount Dilhorne; 443 per Lord Salmon; 446 per Lord Fraser.
[20] Ibid. 433 per Lord Diplock; 443 per Lord Salmon; 446 per Lord Fraser; 451 per Lord Scarman.   [21] Ibid. 443 per Lord Salmon.
[22] Ibid. 432 per Lord Diplock; 443 per Lord Salmon; 445–6 per Lord Fraser.
[23] See M. J. Allen, 'Entrapment: Time for Reconsideration' (1984) 13(4) *Anglo-American Law Review* 57, 65; A. J. Ashworth, 'Defences of General Application—The Law Commission's Report No. 83—(3) Entrapment' [1978] *Criminal Law Review* 137, 138; D. Lanham, 'Entrapment, Qualified Defences and Codification' (1984) 4 *Oxford Journal of Legal Studies* 437, 439; G. F. Orchard, 'Unfairly Obtained Evidence and Entrapment' [1980] *New Zealand Law Journal* 203, 204.
Contra J. D. Watt, 'The Defence of Entrapment' (1970–1) 13 *Criminal Law Quarterly* 313, 336; J. D. Watt, 'Entrapment as a Criminal Defence' (1971) 1 *Queen's Law Journal* 3, 29.
[24] [1987] 1 All ER 771, 777. Lord Hailsham LC endorsed statements that 'the decision of the threatened man whose constancy is overborne so that he yields to the threat, is *a calculated decision to do what he knows to be wrong*, and is therefore that of a man with, perhaps to

Secondly, the House of Lords pointed out that the fact that the commission of an offence had been incited by a person other than an official could not confer a defence upon the defendant. Accordingly, it was said, there was no reason why incitement by an official should make a difference to the defendant's liability: 'It would confuse the law and create unjust distinctions if incitement by a policeman or an official exculpated him whom they incited to crime whereas incitement by others—perhaps exercising much greater influence—did not.'[25] A person who has committed an offence as a result of incitement is obviously less blameworthy and less dangerous than an ordinary offender;[26] however, this diminished culpability will not lead to an acquittal if the incitement has come from a 'lay' person. Thus, in the view of the House of Lords, if the diminished culpability of a defendant incited to crime by a 'lay' person does not constitute sufficient grounds for an acquittal, there is no reason why the diminished culpability of a defendant incited to crime by a policeman or an official should do so.

The House of Lords would appear, therefore, to have regarded the identity of an official inciter as irrelevant. Its reasoning, in essence, is that the actual culpability of an entrapped defendant would be no different from what it would have been had the incitement come from a person unconnected with the executive. As was put by the American Law Institute:

The defendant whose crime results from an entrapment is neither less reprehensible or dangerous nor more reformable or deterrable than other defendants who are properly convicted. Defendants who are aided, deceived or persuaded by police officials stand in the same moral position as those who are aided, deceived or persuaded by other persons.[27]

However, culpability is clearly not the sole consideration here.[28] 'Official' incitement of an offence stands in a completely different position from incitement of an offence by a person unassociated with the executive. The

some exceptionally limited extent, a "guilty mind" ' (emphasis in original); and that 'true duress is not inconsistent with act and will as a matter of legal definition, the maxim being *coactus volui*. Fear of violence does not differ in kind from fear of economic ills, fear of displeasing others, or any other determinant of choice; it would be inconvenient to regard a particular type of motive as negativing of will.'

The defence of provocation is another example: see *Lee Chun-Chuen* v. *R.* [1963] AC 220, in which the Privy Council took the opportunity to reaffirm the law as stated by Lord Goddard in giving the opinion of the Privy Council in *A-G for Ceylon* v. *Perera* [1953] AC 200. Lord Goddard had stated that 'the defence of provocation may arise where a person *does intend to kill or inflict grievous bodily harm* but his intention to do so arises from sudden passion involving loss of self-control by reason of provocation' (ibid. 206 (emphasis added)).

[25] [1980] AC 402, 451 per Lord Scarman.
[26] See R. Park, 'The Entrapment Controversy' (1976) 60 *Minnesota Law Review* 163, 240.
[27] American Law Institute, *Model Penal Code: Tentative Draft No. 9* (1959), 14.
[28] See generally G. P. Fletcher, *Rethinking Criminal Law* (1978), 541–4; Park, 'The Entrapment Controversy', 240–3; P. H. Robinson, 'Criminal Law Defenses: A Systematic Analysis' (1982) 82 *Columbia Law Review* 199, 236–9.

executive has a duty to uphold the law and to prevent crime. Accordingly, it is contrary to the very purpose of the law for the executive to take a hand in crime and to seek to bring to conviction an 'otherwise innocent' individual. The State is seeking, in effect, to bring to conviction a member of the public for an offence for which it has itself 'set her up'. An analogy may be drawn between this situation and the prosecution of a person for an offence in respect of which she has been 'framed' by the police. In both cases the State is prosecuting an individual for an offence which was—in a broad sense—of its own creation.

What the House of Lords fails to recognize, therefore, is that the inappropriateness of convicting an entrapped defendant is not dictated solely by her diminished culpability, but by the fact that this diminished culpability is a consequence of the actions of an official—a consideration absent in the case of 'lay' incitement. To label an entrapped defendant as a criminal, and merely to mitigate her sentence, ignores this crucial fact.

An eloquent and telling comment on the approach to entrapment recommended by the House of Lords has been made in the Supreme Court of Canada:

For the courts to acknowledge at the sentencing stage of the trial a sense of outrage at the position in which the accused and the court have been placed at the instigation of the police, is a wholly unsatisfactory response to the realization that a flagrant abuse of the process of the court has occurred. The harm to both the accused and to the administration of justice is complete with the substantive determination of guilt.[29]

Ironically one of the Law Lords in *Sang*, Lord Salmon, had observed only three years prior to *Sang* that 'for a man to be harassed and put to the expense of perhaps a long trial and then given an absolute discharge is hardly from any point of view an effective substitute for [a stay of proceedings].'[30]

POLICE AND CRIMINAL EVIDENCE ACT 1984, SECTION 78

Entrapment is one area in relation to which the application of section 78 of PACE remains uncertain.[31] The issue has been addressed in three Court of

[29] *Amato* v. R. (1982) 140 DLR (3d) 405, 449 per Estey J. (dissenting). Besides, mitigation or a discharge would obviously be irrelevant in the case of an offence for which the sentence is fixed by law.

[30] *DPP* v. *Humphrys* [1977] AC 1, 46. For a surprising endorsement of the *Sang* approach, see J. Maxton, 'The Judicial Discretion to Exclude Evidence Obtained by Agents Provocateurs' (1980) 9 *New Zealand Universities Law Review* 73.

[31] See generally A. L.-T. Choo, 'Entrapment and Section 78 of PACE' [1992] *Cambridge Law Journal* 236; S. Sharpe, '*Sang* Revisited—Judicial Approval of Police Incitement' (1991) 155 *Justice of the Peace* 761.

Appeal decisions—all reported only in the *Criminal Law Review*—but in spite of this it remains unresolved.

The most recent of the three Court of Appeal decisions is *R. v. Edwards.*[32] It was argued that the police undercover agents involved in the case had been *agents provocateurs* and that their evidence should accordingly have been excluded under section 78. Russell LJ, reading the judgment of the Court of Appeal, held that there was no evidence that the undercover officers were *agents provocateurs*, and that no question of section 78 could therefore arise. In any event there was, he pointed out, conflicting authority in the Court of Appeal as to whether section 78 had any application 'in the event of witnesses being demonstrated to be *agents provocateurs.*' First, there was the decision in *R. v. Harwood.*[33] In *Harwood*, Stocker LJ, giving the judgment of the court, had taken the narrow view that section 78 could not be utilized in entrapment cases. Stocker LJ pointed out that there was no substantive defence of entrapment in English law, and that,

since entrapment is not a defence to a criminal offence, it would seem to us to follow that an Act of Parliament dealing with evidential matters cannot be so interpreted as to bring about the conclusion that the substantive rule of law can be abrogated by evidential means. . . . Trying by evidential means to achieve the same effect as if a substantive rule of law did not exist does not appear to us to be a possible one, bearing in mind the construction of section 78. In our view the rule that entrapment is no defence is a matter of substantive law which cannot be evaded by a procedural device of preventing the prosecution from adducing evidence of the commission of the offence.

However, in the later case of *R. v. Gill and Ranuana*,[34] Lord Lane CJ, reading the judgment of the court, expressed reservations about the correctness of the observations made in *Harwood*.

It is unfortunate that in *Edwards* Russell LJ chose to remain non-committal on this issue, saying simply that

because of our finding that there was not a shred of evidence here to demonstrate that the officers involved in the instant appeal were in truth *agents provocateurs* it is unnecessary for us to resolve the conflict that has arisen in the two unreported cases to which we have just referred and we do not attempt to make any such ruling preferring one case to the other.

EXERCISE OF DISCRETION IN SENTENCING

There is a growing body of reported decisions in which the exercise of the sentencing discretion in cases of entrapment has been considered. It cannot

[32] [1991] Crim. LR 45 (transcript available on LEXIS).
[33] [1989] Crim. LR 285 (transcript available on LEXIS).
[34] [1989] Crim. LR 358 (transcript available on LEXIS).

be said, however, that there has emerged from these decisions a coherent set of principles on which the discretion is to be exercised. In *R. v. Birtles*[35] the defendant pleaded guilty to burglary and carrying an imitation firearm with intent to commit burglary. On the defendant's appeal against sentence it was held that his sentence should be reduced from five to three years. The court took into account, on the one hand, the 'real likelihood' that the defendant 'was encouraged to commit an offence which otherwise he would not have committed', and, on the other, 'the fact that the defendant had been minded to use a real firearm'.[36] Similarly, in *R. v. McCann*, 'a possibility—not perhaps the real possibility of which Lord Parker spoke of the facts of [*Birtles*] but at least some possibility—that McCann might not have carried through this theft had this opportunity not been provided by the police'[37] was sufficient to lead to a reduction in sentence from four to two years. Again, no attempt was made to determine definitively whether the offence *would* otherwise have been committed by the defendant.[38]

However the Court of Appeal in the post-*Sang* case of *R. v. Underhill*, in determining whether the appellant's sentence should be reduced, applied the principle that, 'if a court is satisfied that a crime has been committed *which in truth would not have been committed* but for the activities of the informer or of police officers concerned, it can, if it thinks right so to do, mitigate the penalty accordingly'.[39]

It would, therefore, appear that the protection afforded to an entrapped defendant by the sentencing discretion of the trial judge suffers from lack of certainty in its application. There does not appear to have emerged from the cases[40] a coherent set of principles on which the discretion is to be exercised. *Birtles* and *McCann*, we have seen, suggest that a *possibility or likelihood* that the defendant would not otherwise have committed the offence will be sufficient to lead to a reduction in sentence. But *Underhill* would seem to require definitive proof that the defendant would not otherwise have committed the offence; a possibility or likelihood would appear not to suffice.

---

[35] [1969] 1 WLR 1047. [36] Ibid. 1049.

[37] (1971) 56 Cr. App. R. 359, 365.

[38] In *R. v. Mandica* (1980) 24 SASR 394, the Supreme Court of South Australia apparently adopted a similar approach (ibid. 404 per King CJ): 'In deciding whether to extend leniency by reason of entrapment, the sentencing judge should take a common sense view of the evidence for the purpose of deciding whether there is a *reasonable possibility* that the convicted person would not have committed the offence but for the encouragement involved in the setting of the trap' (emphasis added). [39] (1979) 1 Cr. App. R. (S.) 270, 272 (emphasis added).

[40] See also *R. v. Beaumont* (1987) 9 Cr. App. R. (S.) 342; *R. v. Kelly and Holcroft* (1989) 11 Cr. App. R. (S.) 127; *R. v. Chapman* (1989) 11 Cr. App. R. (S.) 222; *R. v. Perrin* (1991) 13 Cr. App. R. (S.) 518; *R. v. Mackey and Shaw* [1992] Crim. LR 602. Cf. *R. v. Bigley (Stephen) and Bigley (Derek Roy)*, *The Times*, 22 Sept. 1992 (where a defendant's sentence had been reduced on the ground of entrapment, a second defendant who had been recruited by the first was also entitled to a similar reduction).

THE US SUPREME COURT

Having indicated the problems associated with the English approach to the issue of entrapment, we should now consider whether any alternative approaches are available[41] or worthy of consideration. It is appropriate to begin with a discussion of the approaches taken in the US Supreme Court.

The 1932 case of *Sorrells* v. *US*[42] is the first in which the US Supreme Court undertook a thorough and sustained consideration of the issue of entrapment. However, the case produced a division of opinion which has persisted in most of the cases in which the issue of entrapment has subsequently confronted the Court.[43] The debate is as to the relative merits of what may conveniently be termed the 'substantive' and 'procedural' approaches, with academic commentators generally favouring the latter. The 'substantive' approach was for a long time supported only by a majority of the Supreme Court, but in the latest two decisions of the Court it would appear to have gained unanimous support.[44]

THE SUBSTANTIVE APPROACH

It was observed earlier that to convict entrapped defendants is to find them guilty of offences for which the State has, in effect, 'set them up' and then prosecuted them. Recognizing this, followers of the substantive approach have taken the view that, 'when the criminal design originates with the officials of the Government',[45] and the Government by its conduct 'actually implants the criminal design in the mind of the defendant',[46] the defendant must be acquitted. Whether the defence is available to a defendant in a particular case is an issue for determination by the jury.[47]

What is recognized by followers of the substantive approach, therefore, is a substantive defence of entrapment. The focus of an inquiry into whether

---

[41] It should be noted that, in appropriate circumstances, one of the conventional defences may be available to the defendant. In *R.* v. *Woods* (1968) 7 CRNS 1 two off-duty police officers in plain clothes, pretending to be Toronto gangsters, threatened the defendant with violence if he did not commit certain offences. The Ontario Court of Appeal held, apparently on the basis of the defence of duress, that his convictions should be quashed and a verdict of not guilty entered.   [42] 287 US 435 (1932).

[43] The cases in which this division of opinion persisted are *Sherman* v. *US* 356 US 369 (1958); *Masciale* v. *US* 356 US 386 (1958); *US* v. *Russell* 411 US 423 (1973); *Hampton* v. *US* 425 US 484 (1976).

[44] The two cases are *Mathews* v. *US* 108 S. Ct. 883 (1988), in which Brennan J., an advocate of the procedural approach, decided to 'bow to *stare decisis*' and accept the substantive approach (ibid. 889), and *Jacobson* v. *US* 112 S. Ct. 1535 (1992).

[45] *Sorrells* v. *US* 287 US 435, 442 (1932).

[46] *US* v. *Russell* 411 US 423, 436 (1973).

[47] See generally *Sorrells* v. *US* 287 US 435, 452 (1932); *Sherman* v. *US* 356 US 369, 377 (1958).

the defence is available is upon 'the intent or predisposition of the defendant to commit the crime'.[48] 'Where the Government has induced an individual to break the law and the defense of entrapment is at issue . . . the prosecution must prove beyond reasonable doubt that the defendant was disposed to commit the criminal act prior to first being approached by Government agents.'[49] It is said that the rationale of the defence is that, in enacting the statute creating the offence, the legislature could not have intended 'that its processes of detection and enforcement should be abused by the instigation by government officials of an act on the part of persons otherwise innocent in order to lure them to its commission and to punish them'.[50] Accordingly, entrapment 'takes the case out of the purview of the statute'.[51]

The above quotations would suggest that for the defence to succeed the defendant must have had no previous intent to commit the offence charged, doing so only because of 'official' instigation. Yet it can be demonstrated that the actual test applied by those following the substantive approach is altogether different. In *Sherman* v. *US*[52] the defendant had been convicted of three sales of narcotics. The evidence was that a Government informer had asked the defendant to supply him with a source of narcotics, stating that he (the informer) was not responding to treatment for addiction to narcotics. The defendant was initially reluctant but acquiesced after repeated requests involving appeals to sympathy. It was held that the defence of entrapment was available. There was no evidence that the defendant himself had been in the trade, and, when his apartment was searched after his arrest, no narcotics were found. There was in addition no significant evidence that the defendant had even made a profit on any sale to the informer. The defendant's 1942 conviction of illegally selling narcotics and 1946 conviction of illegally possessing them were held to be of no consequence:

a nine-year-old sales conviction and a five-year-old possession conviction are insufficient to prove petitioner had a *readiness to sell narcotics* at the time Kalchinian [the informer] approached him, particularly when we must assume from the record he was trying to overcome the narcotics habit at the time.[53]

Thus it can be seen that the focus of the inquiry was in fact upon the defendant's general readiness to sell narcotics. The defence of entrapment was held to be available on the facts, as the evidence was found to reveal no such 'general readiness'.

This focus on 'general readiness' indicates an unconscious refusal by the

---

[48] *US* v. *Russell* 411 US 423, 429 (1973).
[49] *Jacobson* v. *US* 112 S. Ct. 1535, 1540 (1992).
[50] *Sorrells* v. *US* 287 US 435, 448 (1932).   [51] Ibid. 452.
[52] 356 US 369 (1958).   [53] Ibid. 375–6 (emphasis added).

Court to accept the consequences of a test which focuses on the question of whether the defendant had had the requisite criminal design (that is, had intended to commit the offence in question) prior to the Governmental involvement. The minority in *Sherman* observed:

it is wholly irrelevant to ask if the 'intention' to commit the crime originated with the defendant or government officers . . . *Of course in every case of this kind the intention that the particular crime be committed originates with the police* . . . The intention referred to [by the majority] must be a *general intention or predisposition* to commit, whenever the opportunity should arise, crimes of the kind solicited.[54]

Even though 'predisposition' is crucial to conviction, once inducement by law-enforcement agents is proved, the courts do not require that 'predisposition' be adequately proved. They often permit the admission of general propensity evidence which may otherwise be inadmissible[55] without seriously considering the degree of *relevance* of this evidence to the issue of 'predisposition'. This is demonstrated by a number of decisions of the Court of Appeals,[56] of which *Carlton* v. *US*[57] provides an example. The defendant was charged with the sale of morphine and with the receipt, concealment, and facilitation of the transportation of the morphine. These offences were alleged to have been committed in 1951. Evidence that in 1948 the defendant had been convicted of a misdemeanour narcotics violation was held admissible.[58] *Why* this evidence was sufficiently probative of the defendant's 'predisposition' to warrant admission was not explained. And in *Pulido* v. *US*,[59] where the defendants were charged with narcotics offences, it was held that evidence that one of the defendants had been arrested *twelve years* previously on State narcotics charges (from which no conviction had resulted) was admissible.[60] In some cases evidence of

---

[54] Ibid. 382 (emphasis added). See also W. E. Mikell, 'The Doctrine of Entrapment in the Federal Courts' (1942) 90 *University of Pennsylvania Law Review* 245, 251: 'When it is said that the defendant is entitled to an acquittal if the offense was conceived and planned by the officer, of what "offense" is the court speaking? Presumably the offense for which the defendant is on trial. But in practically every case of entrapment *that* [emphasis in original] offense was "conceived" and "planned" by the officer; that offense, that sale, that mailing, would never have taken place if the officer had not conceived it, planned it and instigated it, for the defendant was unaware even of the existence of the officer before the latter approached him, and therefore could not have "planned" or had the "conception" of dealing with him.'

[55] See W. R. LaFave and J. H. Israel, *Criminal Procedure* (1985), 253.

[56] The relevant cases are conveniently collected in D. E. Feld, 'Admissibility of Evidence of Other Offenses in Rebuttal of Defense of Entrapment' 61 *American Law Reports* 3d 293.

[57] 198 F. 2d 795 (9th Cir. 1952).

[58] See also *Nutter* v. *US* 412 F. 2d 178 (9th Cir. 1969).

[59] 425 F. 2d 1391 (9th Cir. 1970).

[60] See also *Robison* v. *US* 379 F. 2d 338 (9th Cir. 1967). But see *De Jong* v. *US* 381 F. 2d 725 (9th Cir. 1967) (defendant charged with knowingly facilitating the transportation and concealment of marijuana and with knowingly selling the marijuana; *held* that evidence of defendant's previous arrest for *burglary and drunkenness* was not admissible); *US* v. *Daniels* 572 F. 2d 535 (5th Cir. 1978).

doubtful reliability, such as hearsay evidence, has been held admissible. The defendant in *US* v. *Wolffs*[61] was charged with one count of conspiring to possess with intent to distribute marijuana and conspiring to distribute marijuana, and two counts of using a communication facility (a telephone) in the commission of a felony. It was held that the evidence of a detective that he had learnt through informers that the defendant had a reputation for dealing in marijuana was admissible.

The availability of the defence of entrapment in a particular case is, we have seen, an issue for determination by the jury. The dangers of leaving to a jury evidence of a defendant's prior acts of misconduct are well known. There is a possibility that the jury will decide—consciously or sub-consciously—that the defendant is deserving of punishment for her prior misconduct, and find her guilty of the crime charged on this basis.[62] This is the consequence of a substantive approach which is in any event an illusion, as we have just seen.

The substantive approach may, therefore, be summed up as follows. *In theory*, a defendant is to be found not guilty if she would not have committed the offence in question but for the impugned Governmental conduct. But the consequences of applying this test are (implicitly) recognized as being undesirable, and *in practice* the focus of the inquiry is upon the defendant's general intent ('predisposition') to commit crimes of the kind in question. Unfortunately it is apparent that on the whole the courts do not require that this 'predisposition' be adequately proved.

THE PROCEDURAL APPROACH

The procedural approach focuses more upon the issue of the moral integrity of the criminal justice system, and offers the test of whether the impugned official conduct is 'beyond judicial toleration'[63] or, to put it another way, 'falls below standards, to which common feelings respond, for the proper use of governmental power'.[64] This approach subscribes to the idea that a court, out of concern for 'the protection of its own functions and the preservation of the purity of its own temple',[65] cannot countenance the practice of entrapment.[66] Factors to be taken into account in determining

---

[61] 594 F. 2d 77 (5th Cir. 1979). See also *Trice* v. *US* 211 F. 2d 513 (9th Cir. 1954); *Rocha* v. *US* 401 F. 2d 529 (5th Cir. 1968); *US* v. *Brooks* 477 F. 2d 453 (5th Cir. 1973); *US* v. *Simon* 488 F. 2d 133 (5th Cir. 1973).

[62] It is a recognition of this which has led to the evolution of the similar-facts rule in English law: see *DPP* v. *Boardman* [1975] AC 421. See also A. A. S. Zuckerman, 'Similar Fact Evidence—The Unobservable Rule' (1987) 103 *Law Quarterly Review* 187.

[63] *US* v. *Russell* 411 US 423, 443 (1973) per Stewart J.

[64] *Sherman* v. *US* 356 US 369, 382 (1958) per Frankfurter J.

[65] *Sorrells* v. *US* 287 US 435, 457 (1932) per Roberts J.

[66] *Sherman* v. *US* 356 US 369, 380 (1958) per Frankfurter J.

the issue of entrapment vary from case to case, but include the setting in which the inducement took place; the nature, secrecy, and difficulty of detection of the crime involved; and the manner in which the particular criminal activity is usually carried on.[67]

The basis of the entrapment doctrine under the procedural approach is that the need to protect the moral integrity of the criminal justice system requires that the judiciary should not countenance certain Governmental conduct. It follows that the issue of entrapment is one for determination by the trial judge rather than by the jury.[68] Additionally it is said that it is only the court which can, through the gradual evolution of explicit standards in precedents, provide significant guidance for official conduct in the future.[69] Proof of entrapment, at any stage of the proceedings, 'requires the court to stop the prosecution, direct that the indictment be quashed, and the defendant set at liberty'.[70]

According to the procedural approach, the relevant question in determining the issue of entrapment is whether the impugned conduct, objectively considered,[71] would have been likely to instigate or create a criminal offence.[72] Yet, as the judgment of the minority in *US* v. *Russell*[73] (discussed below) demonstrates, this is not the test actually *applied* by followers of the procedural approach. Rather, a close examination is made of all the circumstances of the case to determine the propriety of the Governmental involvement in relation to the commission of the offence. Followers of the procedural approach do not, therefore, embark solely upon a consideration of whether the offence was likely to have been committed as a result of the Governmental involvement.

US v. *Russell* is a useful case for the purposes of illustrating the difference between the substantive and procedural approaches. The defendant was charged with unlawfully manufacturing and selling methamphetamine ('speed'). A Government undercover agent had made an offer to supply the defendants with phenyl-2-propanone—an essential ingredient in the manufacture of methamphetamine—in return for one-half of the drug produced. The manufacturing process having been completed, the agent was given one-half of the drug. The agent agreed to buy, and the defendant agreed to sell, part of the remainder.

The majority of the Supreme Court held, on the basis of the defendant's 'predisposition', that the defence of entrapment was unavailable to him. The minority, however, held that entrapment was established. In his dissenting opinion Douglas J.[74] regarded as immaterial the fact that the chemical

---

[67] Ibid. 384–5.   [68] *Sorrells* v. *US* 287 US 435, 457 (1932) per Roberts J.
[69] *Sherman* v. *US* 356 US 369, 385 (1958) per Frankfurter J.
[70] *Sorrells* v. *US* 287 US 435, 457 (1932) per Roberts J.
[71] *Sherman* v. *US* 356 US 369, 384 (1958) per Frankfurter J.
[72] *US* v. *Russell* 411 US 423, 441 (1973) per Stewart J.
[73] 411 US 423 (1973).   [74] With whom Brennan J. concurred.

supplied by the agent might have been obtained from other sources. He considered that

federal agents play a debased role when they become the instigators of the crime, or partners in its commission, or the creative brain behind the illegal scheme. That is what the federal agent did here when he furnished the accused with one of the chemical ingredients needed to manufacture the unlawful drug.[75]

The other dissenting opinion was delivered by Stewart J.,[76] who regarded as significant the fact that

the Government's agent asked that the illegal drug be produced for him, solved his quarry's practical problems with the assurance that he could provide the one essential ingredient that was difficult to obtain, furnished that element as he had promised, and bought the finished product from the respondent—all so that the respondent could be prosecuted for producing and selling the very drug for which the agent had asked and for which he had provided the necessary component.[77]

It can, therefore, be seen that, in contrast to the substantive approach, the procedural approach to entrapment focuses upon the morality of the impugned Governmental action rather than upon the character of the defendant. In effect, the defendant will be held to have been 'entrapped'[78] if the Governmental involvement in relation to the commission of the offence was such that the need to protect the moral integrity of the criminal justice system requires that the proceedings should not continue.

Due Process

The applicability of due process principles[79] in an 'entrapment case' was considered by the Supreme Court in *Hampton* v. *US*.[80] The defendant in this case was charged with selling heroin to undercover Government agents. The drug had been actually supplied to the defendant by a Government informer. It was argued by the defendant that the case involved a violation of his due-process rights.

In an opinion in which Burger CJ and White J. joined, Rehnquist J. held, in effect, that due-process principles could *never* be invoked to prevent the

---

[75] 411 US 423, 439 (1973).
[76] With whom Brennan and Marshall JJ joined.
[77] 411 US 423, 449 (1973).
[78] Of course, the term 'entrapment' is used by the minority in a wide sense and *not* solely to mean the instigation, by an official of the Government, of an offence which the defendant would not otherwise have committed.
[79] See Ch. 3, n. 74, where the due-process clauses of the Fifth and Fourteenth Amendments are quoted.
[80] 425 US 484 (1976).

conviction of a 'predisposed' defendant.[81] Powell J., with whom Blackmun J. joined, held that there had been no denial of due process *in this case*[82] but was unwilling to conclude that due-process principles could never protect a 'predisposed' defendant.[83] It was emphasized, however, that 'police overinvolvement in crime would have to reach a demonstrable level of outrageousness before it could bar conviction';[84] this would be especially difficult to show in the case of contraband offences, of which detection was difficult in the absence of Government undercover involvement.

The three dissenting judges thought that due-process principles would prevent the defendant being convicted. By, in effect, 'buying contraband from itself through an intermediary and jailing the intermediary', 'the Government's role [had] passed the point of toleration'.[85] Due-process principles, Brennan J. thought, required that conviction be barred in all cases where a defendant was charged with the sale of contraband which had been actually provided by a Government agent.[86]

In sum, five of the eight members of the Court were of the view that due-process principles *could* be engrafted upon the substantive approach to entrapment. It is, therefore, unfortunate that there was no consensus among the five as to the scope of the due-process protection—with the consequence that only three members of the Court considered the protection to be applicable in the case. Of course, this division of opinion or indeterminacy reflects the same kind of indecision we have seen elsewhere in this work. Since *Hampton*, there has been only one 'entrapment case' in which the Court of Appeals has held that the conviction of a defendant should be barred on due-process principles.[87]

It would appear, then, that the procedural and 'due-process' approaches share the same rationale—the protection of the moral integrity of the criminal justice system. In some cases the impugned Governmental involvement in relation to the commission of the offence may be of such a nature that the proceedings should not be allowed to continue. What is lacking, however, is a set of criteria which is of assistance in determining

[81] Ibid. 490–1. Rehnquist J. conceded that the present case differed from *Russell* in that, while in *Russell* the ingredient supplied by the agent could have been obtained from other sources, 'here the drug which the Government informant allegedly supplied to petitioner both was illegal and constituted the corpus delicti for the sale of which the petitioner was convicted' (ibid. 489). This difference was held, however, to be immaterial because of the defendant's 'predisposition'.

[82] Ibid. 491–2. The fact that what was supplied by the Government in this case was contraband whereas the ingredient supplied in *Russell* had not been contraband was held not to be material. 'Although phenyl-2-propanone is not contraband, it is useful only in the manufacture of methamphetamine ("speed"), the contraband involved in *Russell*. Further, it is an essential ingredient in that manufacturing process and is very difficult to obtain' (ibid. 492 n. 1).   [83] Ibid. 493–5.   [84] Ibid. 495 n. 7.

[85] Ibid. 498.   [86] Ibid. 500.

[87] *US* v. *Twigg* 588 F. 2d 373 (3rd Cir. 1978).

whether, in a particular case, the proceedings should be stayed. As we have seen, this absence of guiding principles led to a divergence of opinions in *Hampton* as to the scope of the due-process protection.

CANADIAN SUPREME COURT

For the sake of completeness it should be mentioned that the Supreme Court of Canada has given extensive consideration to the problem of entrapment in the case of *R. v. Mack*.[88] It was said that proof of entrapment should lead to a judicial stay of the proceedings as an abuse of process. The court held that 'entrapment' can occur in two ways. First, it is entrapment for the authorities to offer a person an opportunity to commit a criminal offence unless they have a reasonable suspicion that she is already engaged in criminal activity, or unless such an offer is made pursuant to a bona-fide investigation.[89]

The absence of a reasonable suspicion or a bona fide inquiry is significant in assessing the police conduct because of the risk that the police will attract people who would not otherwise have any involvement in a crime and because it is not a proper use of the police power to simply go out and test the virtue of people on a random basis.[90]

'Reasonable suspicion' can be based on many factors; it is unnecessary for one of these to be a prior criminal record.[91] There must be 'some rational connection and proportionality' between the offence in relation to which the authorities have reasonable suspicion and the offence which they offer the accused the opportunity to commit—the offences cannot, for example, be totally unrelated.[92] There must also be a sufficient temporal connection—'if the reasonable suspicions of the police arise by virtue of the individual's conduct, then this conduct must not be too remote in time.'[93]

The second form of entrapment arises, in the view of the Canadian Supreme Court, where, although having a reasonable suspicion or acting pursuant to a bona-fide investigation, the authorities go beyond offering an opportunity and induce the commission of an offence.[94] The test to be applied is an objective one—the question is 'whether the conduct . . . would have induced *the average person in the position of the accused*, i.e., a person with both strengths and weaknesses, into committing the crime'.[95]

If the recent decision of the Canadian Supreme Court in *R. v. Barnes*[96] is

---

[88] (1988) 67 CR (3d) 1. See also *R. v. Showman* (1988) 67 CR (3d) 61; *R. v. Barnes* (1991) 3 CR (4th) 1.   [89] See e.g., (1988) 67 CR (3d) 1, 44, 49.

[90] Ibid. 50.   [91] Ibid. 44.   [92] Ibid.

[93] Ibid.   [94] See e.g., ibid. 45, 49.   [95] Ibid. 45 (emphasis added).

[96] (1991) 3 CR (4th) 1.

any indication, the existence of a 'bona-fide inquiry' would be much easier to satisfy than the existence of 'reasonable suspicion'. In this case, an undercover officer approached the accused and his friend simply on the basis of a 'hunch' that they might be in possession of illicit drugs, and asked the accused whether he had any 'weed'. He said no. His friend said: 'She wants some weed', and the accused again replied in the negative. The officer persisted, and the accused then agreed to sell her a small quantity of cannabis resin. The Canadian Supreme Court held that the officer did not have 'reasonable suspicion' that the accused was already engaged in unlawful drug-related activity. The factors which drew the officer's attention to the accused (manner of dress and length of hair) were not sufficient to give rise to a reasonable suspicion, and the officer's decision to approach the accused was based on a 'hunch' or 'feeling' rather than extrinsic evidence. However, the Court thought that the officer *was* involved in a bona-fide inquiry: the officer's conduct was motivated by the genuine purpose of investigating and repressing criminal activity, and the police department had directed its investigation at an appropriate part of Vancouver. Given this generous definition of 'bona-fide inquiry', it is difficult to imagine that many cases would arise in which the Court would not need to proceed to a consideration of the second form of entrapment. Clearly, however, the Canadian Supreme Court's definition of 'bona-fide inquiry' is rather too generous: it seems to permit the targeting by the police of *anyone* who is present in an area selected for a police investigation. To illustrate this point, Stober provides the following hypothetical example. Suppose that a six-block area in a city is known to have illegal narcotics activity, but that this area also includes businesses, restaurants, bars, theatres, offices, and government buildings. Stober observes:

To think that the innocent shopper, diner, pedestrian, civil servant or businessman going to see his accountant, may not only be accosted by the odd drug dealer but also by police agents of the state offering them or anyone else within that area, without distinction, and at any time of day or night, the opportunity to commit an offence, appears to be clearly offensive to the community's sense of decency.[97]

OTHER APPROACHES

It has been argued by some commentators that recognition of a discretion to exclude the evidence of an *agent provocateur* on the ground that it was improperly obtained would be an appropriate judicial response to the problem of entrapment.[98] On this basis it may be suggested that an

[97] M. Stober, 'The Limits of Police Provocation in Canada' (1992) 34 *Criminal Law Quarterly* 290, 338.
[98] See e.g., J. D. Heydon, 'The Problems of Entrapment' [1973] *Cambridge Law Journal* 268.

exclusionary discretion (which, as was seen earlier, may not be available in entrapment situations in England) would constitute sufficient weaponry for dealing with entrapment. I would, however, argue that recognition of an exclusionary discretion cannot be regarded as a satisfactory response to the problem of entrapment.

We have seen that in *Sang* the argument of the defendant was that, if entrapment had been established, *all* prosecution evidence of the offences should have been excluded by the trial judge. In *R. v. Ameer and Lucas,*[99] a case overruled by the House of Lords in *Sang,* an application to have all prosecution evidence of the crime excluded in the exercise of discretion, on the ground that this evidence had come about as a result of the activities of an *agent provocateur,* was successful. On other occasions, applications have been made to have only the *evidence of the alleged agent provocateur* excluded.[100] However, this misses the point that the central complaint in a case of entrapment is that the *offence* was, in a broad sense, manufactured by the State. If the only evidence which can be regarded as improperly obtained in a case of entrapment is that obtained by the *agent provocateur,* the exercise of a discretion to exclude improperly obtained evidence would produce arbitrary results. The effect of exclusion on the outcome of the trial would depend on the existence of other prosecution evidence of the crime. If the prosecution has independent evidence of the commission of the crime, or has obtained a confession from the defendant, the defendant could be convicted in spite of the exclusion of the evidence obtained by the *agent provocateur.* If, on the other hand, the evidence of the *agent provocateur* is the only prosecution evidence of the crime, its exclusion would lead to the proceedings being stayed *de facto.*

It is possible that in many cases an *agent provocateur* will not be called as a witness for the prosecution. In *R. v. Burnett and Lee*[101] (which was also overruled by *Sang*) Lee testified that the offences charged had been committed as the result of incitement by a police informer, who was not called to give evidence. The Court held that all evidence against the defendants was inadmissible. It was said that

the absence of Edith's [the informer's] testimony left Lee's account uncontradicted and strengthened the suspicion that her conduct fell on the wrong side of the line. The conduct of Edith could only be regarded as that of an *agent provocateur* and . . . [thus] the case should be withdrawn from the jury on the general ground of unfairness.[102]

If the view had been taken that the entrapment tainted only the evidence obtained by the *agent provocateur,* there would have been no improperly

[99] [1977] Crim. LR 104.
[100] See e.g., *R. v. Murphy* [1965] NI 138; *R. v. Veneman and Leigh* [1970] SASR 506; *R. v. Williams* (1978) 19 SASR 423; *R. v. Coward* (1985) 16 A. Crim. R. 257.
[101] [1973] Crim. LR 748.   [102] Ibid. 748–9.

obtained evidence to exclude. The view taken in this case, however, was that the entrapment tainted *all evidence against the defendants*—with the result that the proceedings were stayed *de facto*.

Thus, it is clear that to exclude the evidence of *agents provocateurs* is an inadequate judicial response to the problem of entrapment. Such exclusion is not directed at the central consideration in a case of entrapment: that the actual commission of the crime, and not merely an item of evidence, can be regarded as having been a fruit of the impropriety.[103] It is inappropriate that the conviction of an entrapped defendant be dependent on such arbitrary factors as the existence of other prosecution evidence of the crime, whether the *agent provocateur* is called as a witness for the prosecution, and so on.[104] For this reason a single judge of the Supreme Court of South Australia, Cox J., held in *R. v. Vuckov and Romeo*[105] that proof of entrapment should lead directly to a stay of the proceedings rather than merely to the exclusion of the evidence of the *agent provocateur*. It was said that

where the court is satisfied in an entrapment case that the prosecution ought to be stopped on policy grounds, it is preferable, in my opinion, that it should avoid the artificiality of evidentiary exclusion and simply make an order that the proceedings be stayed as an abuse of process.[106]

A similar view has been taken recently by Samuels JA,[107] delivering the main judgment of the Court of Criminal Appeal of New South Wales in *R. v. Hsing*,[108] and by the same court in *R. v. Thompson*.[109] However, some other Australian judges have shied away from expressing an unequivocal view as to whether a stay of proceedings should be available in entrapment cases.[110] The time is ripe, therefore, for a consideration of the whole issue by the High Court of Australia.[111]

In New Zealand, too, the position does not appear to be fully settled. It is

---

[103] See Stober, 'The Limits of Police Provocation in Canada', 345 (emphasis added): 'Police provocation which contributes to the commission of a crime is distinguishable from police conduct which infringes Charter rights *after* the commission of an offence by the accused alone, with no participation by the police.'

[104] See also G. Marjoribanks, 'Entrapment—The Juristic Basis' (1990) 6 *Auckland University Law Review* 360, 381.   [105] (1986) 40 SASR 498.

[106] Ibid. 518. See also *R. v. Romeo* (1987) 45 SASR 212.

[107] Hunt J. agreed with Samuels JA.   [108] (1991) 56 A. Crim. R. 88.

[109] (1992) 58 A. Crim. R. 451; noted by A. L.-T. Choo, 'Case and Comment' (1992) 16 *Criminal Law Journal* 356. See also *R. v. Yooyen* (1991) 57 A. Crim. R. 226.

[110] See e.g., *R. v. Romeo* (1987) 45 SASR 212; *R. v. Venn-Brown* [1991] 1 Qd. R. 458; *R. v. Sloane* (1990) 49 A. Crim. R. 270; *R. v. Hsing* (1991) 56 A. Crim. R. 88 per Gleeson CJ. For discussions of *Sloane* and *Hsing*, see A. L.-T. Choo, 'Case and Comment' (1991) 15 *Criminal Law Journal* 220; Choo, 'Case and Comment' (1992) 16, 129.

[111] It is to be noted that none of the Australian judges who has recognized the applicability of the abuse of process discretion in entrapment cases has then gone on to hold that the discretion should have been exercised in the case at hand.

possible to find, in the New Zealand cases on entrapment, references to both the exclusion of evidence and the staying of proceedings as powers available to the trial judge; the exact position has yet to be clarified and properly articulated.[112]

It is arguable that it has not been decided definitively in England that entrapment cannot lead to a stay of the proceedings as being an abuse of the process of the court. The only reference in *Sang* to the concept of abuse of process occurred in the speech of Lord Scarman, who remarked that 'save in the very rare situation, *which is not this case*, of an abuse of the process of the court (against which every court is in duty bound to protect itself), the judge is concerned only with the conduct of the trial'.[113] It is to be noted, however, that another member of the Court, Lord Salmon, stated: 'It is only fair to observe that in the present case there was not a shred of evidence that the police sergeant was an *agent provocateur*.'[114] Consequently it is not inconsistent with *Sang* to hold that proof of entrapment can lead to a stay of the proceedings as being an abuse of the process of the court. It could be argued that it was because there was no evidence of entrapment that the House of Lords considered that this case did not involve an abuse of process. The possibility is therefore left open that proof of entrapment *can* render proceedings an abuse of process, and hence liable to be stayed.

SOME RECOMMENDATIONS

A DEFENCE OF ENTRAPMENT

It has been demonstrated in this chapter that entrapment is of a different dimension from other forms of pre-trial executive misconduct in as much as it has actually caused, in a broad sense, the commission of a crime. In other words, the actual commission of the crime, and not merely the proceedings or an item of evidence, can be regarded as having been a fruit of the impropriety. The judicial response to entrapment should accordingly reflect this fact. What is required is a direct recognition by the law that there is, as we have seen earlier in the chapter,[115] no justification for conviction of an entrapped defendant—in other words, recognition of a defence of entrapment.

It is now timely to consider what form a defence of entrapment in

---

[112] See generally *R. v. Capner* [1975] 1 NZLR 411; *R. v. Pethig* [1977] 1 NZLR 448; *Police v. Lavalle* [1979] 1 NZLR 45; *R. v. Loughlin* [1982] 1 NZLR 236. See also Marjoribanks, 'Entrapment—The Juristic Basis'.

[113] [1980] AC 402, 455 (emphasis added).　　　　　　　　　　　　　　[114] Ibid. 443.

[115] See the text accompanying n. 28 above, and also the discussion of the US 'substantive approach'.

England might take. First, however, it is necessary to consider whether the availability of the defence of entrapment in a particular case should be determined by the court or by the jury.

(a) Court or Jury?

I would suggest that it is more appropriate for the availability of the defence of entrapment in a particular case to be determined by the court than by the jury. As our discussion of the US substantive approach will have made clear, proof of entrapment can raise complex issues. Thus, to leave a jury to convict or acquit a defendant on the basis of whether it is satisfied that entrapment has been adequately proved will cause considerable practical problems, leading to the danger that the defence will not be taken seriously and will be abandoned eventually if it is discovered that the practical problems generated by it are insurmountable. However, if it is accepted that an entrapped defendant must not be convicted, then surely the fact that it may be difficult in particular instances to determine whether entrapment has occurred should not preclude recognition of a defence of entrapment. Interestingly, the US State of Minnesota has taken the innovative step of adopting the US Federal entrapment defence while allowing the defendant to 'elect whether to have his claim of entrapment presented in the traditional manner as a defense to the jury, or to have it heard and decided by the court as a matter of law'.[116] In England the power of a court to stay proceedings makes it possible for the law to recognize a defence of entrapment while leaving the issue to be determined by the court. Hence the court will hear evidence on the issue of entrapment on a voir dire or at a pre-trial hearing, and if it concludes that entrapment is established, order that the proceedings be stayed.

(b) Elements of the Defence

(i) General Intent ('Predisposition')

In their monograph on *Causation in the Law*, Hart and Honoré write:

Whenever it is appropriate to say that one person has acted in consequence of what another has done or said . . . it must be the case that the person so acting should have made up his mind to act only after the first actor's intervention by words or deeds. If before this intervention the second actor had already intended to do the act in question . . . the intervention could not be the second actor's reason for deciding to do what he did, though it may be his reason for persisting in a resolution already formed rather than changing his mind.[117]

It is clear that this point has been appreciated by the US Supreme Court. We have seen that the focus of an inquiry into whether the defence of

[116] *State* v. *Grilli* 230 NW 2d 445 (1975).
[117] H. L. A. Hart and T. Honoré, *Causation in the Law* (2nd edn., 1985), 55.

entrapment is available in a particular case is upon the existence or otherwise of 'predisposition' (general intent) to commit crimes of the type in question should the opportunity to do so arise.[118] If the prosecution proves that the defendant had been 'predisposed' prior to the Governmental intervention, then it cannot be said that she has acted in consequence of the intervention. The shortcoming of the US Federal entrapment defence lies, however, in its failure to address properly the issue of how 'predisposition' should be proved. General intent should not be confused with mere desire. As has been put by the House of Lords: 'intention is something quite distinct from motive or desire.'[119] Possession of a desire to commit crime does not necessarily imply the existence of a general intent to commit it should the opportunity to do so arise. Yasuda observes that 'considerations not wholly laudable may influence behavior, including fear of punishment, pragmatic appreciation of the benefits of a legal course of conduct, or realistic assessment of the difficulty of successfully committing a crime'.[120] Thus the fact that I have a desire to evade paying my fare on a bus does not necessarily imply that I have made up my mind to do so if a relevant opportunity should present itself.[121]

The failure of the US Federal entrapment defence to address properly the issue of how 'predisposition' should be proved has not gone completely unnoticed by other courts in the United States. The Supreme Court of South Dakota, for example, has adopted the Federal entrapment defence while requiring that the defendant's 'predisposition' be more seriously proved. It has decided that evidence that the defendant had previously committed similar crimes, or had the reputation for involvement in the commission of such crimes, or was suspected by the police of criminal activities, is *not* admissible on the issue of 'predisposition'.[122] In so deciding, the Supreme

---

[118] It is to be noted that the fact that an intent to carry out a criminal act is not an 'immediate' one but is conditional upon the appearance of a relevant opportunity to offend does not preclude it from being an intent to carry out that act. In *R. v. Bentham* [1973] QB 357 the Court of Appeal had the task of interpreting s. 16 of the Firearms Act 1968, which prohibits the possession of a firearm *with intent to endanger life*. It was held that it was unnecessary to show an intent immediately and unconditionally to endanger life; it was sufficient that the appellants had been in possession of firearms with a view to using them if and when the occasion arose. See also *R. v. Buckingham* (1976) 63 Cr. App. R. 159 in relation to s. 3 of the Criminal Damage Act 1971 which provides that anyone possessing anything with intent to destroy or damage property is guilty of an offence.

[119] *R. v. Moloney* [1985] AC 905, 926.

[120] T. K. Yasuda, 'Entrapment as a Due Process Defense: Developments after *Hampton* v. *United States*' (1982) 57 *Indiana Law Journal* 89, 128.

[121] For a thoughtful general discussion of intent in criminal law, see N. Lacey, C. Wells, and D. Meure, *Reconstructing Criminal Law: Critical Perspectives on Crime and the Criminal Process* (1990), 30–6.

[122] *State* v. *Nelsen* 228 NW 2d 143 (1975); *State* v. *Nagel* 279 NW 2d 911 (1979); *State* v. *Huber* 356 NW 2d 468 (1984); *State* v. *Iverson* 364 NW 2d 518 (1985); *State* v. *Moeller* 388 NW 2d 872 (1986).

Court of South Dakota has endorsed the approach taken in California prior to 1979.[123]

The following are examples of evidence regarded as admissible in South Dakota, and in California before 1979, on the issue of a defendant's 'predisposition':

1. The nature of the alleged inducement. Appeals to friendship, appeals to sympathy, and offers of excessive sums of money would suggest the lack of predisposition.[124]

2. Whether the defendant first suggested the crime. Such a suggestion would be probative of predisposition, while 'an original contact initiated solely by the police'[125] would not.

3. The response of the defendant to the alleged inducement. A quick or ready response would suggest the existence of predisposition,[126] while a slow, hesitant, or reluctant response, or a response which comes after a considerable lapse of time, would not.[127]

4. Whether the defendant's dealings with the alleged *agent provocateur* indicated that she was already familiar with the criminal activity. Such familiarity would suggest predisposition,[128] while lack of familiarity would not.[129]

5. Whether, prior to the alleged inducement, the defendant would have had a reasonable prospect of being able to commit the offence.[130] In *State v.*

[123] See *People* v. *Benford* 345 P. 2d 928 (1959) and its progeny. In 1979 the Supreme Court of California adopted the procedural approach: *People* v. *Barraza* 591 P. 2d 947 (1979).

[124] See *State* v. *Nelsen* 228 NW 2d 143, 148 (1975).

[125] *People* v. *Marsden* 44 Cal. Rptr. 728, 730 (1965).

[126] See *People* v. *Harris* 26 Cal. Rptr. 850, 852 (1962) ('Defendant readily obliged the officer, not only on the first occasion, but also made a second sale, all with no apparent reluctance or hesitation'); *People* v. *Estrada* 27 Cal. Rptr. 605, 607 (1963) ('lack of any expressed reluctance to effect a sale'); *State* v. *Iverson* 364 NW 2d 518, 528 (1985) ('Iverson was prepared to sell Hammer marijuana within a few hours of Hammer's inquiry').

[127] See *State* v. *Moeller* 388 NW 2d 872, 877 (1986) (Response 'not very ready, in light of Agent's endeavor to obtain a response which continued almost a full year'. 'For up to a whole year, the defendant refused all of the Agent's solicitations to sell marijuana or cocaine. This despite the fact defendant was already a user of marijuana'). See also *Jacobson* v. *US* 112 S. Ct. 1535, 1543 (1992) ('The evidence that petitioner was ready and willing to commit the offense came only after the Government had devoted 2½ years to convincing him that he had or should have the right to engage in the very behavior proscribed by law').

[128] See *People* v. *Estrada* 27 Cal. Rptr. 605, 607 (1963) ('knowledge of the sources of supply . . . knowledge of the going price of a marijuana cigarette').

[129] See *Patty* v. *Board of Medical Examiners* 508 P. 2d 1121, 1130 (1973) ('lack of familiarity with the vernacular—"whites" or "dexies"—used by the Board's agent . . . the doctor apparently did not even know the common names of the drugs').

[130] It is to be noted that in *Cunliffe* v. *Goodman* [1950] 2 KB 237 Asquith LJ made the following comments (ibid. 253): 'An "intention" to my mind connotes a state of affairs which the party "intending"—I will call him X—does more than merely contemplate: it connotes a state of affairs which, on the contrary, he decides, so far as in him lies, to bring about, and which, in point of possibility, he has a *reasonable prospect of being able to bring about*, by his own act of volition. X cannot, with any due regard to the English language, be said to "intend" a result which is wholly beyond the control of his will. . . . If there is a sufficiently formidable

Moeller[131] the absence of evidence that the defendant had had ready access to cocaine was a factor which led the dissenting Justices to hold that entrapment had been established as a matter of law.

Thus there may be some merit in the argument (although the facts of the case as reported make it difficult to assert this with any certainty) that the defendant in *Hampton* v. *US*[132] could not have had a general intent to sell heroin whenever the opportunity to do so arose, given that he had apparently had no access to the substance. It is to be noted that, in contrast, the defendant in *US* v. *Russell*[133] *had* apparently had access to the chemical supplied by the Government.

6. Any relevant testimony and admissible out-of-court statements of the defendant.[134]

The above are merely examples; obviously it is necessary in a given case for *all* relevant factors to be considered and weighed up. Thus in *People* v. *Goree* it was held that the defendant's 'hair-trigger susceptibility' did not of itself negative entrapment as a matter of law.[135] The response of the defendant to the alleged inducement must be weighed against other relevant factors.

This approach represents, then, a serious attempt to overcome the problems which have plagued the application of the entrapment defence in the Federal jurisdiction. The purpose of the prohibition against the admission of evidence of the prior misconduct of the defendant is, of course, to prevent evidence with a high prejudicial effect from going to the jury. As we have seen, the failure of the US Federal courts to regulate carefully the admissibility of such evidence has meant that the defence is in effect unavailable to defendants with a record of prior misconduct. If, however, the availability of the defence in a particular case is to be determined by the court, there is clearly no reason to forbid the adduction by the prosecution of evidence of the defendant's prior misconduct. In appropriate circumstances evidence of prior misconduct may, when considered in conjunction with other evidence, be probative of the defendant's 'predisposition'.

It is obvious that the courts should articulate clear guide-lines in order that a coherent body of criteria which are of relevance to determination of the issue of predisposition will gradually emerge.

---

succession of fences to be surmounted before the result at which X aims can be achieved, it may well be unmeaning to say that X "intended" that result' (emphasis added). In *R.* v. *Hyam* [1975] AC 55, 74 Lord Hailsham said that 'I know of no better judicial interpretation of "intention" or "intent" than that given in a civil case by Asquith LJ (*Cunliffe* v. *Goodman* [1950] 2 KB 237) . . .'.

[131] 388 NW 2d 872 (1986).
[132] 425 US 484 (1976). See above for a discussion of the case.
[133] 411 US 423 (1973). See above for a discussion of the case.
[134] *State* v. *Nelsen* 228 NW 2d 143, 149 (1975).
[135] 49 Cal. Rptr. 392, 395 (1966).

(ii) Objectively Unacceptable Conduct Only

An important question arises as to whether *any* 'official' conduct is capable of constituting entrapment so long as it induces the commission of an offence by a member of the public who has no pre-existing general intent to commit offences of the type whenever the occasion arises. For the purposes of illustration, a hypothetical example formulated by Professor Friedland is appropriate.[136] Suppose that a number of indecent assaults have occurred in a certain park at night, and the police decide to employ pro-active law-enforcement techniques to trap the offender(s). Accordingly, a police agent sits alone in a provocative pose on a park bench. A passer-by sees the woman, decides, *without any pre-existing general intent*, to assault her, and is arrested just as he has begun to do so. Should he have a defence to a charge of assault? Our definition of entrapment would appear to be satisfied: a person who had not already formed a general intent to commit offences of the type whenever the opportunity to do so arose was induced into the commission of the offence charged by the conduct of a police agent. Yet it is far from obvious why a defence should be available to the defendant in the circumstances. As Friedland puts it: 'Society expects people like him to exercise restraint.' The police have engaged in what appear to be perfectly reasonable (and possibly even laudable) actions in discharging their duties; these actions have, however, resulted in the 'creation' of crime because of the unusual susceptibility to temptation of the defendant. To allow him a defence would be to undermine completely the role of the police in law enforcement.

It is clear, therefore, that the conduct alleged to constitute entrapment must first be shown to be objectively unacceptable. The determination of this issue should be made in isolation of the 'predisposition' issue. Thus, what has to be determined is whether—taking into consideration the crime(s) being investigated—the impugned conduct was objectively reasonable. In relation to the above example the issue would therefore be whether it was objectively reasonable for the police, in investigating sexual assaults which had taken place in a park, to use a female decoy in the way in which they did. The answer, clearly, is yes.

(iii) Entire Course of Conduct

In determining whether entrapment has been proved, it is important that the entire course of official or Governmental conduct, and not just the actual act of solicitation, be considered. This point is demonstrated clearly by the most recent decision on entrapment handed down by the US Supreme Court, *Jacobson* v. *US*.[137] In 1984, before such conduct was criminalized,

---

[136] See M. L. Friedland, 'Controlling Entrapment' (1982) 32 *University of Toronto Law Journal* 1, 24.   [137] 112 S. Ct. 1535 (1992).

Jacobson ordered and received from a bookstore two magazines containing photographs of naked preteen and teenage boys. The receipt through the mail of such material was subsequently made illegal, and, on finding Jacobson's name on the bookstore mailing list, two Government agencies sent mail to him through five fictitious organizations and a bogus pen pal. Many of these organizations professed to having been founded to protect and promote sexual freedom and freedom of choice, and claimed to be promoting lobbying efforts through catalogue sales. After two and a half years on the Government mailing list, Jacobson was finally solicited to order child pornography, and did so.

By a majority, the US Supreme Court upheld Jacobson's plea of entrapment. Unlike the minority, who considered the Governmental conduct prior to the actual solicitation to be irrelevant, the majority treated the entire course of conduct, from the time of the initial Governmental intervention, as relevant. Thus it was held that the Government had failed to prove that Jacobson was predisposed before the Government intervened. The evidence of Jacobson's 1984 order and receipt of the magazines 'may indicate a predisposition to view sexually-oriented photographs that are responsive to his sexual tastes; but evidence that merely indicates a generic inclination to act within a broad range, not all of which is criminal, is of little probative value in establishing predisposition.'[138]

The approach of the majority of the US Supreme Court in *Jacobson* is clearly superior to that of the minority; it is extremely artificial, and there is no reason, in principle, to confine examination of the official or Governmental conduct to the actual solicitation only. The entire course of conduct from the time of the first intervention by the Government should be regarded as relevant.

(iv) Onus of Proof

In respect of onus of proof the defence should be similar to the substantive common-law defences in English criminal law, with the exception of insanity. Thus, the defendant must first adduce sufficient evidence to put the defence of entrapment in issue—that is, she carries the evidential burden—unless such evidence has already emerged in the course of the prosecution case. It should be sufficient for the defendant to discharge this burden by demonstrating, for example, that 'the government had a meaningful presence, directly or indirectly, in the alleged criminal enterprise or affair which *could reasonably have influenced defendant's conduct* to commit the offenses charged against him.'[139] The burden then falls on the prosecution

---

[138] Ibid. 1541.

[139] J. B. Ehrlich, 'Sorrells—Entrapment or Due Process? A Redefinement of the Entrapment Defense: Part II' (1983) 55(6) *New York State Bar Journal* 42, 46 (emphasis added).

to negate this evidence, which it must do beyond reasonable doubt. In other words, the prosecution bears the legal burden of proof.

(v) Identity of Alleged Inducer

As a final point it should be noted that the concept of official or Governmental conduct should extend to all conduct which is sufficiently linked to the executive—in particular, the conduct of lay persons who were co-operating with the State, or who were acting either in expectation of or in the hope for a reward or immunity from prosecution. In *Sherman* the following comments were made by the Supreme Court:

The Government cannot disown Kalchinian and insist it is not responsible for his actions. Although he was not being paid, Kalchinian was an active government informer who had but recently been the instigator of at least two other prosecutions. Undoubtedly the impetus for such achievements was the fact that in 1951 Kalchinian was himself under criminal charges for illegally selling narcotics and had not yet been sentenced.[140]

(c) Conclusion

As we have seen, the attitude to entrapment of the House of Lords reflects the extreme reluctance of the English judiciary to become involved with the issue of the consequences for a criminal trial of pre-trial executive misconduct. By contrast, the US Supreme Court has paid far greater attention to the problems associated with entrapment. In the light of the US experience, it is unlikely that such problems are not encountered in England. The recommendations which I have made in relation to recognition of a defence of entrapment provide at least a starting point for serious judicial consideration in this country of the topic of entrapment.

DISCLOSURE REQUIREMENTS

An issue which should not be overlooked in the context of entrapment relates to whether, and to what extent, the prosecution should disclose relevant aspects of State involvement in relation to the offence. In the English case of *R. v. Macro*[141] the defendant pleaded guilty to robbing (together with a 'man unknown', S) a postmaster. S was in fact an informer who together with the police had warned the postmaster of the intended crime. The postmaster was accordingly aware that a raid was to take place and a police officer was placed on hand to protect him. The Court of Appeal held that the defendant's conviction of robbery with violence should be quashed, since it might well have been the case that the postmaster was not

---

[140] 356 US 369, 373–4 (1958).　　　　[141] [1969] Crim. LR 205.

in fear of violence.[142] (The offence which was in fact committed by the defendant might well, therefore, have amounted to no more than larceny or theft.) The Court 'hoped' that such a situation would not arise again, since judges could not be expected to exercise their functions properly if they were not permitted to know the true and complete facts. In *R. v. Birtles*, decided three months later, *Macro* was cited by the Court of Appeal for the proposition that 'there is of course no harm in not revealing the fact that there is an informer, but it is quite another thing to conceal facts which go to the *quality of the offence*.'[143] More recently, the Court has stated, *obiter*, that

a mere failure on the part of the prosecution to disclose the fact that one of their witnesses is an informer is not on the face of it irregular conduct or any ground for upsetting a subsequent conviction. Different situations may arise where the effect of the conduct of the prosecution is to mislead the Court in some *vital feature of the charge* which is being tried, or if the non-disclosure of the evidence, as Lord Parker CJ put it [in *Birtles*], effects [*sic*] the *quality of the offence*.[144]

Defence counsel's argument that his cross-examination of the witness—and indeed the course of the trial—would have been very different if disclosure had been made stirred no emotions in the Court.

That the principles articulated by the Court of Appeal simply do not go far enough is obvious. Disclosure of State involvement is relevant in a number of other respects. It may, for example, inform the defendant that she had in fact been entrapped into committing the offence. Since there would not have been an entrapment if the commission had been incited by someone unassociated with the executive, knowledge that the inciter was—for instance—a police officer is crucial.

The problem of disclosure may also arise where the fact of State involvement is known but the identity of the individual concerned (usually a lay informer) is not. It has been affirmed by the Court of Appeal that, on the grounds of public interest, 'police and other investigating officers cannot be asked to disclose the sources of their information'.[145] This rule of exclusion is, however, 'subject to a duty to admit in order to avoid a miscarriage of

---

[142] For similar situations see *R. v. Martin* (1811) Russ. & R. 196 (no offence of aiding a prisoner at war to escape if the prisoner had been acting merely to detect the defendant and consequently neither escaped nor intended to escape); *R. v. Mills* (1857) 7 Cox CC 263 (no offence of obtaining money by false pretences if the prosecutor knew when he parted with his money that the representation was false; cf. *R. v. Hensler* (1870) 11 Cox CC 570: attempt to obtain money by false pretences).

[143] [1969] 1 WLR 1047, 1049 (emphasis added).

[144] *R. v. O'Brien* (1974) 59 Cr. App. R. 222, 227 (emphasis added).

[145] *R. v. Rankine* [1986] 2 All ER 566, 568. See also *A-G v. Briant* (1846) 15 M. & W. 169; *R. v. Brown* (1987) 87 Cr. App. R. 52; *R. v. Hardy* [1988] Crim. LR 687; *R. v. Agar* (1989) 90 Cr. App. R. 318; *R. v. Langford* [1990] Crim. LR 653; *R. v. Slowcombe* [1991] Crim. LR 198; *R. v. Vaillencourt, The Times,* 12 June 1992.

justice'.[146] These principles had been endorsed previously in guide-lines issued by the Attorney-General on the disclosure of information to the defence in cases to be tried on indictment.[147]

The principles articulated in *Dallison* v. *Caffery*[148] may also be relevant. Diplock LJ held there that, if a prosecutor 'happens to have information from a *credible witness* which is *inconsistent with the guilt of the accused*, or, although not inconsistent with his guilt, is *helpful to the accused*, the prosecutor should make such witness available to the defence'.[149] Lord Denning MR similarly thought that the prosecution should call a credible witness who could give evidence which would tend to show the defendant to be innocent,[150] or should make her statement available to the defence. Lord Denning added, however, that, even where the prosecution knew of witnesses whom it did *not* accept as credible, it should inform the defence about them so that the defence could call them if it wished.[151] However, it should be realized that Diplock LJ and Lord Denning MR were not addressing the specific issue of the disclosure of the identity of *informers*, and the question arises whether in cases concerning informers the interests of crime control are not overriding.

The specific issue of the disclosure of the identity of lay informers was the subject of consideration by the US Supreme Court in *Roviaro* v. *US*.[152] The Court stated that what was known as the 'informer's privilege' was in reality an acknowledgement that, by the preservation of their anonymity, members of the public would be encouraged to perform their obligation of communicating any knowledge of the commission of crimes to law-enforcement officials.[153] Accordingly there must be limitations on the applicability of the privilege, such as

where the disclosure of an informer's identity, or of the contents of his communication, is *relevant and helpful to the defense of an accused, or is essential to a fair determination of a cause* . . . In these situations the trial court may require disclosure and, if the Government withholds the information, dismiss the action.[154]

---

[146] *R.* v. *Rankine* [1986] 2 All ER 566, 569. See also *Marks* v. *Beyfus* (1890) 25 QBD 494 and *R.* v. *Richardson* (1863) 3 F. & F. 693, in which the defendant was indicted for administering poison with intent to murder. The police had, on the receipt of certain information, found the bottle containing the poison in a place used only by the defendant. It was held that they were obliged to disclose the names of the persons from whom they had received the information.
[147] See Practice Note [1982] 1 All ER 734. See also K. Vaughan, 'Protecting Those Who Grass' (1990) 87(34) *Law Society's Guardian Gazette* 16 and, generally, P. O'Connor, 'Prosecution Disclosure: Principle, Practice and Justice' [1992] *Criminal Law Review* 464.
[148] [1965] 1 QB 348.   [149] Ibid. 375–6 (emphasis added).
[150] Unlike Diplock LJ, Lord Denning made no mention of evidence which would be otherwise helpful to the defendant.
[151] [1965] 1 QB 348, 369. See also *R.* v. *Lawson* (1989) 90 Cr. App. R. 107.
[152] 353 US 53 (1957).   [153] Ibid. 59.   [154] Ibid. 60–1 (emphasis added).

The issue of disclosure, the Court held, was to be determined by 'balancing the public interest in protecting the flow of information against the individual's right to prepare his defense'; relevant factors in this determination might include a consideration of the crime charged, the *possible defences*, and the possible significance of the informer's testimony.[155] Thus the fact that in *Roviaro* the informer's testimony might have disclosed an entrapment[156] was one of the factors which led the Court to hold that disclosure should have been made.[157]

In determining the issue of disclosure, trial courts in the United States have generally utilized in-camera interviews of the informer 'to assess the relevance and possible helpfulness of the informant's testimony to the defense'.[158] Where the defendant claims entrapment, she must adduce some evidence of entrapment. Thus in *US* v. *Sharp* it was found that there had been

an abuse of discretion in the trial court's ordering disclosure based solely on defense counsel's representations, without conducting an *in camera* interview of the informant, and without first requiring that the defendant adduce some evidence of entrapment. We emphasize that it is ordinarily not even appropriate for the trial court to compel the production of the suspected informant for an *in camera* interview unless the defendant has first borne his burden of producing some evidence supportive of his entrapment defense, and not merely unsworn assertions of his counsel.[159]

In some US States the in-camera hearing procedure has been the subject of statutory provision.[160]

In England, the House of Lords has acknowledged that a court may in the exercise of its inherent jurisdiction order that a hearing be conducted in

---

[155] Ibid. 62.

[156] Ibid. 64. See also *US* v. *Price* 783 F. 2d 1132 (4th Cir. 1986).

[157] Recent decisions of the US Court of Appeals on the disclosure of the identity of informers include *US* v. *Nixon* 777 F. 2d 958 (5th Cir. 1985); *US* v. *Sharp* 778 F. 2d 1182 (6th Cir. 1985); *US* v. *Price* 783 F. 2d 1132 (4th Cir. 1986); *US* v. *Zamora* 784 F. 2d 1025 (10th Cir. 1986); *US* v. *Reardon* 787 F. 2d 512 (10th Cir. 1986); *US* v. *Giry* 818 F. 2d 120 (1st Cir. 1987); *US* v. *De Los Santos* 819 F. 2d 94 (5th Cir. 1987); *US* v. *Cerone* 830 F. 2d 938 (8th Cir. 1987); *US* v. *Smith* 857 F. 2d 682 (10th Cir. 1988); *US* v. *Parikh* 858 F. 2d 688 (11th Cir. 1988); *US* v. *Yunis* 867 F. 2d 617 (DC Cir. 1989); *US* v. *Fryar* 867 F. 2d 850 (5th Cir. 1989); *US* v. *Vizcarra-Porras* 889 F. 2d 1435 (5th Cir. 1989); *US* v. *Eniola* 893 F. 2d 383 (DC Cir. 1990); *US* v. *Moralez* 908 F. 2d 565 (10th Cir. 1990); *US* v. *Vargas* 931 F. 2d 112 (1st Cir. 1991); *DiBlasio* v. *Keane* 932 F. 2d 1038 (2nd Cir. 1991); *US* v. *Evans* 941 F. 2d 267 (5th Cir. 1991); *US* v. *Straughter* 950 F. 2d 1223 (6th Cir. 1991); *US* v. *Formanczyk* 949 F. 2d 526 (1st Cir. 1991); *US* v. *Cooper* 949 F. 2d 737 (5th Cir. 1991); *US* v. *Moore* 954 F. 2d 379 (6th Cir. 1992); *US* v. *Blevins* 960 F. 2d 1252 (4th Cir. 1992).

[158] *US* v. *Sharp* 778 F. 2d 1182, 1187 (6th Cir. 1985).

[159] 778 F. 2d 1182, 1187 (6th Cir. 1985).

[160] See e.g., California Evidence Code, ss. 1041, 1042.

camera where this is required in the interests of justice.[161]

In sum, the recommendations made earlier in this chapter as to how problems of entrapment should be approached would be largely ineffective in the absence of prosecutorial disclosure of all relevant aspects of State involvement in relation to the offence. It is only with the benefit of such knowledge that defence counsel can properly assess what arguments she might raise. Where the fact of State involvement is known but the identity of the individual concerned is not, the court should be prepared to determine the issue of the disclosure of her identity if called upon to do so. In determining the issue, an approach of balancing the public interest in protecting the flow of information against the public interest in ensuring that defendants are able to prepare their defence should be adopted.

Pro-Active Techniques not Culminating in Entrapment

As we saw at the beginning of the chapter, it is to obtain evidence of certain crimes that pro-active law-enforcement techniques are typically employed. Entrapment occurs when the use of such techniques actually causes, in a broad sense, the commission of an offence. However, even in the absence of entrapment, the obtaining of evidence by the use of pro-active law-enforcement techniques may in certain circumstances be regarded as objectionable. The question therefore arises as to whether such evidence should be excluded. Pro-active law-enforcement techniques often place police agents in situations where they are forced, so as not to 'blow their cover', to commit or participate in crime.[162] Accordingly it is generally accepted that orthodox crime-detection methods should be employed wherever possible, with pro-active techniques being resorted to only where they prove necessary. But, in practice, it appears that pro-active techniques may on occasion be employed not because they are necessary but merely because they provide a relatively easy means of investigation. Another important consideration is that the use of pro-active law-enforcement techniques may on occasion carry the risk of injury to innocent members of the public. This may happen, for example, where an undercover operation involving a violent or dangerous suspect is set up in a public place.

The issue has arisen in England on a number of occasions as to whether

---

[161] *A-G* v. *Leveller Magazine* [1979] AC 440, 450 per Lord Diplock; 457 per Viscount Dilhorne. See also *D* v. *D* [1903] P. 144; *Scott* v. *Scott* [1913] AC 417; *R.* v. *Governor of Lewes Prison, ex p. Doyle* [1917] 2 KB 254, 271 per Viscount Reading CJ; *R.* v. *Malvern JJ, ex p. Evans* [1988] 2 WLR 218.

[162] In *R.* v. *Pethig* [1977] 1 NZLR 448 an undercover police officer, for the purpose of detecting drug offenders, 'took up residence with a young man named Stewart and two girls, those three being users of marijuana, and in fact entered upon a sexual liaison with one of the girls. It was also not in dispute that he joined with them from time to time in smoking marijuana' (ibid. 449).

evidence obtained by the use of pro-active law-enforcement techniques should be excluded under section 78 of PACE.[163] In *DPP* v. *Marshall*[164] the respondents were charged with selling lager and wine without having the appropriate justices' licence to do so. The case for the prosecution rested entirely on 'test purchases' made by plain-clothes police officers. It was argued that the police officers' evidence should be excluded under section 78 because the officers had not at the time of the purchase revealed that they were police officers. This argument was not accepted by the Divisional Court: 'it is difficult to see how the fact that the police officers did not reveal their identity could have any effect on the trial', and the mere fact 'that the police officers obtained the evidence by taking part themselves in a sale which contravened the law' was insufficient.[165]

The 1992 case of *R.* v. *Christou and Wright*[166] arose from an undercover police operation described as unique in England. In 1990 a shop called 'Stardust Jewellers' was set up by the police in London. This shop purported to conduct the business of buying and selling jewellery on a commercial basis, but was in reality an undercover police operation and staffed solely by two undercover officers who purported to be shady jewellers willing to buy stolen property. The purpose of the operation was to recover stolen property for the owners, and to obtain evidence against those who had either stolen it or dishonestly handled it. As a result of the operation the two appellants were charged with handling stolen goods. They argued, *inter alia*, that evidence of the conversations resulting from the undercover operation should be excluded under section 78 on the basis that the caution required by paragraph 10.1 of Code C of the Codes of Practice had not been administered. This contention was rejected: the appellants were not being questioned by police officers acting as such, conversation was on equal terms, and there was no pressure or intimidation by the officers as persons actually in authority or believed to be. The Code, the Court concluded, was simply not intended to apply in such a context.

The Court was careful, however, to enter the following caveat:

It would be wrong for police officers to adopt or use an undercover pose or disguise to enable themselves to ask questions about an offence uninhibited by the requirements of the Code and with the effect of circumventing it. . . . Were they to do so, it would be open to the judge to exclude the questions and answers under section 78 of the Act of 1984.[167]

---

[163] See also the judgment of the European Court of Human Rights in *Lüdi* v. *Switzerland* (17/1991/269/340).
[164] [1988] 3 All ER 683.
[165] Ibid. 685.
[166] [1992] 3 WLR 228.
[167] Ibid. 237. Note that the Court of Appeal refused leave to appeal to the House of Lords, but certified, under s. 33(2) of the Criminal Appeal Act 1968, that the following point of law of general public importance was involved in its decision ((1992) 95 Cr. App. R. 457): '(1)

Just one month after the decision in *Christou and Wright* this caveat was applied by the Court of Appeal in *R. v. Bryce*.[168]

It is clear that, in determining whether evidence obtained by the use of pro-active techniques should be excluded, a number of special factors need to be taken into account in addition to general factors of the type identified in Chapter 4 as relevant to application of the principle of judicial legitimacy in the context of investigatory impropriety. First, one should consider whether it was necessary for the police to resort to pro-active law-enforcement techniques in the circumstances. That is to say, is the offence charged one which, by its nature, generally necessitates executive involvement prior to its commission to ensure enforcement of the law? Victimless crimes, as we have seen, fall into this category. On the other hand, evidence of crimes of violence is usually provided by complaining victims and eyewitnesses.[169]

Secondly, even if executive involvement prior to the commission of the offence was necessary in the circumstances, would a lesser degree of involvement have sufficed?[170]

Thirdly, it is necessary to consider whether the pro-active law enforcement techniques employed actually posed a danger to society. This point has been noted succinctly by Klar:

If the police know that a particular person is violent, the risk that others might be injured during the course of the criminal acts allowed outweighs the benefit of gathering the evidence needed to gain a conviction. For example, the risk that innocent bystanders might be hurt is too great to allow the police to set up an undercover drug purchase in a public place with a person known to carry and use weapons.[171]

---

whether evidence obtained by a trick consisting of words spoken by a defendant in conversation with undercover police officers should be excluded at common law or under section 78 of the Police and Criminal Evidence Act 1984; and (2) whether the Codes of Practice . . . for the detention, treatment and questioning of persons by police officers . . . apply to conversation between an undercover police officer and a suspect.'

[168] [1992] 4 All ER 567.

[169] See generally B. L. Gershman, 'Entrapment, Shocked Consciences, and the Staged Arrest' (1982) 66 *Minnesota Law Review* 567, 617.

[170] Cf. *DPP v. Marshall* [1988] 3 All ER 683, 684: 'In regard to the particular offences which were alleged in this information, one can conceive that by keeping the premises under observation the police could have obtained the evidence without adopting the stratagem which was adopted in this case. Clearly, while that could have been done it would have been much more time consuming and difficult than adopting the simple procedure which was adopted in this case of trying to make a purchase which would contravene the law in the way alleged in the information.'

[171] J. N. Klar, 'The Need for a Dual Approach to Entrapment' (1981) 59 *Washington University Law Quarterly* 199, 220–1. See also Gershman, 'Entrapment, Shocked Consciences, and the Staged Arrest', 626–8.

Finally, did the pro-active law-enforcement techniques involve illegality? Obviously, courts should be slow to turn a blind eye to the use of pro-active techniques which involve the commission of, or participation in, crime by police agents.[172]

---

[172] Cf. *Brannan* v. *Peek* [1948] 1 KB 68, 72 per Lord Goddard CJ: 'If the police authorities have reason to believe that offences are being committed in public houses, it is right that they should cause watch to be kept by detective officers, but it is not right that they should instruct, allow or permit a detective officer or constable in plain clothes to commit an offence so that they can say that another person in that house committed an offence.'

7

Conclusion: Rationalization and Reform

The existence of a judicial discretion to stay criminal proceedings which are an abuse of the process of the court is no longer doubted in England. More uncertain, however, is precisely what makes proceedings an abuse of process. Clearly, the term 'abuse of process' is not one which should be taken literally. The circumstances in which stays may be ordered are certainly not confined to situations where the proceedings represent an abuse, in the sense of a misuse, of the legal process.[1] Indeed, the courts are not even consistent in their use of the term 'abuse of process'. While it is typically used as a label for *proceedings* which should be stayed, courts have on occasion used it as a label for *particular pre-trial actions* of the executive which should lead to a stay.[2]

I have argued that, in determining whether a particular prosecution is to be stayed, the court should apply what I have called the principle of judicial legitimacy. This principle is premised on the notion that a court is not behaving in a legitimate manner unless it discharges its public duty of protecting the innocent from wrongful conviction and of protecting the moral integrity of the criminal process, while at the same time keeping in mind the public interest in the conviction of the guilty. The idea that protection of the moral integrity of the criminal process should be of fundamental concern to a criminal court is one which has been defended at some length in this work. Criminal justice has a clear public dimension as well as a moral dimension. The conviction of an offender imposes upon her a special moral stigma of community condemnation, and has the effect of warning the public against engaging in illegal actions. It is precisely because of this public dimension of criminal justice that criminal justice has also acquired a moral dimension: the law has recognized that it is inappropriate to expose an offender to the stigmatic effects of conviction and punishment unless the values attached to dignity and freedom have been respected in the course of bringing her to conviction. This philosophy is reflected in the doctrine of mens rea, and in the law's articulation of 'fair-process norms'

---

[1] See the discussion by D. M. Paciocco, 'The Stay of Proceedings as a Remedy in Criminal Cases: Abusing the Abuse of Process Concept' (1991) 15 *Criminal Law Journal* 315.

[2] See *R. v. Heston-Francois* [1984] 1 All ER 785.

which place substantive and procedural limits on the State's exercise of power. Thus, the public interest in maintaining the moral integrity of the criminal process is an accepted and entrenched notion in the criminal law. It follows that the principle of judicial legitimacy should be recognized even on concepts of criminal justice as currently accepted in England.

We have seen that, in England at present, the abuse of process discretion is regarded as definitely exercisable in double-jeopardy situations and in cases of delay, but is apparently unavailable in cases of illegal extradition. Is it merely coincidental that protection of the innocent from wrongful conviction may be a relevant issue in cases of double jeopardy and delay, while in cases of illegal extradition the sole issue is the protection of the moral integrity of the criminal process? We have seen that the apparent unwillingness of English courts to stay proceedings on account of illegal extradition is anomalous when viewed against the increasing willingness of the courts to exclude reliable evidence on the ground that it was improperly obtained. There is some evidence that the English Court of Appeal is already moving towards an implicit adoption of the judicial legitimacy principle in its section 78 jurisprudence. Thus, consistency requires a reform of the law relating to the consequences of illegal extradition. The public interest in the moral integrity of the criminal process requires that a court disassociate itself from pre-trial executive impropriety and refrain from bringing such impropriety to fruition; this may be achieved by a stay of any proceedings commenced in consequence of the impropriety. Thus, a decision as to whether proceedings should be stayed on account of illegal extradition should be reached by weighing the public interest in the conviction of the guilty against the public interest in the moral integrity of the criminal process. It is entirely inappropriate to regard a criminal trial as being concerned solely with determination of the 'truth'. The criminal trial is an integral part of the entire criminal justice system, and by allowing 'tainted' proceedings to continue a court effectively becomes implicated in the conduct of the executive. As the two competing interests to be weighed are both public interests, a court would not be weighing incommensurables. If, on the other hand, the compensatory rationale for a stay were adopted, a court would then be attempting to weigh incommensurables: the public interest in the conviction of the guilty on the one hand, and individual rights on the other. The deterrent rationale for a stay is also problematic, as it would require the public interest in the conviction of the guilty to be weighed against the speculative future benefits of a stay.

Of course, a stay of proceedings should not be ordered in any circumstances unless judicial legitimacy would be compromised *if the proceedings were allowed to continue*. In many cases, less drastic measures than a stay would suffice to prevent judicial legitimacy from being compromised. Examples of such measures might include adverse judicial comment on the conduct of the executive,[3] a direction to the jury, the exclusion of evidence, and the imposition of a lower sentence than would otherwise have been imposed. Take, for example, the issue of delay. Suppose that there is a substantial danger that the continuation of the proceedings in their present form would result in the conviction of an innocent person. Yet a stay of the proceedings is not necessarily the appropriate solution. If the danger of wrongful conviction stems from the likely unreliability of the testimony of a particular witness or particular witnesses, then it may be possible to eliminate this danger simply by the exclusion of the evidence of the witness or witnesses.

Police impropriety at the investigatory stage provides the best example of a situation in relation to which exclusion, rather than a stay, may represent the appropriate solution. A stay should be ordered where the proceedings have been 'tainted' by the impropriety to such an extent that judicial legitimacy would be compromised if the proceedings were allowed to continue. In other cases, however, the exclusion of an item of 'tainted' evidence may be sufficient to prevent judicial legitimacy from being compromised. Again, it is all a matter of degree.

Application of the judicial legitimacy principle would inevitably involve the exercise of judicial discretion, in the sense that there can be no automatic way of determining whether, in a particular case, a stay should be ordered. On the one hand, it is clear that a measure of judicial discretion is necessary to enable all relevant circumstances to be taken into account in the individual case. On the other hand, the flexibility inherent in judicial discretion may produce considerable uncertainty of application. However, problems of unpredictability and of uncertainty of application may be minimized if the discretion is appropriately confined, structured, and checked. We have drawn attention to two ways in which confinement of the abuse of process discretion may be achieved. The first relates to the double-jeopardy principle, and involves the expansion of the scope of the pleas in bar and the revival of the doctrine of criminal issue estoppel, while reserving the abuse of process discretion for deployment in exceptional cases not covered by legal principle. The second relates to police impropriety at the investigatory stage, and involves the adoption of a rule of law that any prosecution 'tainted' by a very serious infringement of rights—for example, torture by UK authorities—must be automatically stayed. This would

---

[3] Note the following comments by the Court of Appeal in R. v. *Mackintosh* (1982) 76 Cr. App. R. 177, 182: 'It is most important that the police should bear in mind that it is stupid as well as unlawful to keep someone in custody for a minute longer than they should. It is to be hoped that such behaviour by the police will not occur in future. . . . Nothing is more likely to muddy the waters of the administration of justice than this kind of behaviour by police officers.'

confine discretion to situations where no such infringement has occurred, which presumably would account for the vast majority of cases.

The main way in which the abuse of process discretion may be structured is through the recognition of guide-lines for its exercise. Much of this work has been devoted to the identification of appropriate guide-lines for the exercise of the discretion in specific contexts. The specific issue of the circumstances in which proceedings should be stayed on account of improper pre-trial executive delay was examined in Chapter 3. We saw that there are two independent bases on which the principle of judicial legitimacy would require improperly delayed proceedings to be stayed. First, it is necessary to consider the possibility that the delay may have left the defendant without a fair opportunity to defend herself. Some of the factors which might be taken into account in relation to this were identified. These include the length of the delay since the time of the alleged offence; whether the offence is to be proven primarily by testimonial rather than documentary evidence; whether the delay occurred before or after the defendant had been alerted to the prospect of litigation against her; the death or disappearance during the delay of a person who would otherwise have been a vital witness; and the prior attitude of the defendant to the delay. The existence or otherwise of a substantial risk that the defendant has been left by the delay without a fair opportunity to defend herself is the crucial issue. But, if it is considered that the proceedings ought not to be stayed on this basis, then the second basis on which a stay may be ordered must be considered. This second basis is analogous to that on which, for example, proceedings may be stayed on account of illegal extradition. That is, even though there is no danger of wrongful conviction, the delay may, by causing the defendant to suffer oppression, anxiety, and concern, have compromised the moral integrity of the criminal process to such an extent that the public interest requires a stay of the proceedings.

In Chapter 4 a number of guide-lines which may be relevant to application of the judicial legitimacy principle to determine whether proceedings should be stayed on account of police impropriety at the investigatory stage were identified. These involve a consideration of factors such as whether a serious infringement of rights was involved; whether the police acted in good faith; the presence or otherwise of circumstances of urgency, emergency, or necessity; the gravity of the offence charged; and the availability or otherwise of a direct sanction against the person(s) responsible for the impropriety. It was also argued that the onus of proof should lie on the prosecution once the relevant pre-trial executive impropriety is established. In other words, the onus should lie on the prosecution to satisfy the judge that the proceedings should not be stayed.

Checks of discretion would be provided primarily by appeals to the Court of Appeal (or applications to the Divisional Court for judicial review) on the basis of incorrect application of the judicial legitimacy principle. The Court of Appeal (or the Divisional Court) should not hesitate to formulate principles which provide sufficient guidance as to how the discretion should be exercised in individual cases. At the same time, however, it is important that the discretion be left sufficiently unfettered to enable it to be adapted to new factual circumstances. The basic consideration is that a careful balance must be reached between flexibility and predictability.

The problem of entrapment deserves special mention. The English approach to entrapment reflects the same conservatism and lack of sustained analysis which has pervaded most other judicial considerations in England of the implications for criminal proceedings of investigatory impropriety. I have argued that it is entirely appropriate that a stay of proceedings should be ordered where entrapment is established. Thus, the abuse of process discretion is totally irrelevant in entrapment situations; what is required is recognition of a principle of law that proof of entrapment must lead automatically to a stay of the proceedings. As entrapment actually causes (in a broad sense) the commission of a crime, it is obviously of a totally different dimension from other forms of investigatory impropriety. In a case of entrapment, the 'fruit' of the executive action is not merely a specific item of prosecution evidence, or even the proceedings as a whole, but the actual commission of the offence. If the use of pro-active law-enforcement techniques has resulted merely in the obtaining of evidence, then the judicial legitimacy principle should be applied to determine whether the evidence should be excluded under section 78. If, however, there is a likelihood that the pro-active techniques may have lured the defendant into the actual commission of the offence, then the recommendations made in Chapter 6 should be drawn upon in determining whether the defendant should have a defence to liability. The main problems with recognition of a defence of entrapment are likely to arise in relation to the determination of whether entrapment has actually occurred. Leaving the responsibility for determining the issue of entrapment to the trial judge rather than to the jury will ensure that difficulties with the practical application of the defence do not arise.

The extent to which Crown Courts are faced with applications for stays of proceedings on the ground of abuse of process is uncertain. The reality is that some trial judges may in fact be adopting a relatively liberal approach in considering applications for stays of proceedings, mindful of the fact that no prosecution appeal to the Court of Appeal is available.[4] However, what

---

[4] Note also that the binding effect of Crown Court decisions is doubtful: see 'The Binding Effect of Crown Court Decisions' [1980] *Criminal Law Review* 402.

is required is acceptance by the appellate courts of the need for reform of the area, in order that a coherent body of law will develop. It is to be hoped that the recommendations made in this work provide at least an indication of the sorts of issues which should be addressed by all courts in considering the abuse of process discretion.

Bibliography

ARTICLES

ALLEN, C. J. W., 'Discretion and Security: Excluding Evidence under Section 78(1) of the Police and Criminal Evidence Act 1984' [1990] *Cambridge Law Journal* 80.

ALLEN, D. K., 'Entrapment and Exclusion of Evidence' (1980) 43 *Modern Law Review* 450.

ALLEN, M. J., 'Judicial Discretion and the Exclusion of Evidence in Entrapment Situations in Light of the House of Lords Decision in R. v. Sang' (1982) 33 *Northern Ireland Legal Quarterly* 105.

—— 'Entrapment: Time for Reconsideration' (1984) 13(4) *Anglo-American Law Review* 57.

ALSCHULER, A. W., 'Courtroom Misconduct by Prosecutors and Trial Judges' (1972) 50 *Texas Law Review* 629.

AMSTERDAM, A. G., 'Perspectives on the Fourth Amendment' (1974) 58 *Minnesota Law Review* 349.

ANDREWS, J. A., 'Involuntary Confessions and Illegally Obtained Evidence in Criminal Cases—I' [1963] *Criminal Law Review* 15.

—— 'Involuntary Confessions and Illegally Obtained Evidence in Criminal Cases—II' [1963] *Criminal Law Review* 77.

ARENELLA, P., 'Rethinking the Functions of Criminal Procedure: The Warren and Burger Courts' Competing Ideologies' (1983) 72 *Georgetown Law Journal* 185.

ASHWORTH, A. J., 'Excluding Evidence as Protecting Rights' [1977] *Criminal Law Review* 723.

—— 'Defences of General Application—The Law Commission's Report No. 83—(3) Entrapment' [1978] *Criminal Law Review* 137.

—— 'Concepts of Criminal Justice' [1979] *Criminal Law Review* 412.

—— 'The Court's Discretion to Exclude Evidence' (1979) 143 *Justice of the Peace* 558.

BAKER, R. W., 'Confessions and Improperly Obtained Evidence' (1956) 30 *Australian Law Journal* 59.

BALDIGA, W. R., 'Excluding Evidence to Protect Rights: Principles Underlying the Exclusionary Rule in England and the United States' (1983) 6 *Boston College International and Comparative Law Review* 133.

BALDWIN, F. N., jun., 'Due Process and the Exclusionary Rule: Integrity and Justification' (1987) 39 *University of Florida Law Review* 505.

BALDWIN, R., 'Why Accountability?' (1987) 27 *British Journal of Criminology* 97.

BANCROFT, D. P., 'Administration of the Affirmative Trap and the Doctrine of Entrapment: Device and Defense' (1963) 31 *University of Chicago Law Review* 137.

BARLOW, N. L. A., 'Recent Developments in New Zealand in the Law Relating to Entrapment: 1' [1976] *New Zealand Law Journal* 304.

—— 'Recent Developments in New Zealand in the Law Relating to Entrapment: 2' [1976] *New Zealand Law Journal* 328.

—— 'Entrapment and the Common Law: Is There a Place for the American Doctrine of Entrapment?' (1978) 41 *Modern Law Review* 266.

BAYLES, M., 'Principles for Legal Procedure' (1986) 5 *Law and Philosophy* 33.

BENNETT, F. G., 'Judicial Integrity and Judicial Review: An Argument for Expanding the Scope of the Exclusionary Rule' (1973) 20 *University of California Los Angeles Law Review* 1129.

BENNION, F., 'The New Prosecution Arrangements: (1) The Crown Prosecution Service' [1986] *Criminal Law Review* 3.

BENTIL, J. K., 'When Extradition Masquerades as Deportation' (1983) 127 *Solicitors' Journal* 604.

BERNARDI, F. A., 'The Exclusionary Rule: Is a Good Faith Standard Needed to Preserve a Liberal Interpretation of the Fourth Amendment?' (1980) 30 *DePaul Law Review* 51.

BILLY, M., jun., and REHNBORG, G. A., jun., 'The Fourth Amendment Exclusionary Rule: Past, Present, No Future' (1975) 12 *American Criminal Law Review* 507.

'The Binding Effect of Crown Court Decisions' [1980] *Criminal Law Review* 402.

BIRCH, D., 'The PACE Hots Up: Confessions and Confusions under the 1984 Act' [1989] *Criminal Law Review* 95.

BLECKER, R. I., 'Beyond 1984: Undercover in America—Serpico to Abscam' (1984) 28 *New York Law School Law Review* 823.

BRADLEY, C. M., 'The Exclusionary Rule in Germany' (1983) 96 *Harvard Law Review* 1032.

—— 'The "Good Faith Exception" Cases: Reasonable Exercises in Futility' (1985) 60 *Indiana Law Journal* 287.

—— 'Enforcing the Rules of Criminal Procedure: An American Perspective' (1988–9) 18 *Federal Law Review* 188.

BRADLEY, G. V., 'Present at the Creation? A Critical Guide to *Weeks v. United States* and its Progeny' (1986) 30 *St Louis University Law Journal* 1031.

BRITTAIN, R. P., ' "Entrapment"—the English Approach' (1974) 124 *New Law Journal* 1072.

BRYANT, A. W., GOLD, M., STEVENSON, H. M., and NORTHRUP, D., 'Public Attitudes toward the Exclusion of Evidence: Section 24(2) of the Canadian Charter of Rights and Freedoms' (1990) 69 *Canadian Bar Review* 1.

BYRNE, P., 'The Right to a Speedy Trial' (1988) 62 *Australian Law Journal* 160.

C., J. A., 'The So-Called Defence of Entrapment' (1980) 44 *Journal of Criminal Law* 38.

C., J. T., 'Evidence Obtained by Means Considered Irregular' [1969] *Juridical Review* 55.

CANON, B. C., 'Is the Exclusionary Rule in Failing Health? Some New Data and a Plea against a Precipitous Conclusion' (1974) 62 *Kentucky Law Journal* 681.

CHOO, A. L.-T., 'Abuse of Process and Pre-Trial Delay: A Structured Approach' (1989) 13 *Criminal Law Journal* 178.

CHOO, A. L.-T., 'Improperly Obtained Evidence: A Reconsideration' (1989) 9 *Legal Studies* 261.

—— 'A Defence of Entrapment' (1990) 53 *Modern Law Review* 453.

—— 'Case and Comment' (1991) 15 *Criminal Law Journal* 220.

—— 'Case and Comment' (1992) 16 *Criminal Law Journal* 129.

—— 'The Consequences of Illegal Extradition' [1992] *Criminal Law Review* 490.

—— 'Entrapment and Section 78 of PACE' [1992] *Cambridge Law Journal* 236.

—— 'Case and Comment' (1992) 16 *Criminal Law Journal* 356.

—— 'Delay and Abuse of Process' (1992) 108 *Law Quarterly Review* 565.

—— 'Joint Unlawful Enterprises and Murder' (1992) 55 *Modern Law Review* 870.

CODE, M., 'American Cadillacs or Canadian Compacts: What is the Correct Criminal Procedure for S. 24 Applications under the Charter of Rights?: Part I' (1991) 33 *Criminal Law Quarterly* 298.

—— 'American Cadillacs or Canadian Compacts: What is the Correct Criminal Procedure for S. 24 Applications under the Charter of Rights?: Part II' (1991) 33 *Criminal Law Quarterly* 407.

COLE, C. V., 'Extradition Treaties Abound but Unlawful Seizures Continue' (1975) 9 *Law Society Gazette* 177.

Comment, 'Police Perjury in Narcotics "Dropsy" Cases: A New Credibility Gap' (1971) 60 *Georgetown Law Journal* 507.

Comment, 'The Tort Alternative to the Exclusionary Rule in Search and Seizure' (1972) 63 *Journal of Criminal Law, Criminology and Police Science* 256.

CONWAY, R., 'The Right to Counsel and the Admissibility of Evidence' (1985) 28 *Criminal Law Quarterly* 28.

CORBETT, C. and KORN, Y., 'Custody Time Limits in Serious and Complex Cases: Will they Work in Practice?' [1987] *Criminal Law Review* 737.

CORRE, N., 'Abuse of Process and the Power to Stay a Prosecution' (1991) 155 *Justice of the Peace* 469, 486, 501.

—— 'Further Observations on Abuse of Process' (1992) 156 *Justice of the Peace* 115.

COUGHLAN, S. G., 'R. v. Askov—A Bold Step Not Boldly Taken' (1991) 33 *Criminal Law Quarterly* 247.

—— 'Good Faith and Exclusion of Evidence under the *Charter*' (1992) 11 *Criminal Reports* (4th) 304.

—— 'Trial within a Reasonable Time: Does the Right Still Exist?' (1992) 12 *Criminal Reports* (4th) 34.

COWLEY, D., 'Discouraging the Unfair Cop' (1980) 124 *Solicitors' Journal* 690.

COWLING, M. G., 'Unmasking "Disguised" Extradition—Some Glimmer of Hope' (1992) 109 *South African Law Journal* 241.

CRAGG, S., 'Putting the Police on Trial' (1992) 89(20) *Law Society's Guardian Gazette* 17.

DAMAŠKA, M., 'Evidentiary Barriers to Conviction and Two Models of Criminal Procedure: A Comparative Study' (1973) 121 *University of Pennsylvania Law Review* 506.

DAVIES, F. G., 'Abuse of Process—An Expanding Doctrine' (1991) 55 *Journal of Criminal Law* 374.

DAWSON, J. B., 'Death of a Discretion' (1980) 4 *Otago Law Review* 503.

DENNIS, I. H., 'Reconstructing the Law of Criminal Evidence' (1989) 42 *Current Legal Problems* 21.

DICKINSON, E. D., 'Jurisdiction Following Seizure or Arrest in Violation of International Law' (1934) 28 *American Journal of International Law* 231.

DODDS, M. D., 'The Restrictions on Custodial Sentences in the Criminal Justice Act 1991—Sentencing Guidelines from the Criminal Justice Act 1982' (1992) 156 *Justice of the Peace* 691, 710, 726.

DONNELLY, R. C., 'Judicial Control of Informants, Spies, Stool Pigeons, and Agent Provocateurs' (1951) 60 *Yale Law Journal* 1091.

DONOVAN, B., 'The Role of Causation under S. 24(2) of the *Charter*: Nine Years of Inconclusive Jurisprudence' (1991) 49(2) *University of Toronto Faculty of Law Review* 233.

DOWLER, P. C. and DUNCAN, E. W., 'The Defense of Entrapment in California' (1968) 19 *Hastings Law Journal* 825.

DOWNEY, B., 'Judicial Discretion and the Fruit of the Poisoned Tree' (1978) 8 *Hong Kong Law Journal* 43.

DOYLE, M. W., 'The Discretion to Exclude Unfairly Obtained Evidence' [1978] *New Zealand Law Journal* 25.

DRISCOLL, J., 'Excluding Illegally Obtained Evidence in the United States' [1987] *Criminal Law Review* 553.

DUNHAM, D. S., '*Hampton* v. *United States*: Last Rites for the "Objective" Theory of Entrapment?' (1977) 9 *Columbia Human Rights Law Review* 223.

DWORKIN, G., 'The Serpent Beguiled Me and I Did Eat: Entrapment and the Creation of Crime' (1985) 4 *Law and Philosophy* 17.

Editorial, 'The Criminal Investigation Bill [1977]' (1977) 1 *Criminal Law Journal* 117.

Editorial, 'The Criminal Investigation Bill 1981' (1982) 6 *Criminal Law Journal* 65.

EDWARDS, J. LL. J., 'Bora Laskin and the Criminal Law' (1985) 35 *University of Toronto Law Journal* 325.

'Effect of *Mapp* v. *Ohio* on Police Search-and-Seizure Practices in Narcotics Cases' (1968) 4 *Columbia Journal of Law and Social Problems* 87.

EHRLICH, J. B., 'Sorrells—Entrapment or Due Process? A Redefinement of the Entrapment Defense: Part I' (1983) 55(5) *New York State Bar Journal* 33.

—— 'Sorrells—Entrapment or Due Process? A Redefinement of the Entrapment Defense: Part II' (1983) 55(6) *New York State Bar Journal* 42.

FAWCETT, J. E. S., 'The *Eichmann* Case' (1962) 38 *British Yearbook of International Law* 181.

FELD, D. E., 'Admissibility of Evidence of Other Offenses in Rebuttal of Defense of Entrapment' 61 *American Law Reports* 3d 293.

FELDMAN, D., 'Regulating Treatment of Suspects in Police Stations: Judicial Interpretation of Detention Provisions in the Police and Criminal Evidence Act 1984' [1990] *Criminal Law Review* 452.

FLETCHER, W. A., 'The Discretionary Constitution: Institutional Remedies and Judicial Legitimacy' (1982) 91 *Yale Law Journal* 635.

FOOTE, C., 'Tort Remedies for Police Violations of Individual Rights' (1955) 39 *Minnesota Law Review* 493.

Fox, R. G., 'Criminal Delay as Abuse of Process' (1990) 16 *Monash University Law Review* 64.

France, S., 'Problems in the Defence of Entrapment' (1988) 22 *University of British Columbia Law Review* 1.

Franck, T., 'Case and Comment' (1955) 33 *Canadian Bar Review* 721.

Frankel, S. D., 'Entrapment: Recent Happenings' (1985) 43 *Advocate* 505.

Friedland, M. L., 'Controlling Entrapment' (1982) 32 *University of Toronto Law Journal* 1.

G., F., 'Agent Provocateur?' (1968) 112 *Solicitors' Journal* 185.

Galligan, D. J., 'Regulating Pre-Trial Decisions', in I. H. Dennis (ed.), *Criminal Law and Justice: Essays from the W. G. Hart Workshop, 1986* (London: Sweet & Maxwell, 1987).

—— 'More Scepticism about Scepticism' (1988) 8 *Oxford Journal of Legal Studies* 249.

Gee, D., 'The Independent Source Exception to the Exclusionary Rule: The Burger Court's Attempted Common-Sense Approach and Resulting "Cure-All" to Fourth Amendment Violations' (1985) 28 *Howard Law Journal* 1005.

Gelowitz, M. A., 'Section 78 of the Police and Criminal Evidence Act 1984: Middle Ground or No Man's Land?' (1990) 106 *Law Quarterly Review* 327.

Gershman, B. L., 'Abscam, the Judiciary, and the Ethics of Entrapment' (1982) 91 *Yale Law Journal* 1565.

—— 'Entrapment, Shocked Consciences, and the Staged Arrest' (1982) 66 *Minnesota Law Review* 567.

Ghandhi, P. R., 'Punitive Damages against the Police' (1990) 134 *Solicitors' Journal* 357.

Gilchrist, S., 'Crime Reporter' (1992) 136 *Solicitors' Journal* 410.

—— 'Crime Reporter' (1992) 136 *Solicitors' Journal* 888.

Gilvarry, E., 'Speeding Up Crime Cases' (1991) 88(8) *Law Society's Guardian Gazette* 3, 5.

Glicksman, E. B., 'Reform of English Criminal Procedure—Fact or Fiction?' (1986) 15 *Anglo-American Law Review* 1.

Goldstein, A. S., 'Reflections on Two Models: Inquisitorial Themes in American Criminal Procedure' (1974) 26 *Stanford Law Review* 1009.

Gordon, R., '*United States v. Leon*: The "Good Faith" Evisceration of the Exclusionary Rule and the Fourth Amendment' (1985) 28 *Howard Law Journal* 1051.

Grassie, Y. G., 'Federally Sponsored International Kidnapping: An Acceptable Alternative to Extradition?' (1986) 64 *Washington University Law Quarterly* 1205.

Greer, S. C., 'Supergrasses and the Legal System in Britain and Northern Ireland' (1986) 102 *Law Quarterly Review* 198.

Griffiths, J., 'Ideology in Criminal Procedure *or* A Third "Model" of the Criminal Process' (1970) 79 *Yale Law Journal* 359.

Griswold, E. N., 'Sed Quis Custodiet Ipsos Custodies? Some Reflections on ABSCAM', in A. R. Blackshield (ed.), *Legal Change: Essays in Honour of Julius Stone* (Sydney: Butterworths, 1983).

Hall, A., 'Time for a Change?' [Aug. 1990] *Legal Action* 7.

—— 'Still Time for a Change?' [June 1991] *Legal Action* 9.

HARPER, T., 'Entrapment' (1975) 125 *New Law Journal* 347.

HART, H. M., jun., 'The Aims of the Criminal Law' (1958) 23 *Law and Contemporary Problems* 401.

HEFFERNAN, W. C. and LOVELY, R. W., 'Evaluating the Fourth Amendment Exclusionary Rule: The Problem of Police Compliance with the Law' (1991) 24 *University of Michigan Journal of Law Reform* 311.

HERRICK, J. M., 'Double Jeopardy Analysis Comes Home: The "Same Conduct" Standard in *Grady v. Corbin*' (1991) 79 *Kentucky Law Journal* 847.

HEYDON, J. D., 'Illegally Obtained Evidence (2)' [1973] *Criminal Law Review* 690.

—— 'The Problems of Entrapment' [1973] *Cambridge Law Journal* 268.

—— 'Current Trends in the Law of Evidence' (1977) 8 *Sydney Law Review* 305.

—— 'Entrapment and Unfairly Obtained Evidence in the House of Lords' [1980] *Criminal Law Review* 129.

HICKEY, T. J., 'Double Jeopardy after *Grady* v. *Corbin*' (1992) 28 *Criminal Law Bulletin* 3.

HIRST, M., 'Contradicting Previous Acquittals' [1991] *Criminal Law Review* 510.

HODGE, A. S., 'The Process of Abuse' (1990) 20 *Hong Kong Law Journal* 195.

HOFFMANN, L. H., 'Similar Facts after Boardman' (1975) 91 *Law Quarterly Review* 193.

HUNTER, J., 'The Development of the Rule against Double Jeopardy' (1984) 5 *Journal of Legal History* 3.

—— ' "Tainted" Proceedings: Censuring Police Illegalities' (1985) 59 *Australian Law Journal* 709.

HUTCHINSON, A. C. and WITHINGTON, N. R., 'Comment' (1980) 58 *Canadian Bar Review* 376.

ISAACS, N., 'The Limits of Judicial Discretion' (1923) 32 *Yale Law Journal* 339.

JACKSON, J. D., 'Unfairness and the Judicial Discretion to Exclude Evidence' (1980) 130 *New Law Journal* 585.

JACOB, I. H., 'The Inherent Jurisdiction of the Court' (1970) 23 *Current Legal Problems* 23.

JAMES, Lord Justice, 'A Judicial Note on the Control of Discretion in the Administration of Criminal Justice', in R. Hood (ed.), *Crime, Criminology and Public Policy: Essays in Honour of Sir Leon Radzinowicz* (London: Heinemann, 1974).

JENNEX, D., 'Dworkin and the Doctrine of Judicial Discretion' (1992) 14 *Dalhousie Law Journal* 473.

JOCHUM, R. A., 'I Come Not to Praise the Exclusionary Rule but to Bury it' (1985) 18 *Creighton Law Review* 819.

JOLOWICZ, J. A., 'Abuse of the Process of the Court: Handle with Care' (1990) 43 *Current Legal Problems* 77.

KAMISAR, Y., 'Is the Exclusionary Rule an "Illogical" or "Unnatural" Interpretation of the Fourth Amendment?' (1978) 62 *Judicature* 66.

—— 'Does the Exclusionary Rule Affect Police Behavior?' (1978) 62 *Judicature* 70.

—— ' "Comparative Reprehensibility" and the Fourth Amendment Exclusionary Rule' (1987) 86 *Michigan Law Review* 1.

KAPLAN, J., 'The Limits of the Exclusionary Rule' (1974) 26 *Stanford Law Review* 1027.

KAPNOULLAS, S., 'Entrapment Defence Rejected by Supreme Court' (1989) 63 *Law Institute Journal* 607.

KHAN, A. N., 'Extradition in the Guise of Deportation' (1986) 130 *Solicitors' Journal* 657.

—— 'Trial without Extradition—Abuse of Court's Process' [1986] *New Zealand Law Journal* 123.

KING, R. L., 'The International Silver Platter and the "Shocks the Conscience" Test: US Law Enforcement Overseas' (1989) 67 *Washington University Law Quarterly* 489.

KLAR, J. N., 'The Need for a Dual Approach to Entrapment' (1981) 59 *Washington University Law Quarterly* 199.

KLINCK, D. R., 'The Quest for Meaning in *Charter* Adjudication: Comment on R. v. *Therens*' (1985) 31 *McGill Law Journal* 104.

KODILINYE, G., 'Setting in Motion Malicious Prosecutions: The Commonwealth Experience' (1987) 36 *International and Comparative Law Quarterly* 157.

KOVACEVICH, J., 'The Inherent Power of the District Court: Abuse of Process, Delay and the Right to a Speedy Trial' [1989] *New Zealand Law Journal* 184.

LSE Jury Project, 'Jurors and the Rules of Evidence' [1973] *Criminal Law Review* 208.

L., F. D., jun., 'The Lagging Right to a Speedy Trial' (1965) 51 *Virginia Law Review* 1587.

LANGBEIN, J. H., 'Controlling Prosecutorial Discretion in Germany' (1974) 41 *University of Chicago Law Review* 439.

LANHAM, D., 'Entrapment, Qualified Defences and Codification' (1984) 4 *Oxford Journal of Legal Studies* 437.

—— 'Informal Extradition in Australian Law' (1987) 11 *Criminal Law Journal* 3.

LAWTON, The Hon. Sir F., 'The Role and Responsibility of the Judge' (1968) 8 *Medicine, Science and the Law* 243.

LEVY, J. C., 'Police Entrapment—A Note on Recent Developments' (1970) 35 *Saskatchewan Law Review* 180.

LEWIS, C. E., 'Unlawful Arrest: A Bar to the Jurisdiction of the Court, or Mala Captus Bene Detentus? Sidney Jaffe: A Case in Point' (1986) 28 *Criminal Law Quarterly* 341.

LIDSTONE, K. W., 'The Reformed Prosecution Process in England: A Radical Reform?' (1987) 11 *Criminal Law Journal* 296.

LOEWENTHAL, M. A., 'Evaluating the Exclusionary Rule in Search and Seizure' (1980) 9 *Anglo-American Law Review* 238.

LOEWY, A. H., 'The Fourth Amendment as a Device for Protecting the Innocent' (1983) 81 *Michigan Law Review* 1229.

McCLEAN, J. D., 'Informers and Agents Provocateurs' [1969] *Criminal Law Review* 527.

MacCRIMMON, M. T., 'Developments in the Law of Evidence: The 1984–85 Term' (1986) 8 *Supreme Court Law Review* 249.

MACDOUGALL, D. V., 'The Exclusionary Rule and its Alternatives—Remedies for

Constitutional Violations in Canada and the United States' (1985) 76 *Journal of Criminal Law and Criminology* 608.

McGINNIS, L. A., '*Grady v. Corbin*: Doubling the Scope of the Double Jeopardy Clause?' (1991) 17 *Ohio Northern University Law Review* 873.

MARJORIBANKS, G., 'Entrapment—The Juristic Basis' (1990) 6 *Auckland University Law Review* 360.

MASON, K., 'The Inherent Jurisdiction of the Court' (1983) 57 *Australian Law Journal* 449.

MAXTON, J., 'The Judicial Discretion to Exclude Evidence Obtained by Agents Provocateurs' (1980) 9 *New Zealand Universities Law Review* 73.

MAY, R., 'Admissibility of Confessions: Recent Developments' (1991) 55 *Journal of Criminal Law* 366.

MIERS, D. R., 'Informers and Agents Provocateurs' (1970) 120 *New Law Journal* 577.

—— 'Agents Provocateurs—The Judicial Response' (1970) 120 *New Law Journal* 597.

MIKELL, W. E., 'The Doctrine of Entrapment in the Federal Courts' (1942) 90 *University of Pennsylvania Law Review* 245.

MIRFIELD, P., 'Shedding a Tear for Issue Estoppel' [1980] *Criminal Law Review* 336.

—— 'The Police and Criminal Evidence Act 1984: (4) The Evidence Provisions' [1985] *Criminal Law Review* 569.

—— 'Similar Facts—*Makin* Out?' [1987] *Cambridge Law Journal* 83.

—— 'The Early Jurisprudence of Judicial Disrepute' (1988) 30 *Criminal Law Quarterly* 434.

MORGENSTERN, F., 'Jurisdiction in Seizures Effected in Violation of International Law' (1952) 29 *British Yearbook of International Law* 265.

MORISSETTE, Y.-M., 'The Exclusion of Evidence under the *Canadian Charter of Rights and Freedoms*: What to Do and What Not to Do' (1984) 29 *McGill Law Journal* 521.

MORRIS, A. A., 'The Exclusionary Rule, Deterrence and Posner's Economic Analysis of Law' (1982) 57 *Washington Law Review* 647.

MULLOCK, P., 'The Logic of Entrapment' (1985) 46 *University of Pittsburgh Law Review* 739.

NEASEY, F. M., 'The Rights of the Accused and the Interests of the Community' (1969) 43 *Australian Law Journal* 482.

NESSON, C., 'The Evidence or the Event? On Judicial Proof and the Acceptability of Verdicts' (1985) 98 *Harvard Law Review* 1357.

Note (1967) 83 *Law Quarterly Review* 472.

Note, 'The Extraterritorial Applicability of the Fourth Amendment' (1989) 102 *Harvard Law Review* 1672.

Note, 'The Nature and Consequences of Forensic Misconduct in the Prosecution of a Criminal Case' (1954) 54 *Columbia Law Review* 946.

OAKS, D. H., 'Studying the Exclusionary Rule in Search and Seizure' (1970) 37 *University of Chicago Law Review* 665.

O'CONNOR, P., 'Prosecution Disclosure: Principle, Practice and Justice' [1992] *Criminal Law Review* 464.

O'HIGGINS, P., 'Unlawful Seizure and Irregular Extradition' (1960) 36 *British Yearbook of International Law* 279.

ORCHARD, G. F., 'A Rejection of Unfairly Obtained Evidence: A Commentary on Hall v. Police' [1976] *New Zealand Law Journal* 434.

—— 'Unfairly Obtained Evidence and Entrapment' [1980] *New Zealand Law Journal* 203.

ORFIELD, M. W., jun., 'The Exclusionary Rule and Deterrence: An Empirical Study of Chicago Narcotics Officers' (1987) 54 *University of Chicago Law Review* 1016.

—— 'Deterrence, Perjury, and the Heater Factor: An Exclusionary Rule in the Chicago Criminal Courts' (1992) 63 *University of Colorado Law Review* 75.

OSBOROUGH, N., 'Deception on the Part of the Police in the Detection of Crime' [1968] *Irish Jurist* 233.

OSCAPELLA, E., 'A Study of Informers in England' [1980] *Criminal Law Review* 136.

PACIOCCO, D. M., 'The Judicial Repeal of S. 24(2) and the Development of the Canadian Exclusionary Rule' (1990) 32 *Criminal Law Quarterly* 326.

—— 'The Stay of Proceedings as a Remedy in Criminal Cases: Abusing the Abuse of Process Concept' (1991) 15 *Criminal Law Journal* 315.

PAKTER, W., 'Exclusionary Rules in France, Germany, and Italy' (1985) 9 *Hastings International and Comparative Law Review* 1.

PANAGOPOULOS, N. V., '*Amato v. The Queen*: A Precedent for Entrapment' (1983) 32 *University of New Brunswick Law Journal* 261.

PARK, R., 'The Entrapment Controversy' (1976) 60 *Minnesota Law Review* 163.

PARKER, G., 'Comment' (1970) 48 *Canadian Bar Review* 178.

PATERSON, R. K., 'Towards a Defence of Entrapment' (1979) 17 *Osgoode Hall Law Journal* 261.

PATTENDEN, R., 'The Exclusion of Unfairly Obtained Evidence in England, Canada and Australia' (1980) 29 *International and Comparative Law Quarterly* 664.

—— 'The Power of the Courts to Stay a Criminal Prosecution' [1985] *Criminal Law Review* 175.

—— 'Abuse of Process in Criminal Litigation' (1989) 53 *Journal of Criminal Law* 341.

PAULSEN, M. G., 'The Exclusionary Rule and Misconduct by the Police' (1961) 52 *Journal of Criminal Law, Criminology and Police Science* 255.

PERELLI-MINETTI, C. R., 'Causation and Intention in the Entrapment Defense' (1981) 28 *University of California Los Angeles Law Review* 859.

PERRY, G., 'Excluding Evidence in a Criminal Case—The Court's Discretionary Power' (1989) 108 *Law Notes* 105.

PHILLIPS, Mr Justice J. H., 'The Voir Dire' (1989) 63 *Australian Law Journal* 46.

PLUMB, W. T., jun., 'Illegal Enforcement of the Law' (1939) 24 *Cornell Law Quarterly* 337.

POLYVIOU, P. G., 'Illegally Obtained Evidence and R. v. Sang', in C. F. H. Tapper (ed.), *Crime, Proof and Punishment: Essays in Memory of Sir Rupert Cross* (London: Butterworths, 1981).

POSNER, R. A., 'Excessive Sanctions for Governmental Misconduct in Criminal Cases' (1982) 57 *Washington Law Review* 635.

PRICE, D., 'Recent Development' (1980) 14 *Law Teacher* 52.

QUICK, B., 'Recent Case' (1976) 53 *North Dakota Law Review* 284.

QUINLAN, P., 'Askov: Lowering the Boom' (1990) 79 *Criminal Reports* (3d) 321.

RAWLS, J., 'Two Concepts of Rules' (1955) 64 *Philosophical Review* 3.

RILEY, M., 'A Proposed Defence of Entrapment' (1977) 121 *Solicitors' Journal* 384.

ROBERTSON, B., 'The Looking-Glass World of Section 78' (1989) 139 *New Law Journal* 1223.

ROBINSON, P. H., 'Criminal Law Defenses: A Systematic Analysis' (1982) 82 *Columbia Law Review* 199.

SALTZBURG, S. A., 'The Reach of the Bill of Rights Beyond the *Terra Firma* of the United States', in R. B. Lillich (ed.), *International Aspects of Criminal Law: Enforcing United States Law in the World Community (Fourth Sokol Colloquium)* (Charlottesville, Va: Michie Company, 1981).

SAMUELS, A., 'Criminal Evidence—"It's Unfair: Keep it Out" ' (1989) 153 *Justice of the Peace* 151.

—— 'Serious: What is a Serious Offence?' (1992) 156 *Justice of the Peace* 59.

SAVAGE, S. R., 'Criminal Justice Act 1991—Sentenced by Seriousness' (1992) 156 *Justice of the Peace* 550.

SCHNEIDER, A. L., 'The Right to a Speedy Trial' (1968) 20 *Stanford Law Review* 476.

SCHROCK, T. S. and WELSH, R. C., 'Up from Calandra: The Exclusionary Rule as a Constitutional Requirement' (1974) 59 *Minnesota Law Review* 251.

SCHWARTZ, H., 'Retroactivity, Reliability, and Due Process: A Reply to Professor Mishkin' (1966) 33 *University of Chicago Law Review* 719.

SEGAL, M. D., 'The Impact of R. v. Therens on Various Forms of State Constraint' (1986) 38 *Motor Vehicle Reports* 71.

SEIDMAN, L. M., 'The Supreme Court, Entrapment, and Our Criminal Justice Dilemma' [1981] *Supreme Court Review* 111.

SHAFER, J. and SHERIDAN, W. J., 'The Defence of Entrapment' (1970) 8 *Osgoode Hall Law Journal* 277.

SHANKS, B. F., 'Comparative Analysis of the Exclusionary Rule and its Alternatives' (1983) 57 *Tulane Law Review* 648.

SHARPE, S., '*Sang* Revisited—Judicial Approval of Police Incitement' (1991) 155 *Justice of the Peace* 761.

SINGER, R. G., 'Forensic Misconduct by Federal Prosecutors—and How it Grew' (1968) 20 *Alabama Law Review* 227.

SMITH, K. J. M., 'The Law Commission Working Paper No. 55 on Codification of the Criminal Law, Defences of General Application: Official Instigation and Entrapment' [1975] *Criminal Law Review* 12.

SMITH, R., 'Is Anybody Listening?' (1992) 142 *New Law Journal* 816.

SNEIDEMAN, B. M., 'A Judicial Test for Entrapment: The Glimmerings of a Canadian Policy on Police-Instigated Crime' (1973–4) 16 *Criminal Law Quarterly* 81.

SPIOTTO, J. E., 'Search and Seizure: An Empirical Study of the Exclusionary Rule and its Alternatives' (1973) 2 *Journal of Legal Studies* 243.

STOBER, M., 'The Limits of Police Provocation in Canada' (1992) 34 *Criminal Law Quarterly* 290.

SUMMERS, R. S., 'Evaluating and Improving Legal Processes—A Plea for "Process Values" ' (1974) 60 *Cornell Law Review* 1.

TAPPER, C., 'Proof and Prejudice' in E. Campbell and L. Waller (eds.), *Well and Truly Tried* (Sydney: Law Book Co., 1982).

TEMKIN, J., 'Police Traps' (1974) 37 *Modern Law Review* 102.

THEISEN, S. H., 'Evidence Seized in Foreign Searches: When Does the Fourth Amendment Exclusionary Rule Apply?' (1983) 25 *William and Mary Law Review* 161.

THOMAS, G. C. III, 'A Modest Proposal to Save the Double Jeopardy Clause' (1991) 69 *Washington University Law Quarterly* 195.

THOMSON, C., 'Abuse of Process and Public Interests: Implications of Herron v. McGregor and Others' (1987) 11 *Criminal Law Journal* 206.

TREGILGAS-DAVEY, M., 'The Police and Accountability: Part 1' (1990) 140 *New Law Journal* 697.

—— 'The Police and Accountability: Part 2' (1990) 140 *New Law Journal* 738.

TWINING, W., 'The Rationalist Tradition of Evidence Scholarship', in E. Campbell and L. Waller (eds.), *Well and Truly Tried* (Sydney: Law Book Co., 1982).

UVILLER, H. R., '*Barker* v. *Wingo*: Speedy Trial Gets a Fast Shuffle' (1972) 72 *Columbia Law Review* 1376.

VAUGHAN, K., 'Protecting Those Who Grass' (1990) 87(34) *Law Society's Guardian Gazette* 16.

VENNARD, J., 'COURT DELAY AND SPEEDY TRIAL PROVISIONS' [1985] *Criminal Law Review* 73.

WADHAM, J., 'Abuse of Process through Delay in the Criminal Courts' [Feb. 1991] *Legal Action* 15.

WALLER, L., 'Evidence' in R. Baxt (ed.), *An Annual Survey of Law 1979* (Sydney: Law Book Co., 1980).

WASIK, M., 'The Grant of an Absolute Discharge' (1985) 5 *Oxford Journal of Legal Studies* 211.

WASSERSTROM, S. and MERTENS, W. J., 'The Exclusionary Rule on the Scaffold: But was it a Fair Trial?' (1984) 22 *American Criminal Law Review* 85.

WATT, J. D., 'The Defence of Entrapment' (1970–1) 13 *Criminal Law Quarterly* 313.

—— 'Entrapment as a Criminal Defence' (1971) 1 *Queen's Law Journal* 3.

WEBRE, C. J., '*Grady* v. *Corbin*: Successive Prosecutions Must Survive Heightened Double Jeopardy Protection' (1991) 36 *Loyola Law Review* 1171.

WEINBERG, M. S., 'The Judicial Discretion to Exclude Relevant Evidence' (1975) 21 *McGill Law Journal* 1.

WHELAN, M. F. J., 'Lead Us Not into (Unwarranted) Temptation: A Proposal to Replace the Entrapment Defense with a Reasonable-Suspicion Requirement' (1985) 133 *University of Pennsylvania Law Review* 1193.

WIGMORE, J. H., 'Using Evidence Obtained by Illegal Search and Seizure' (1922) 8 *American Bar Association Journal* 479.

WILLIAMS, G., 'Theft, Consent and Illegality' [1977] *Criminal Law Review* 327.

WILLIAMS, S. A., 'Comment' (1975) 53 *Canadian Bar Review* 404.

WILLIAMS, S., 'Exclusion of Illegally Obtained Evidence: A Comparison of English and American Law' (1989) 57 *University of Missouri Kansas City Law Review* 315.

WYLIE, J. C. W., 'Judicial Control of Police Evidence: Agents Provocateurs' (1966) 17 *Northern Ireland Legal Quarterly* 142.

YASUDA, T. K., 'Entrapment as a Due Process Defense: Developments after *Hampton* v. *United States*' (1982) 57 *Indiana Law Journal* 89.

YEO, M. H., 'The Discretion to Exclude Illegally and Improperly Obtained Evidence: A Choice of Approaches' (1981) 13 *Melbourne University Law Review* 31.

—— 'At the Crossroads of R. v. Sang and Bunning v. Cross' (1982) 6 *Criminal Law Journal* 89.

—— 'Inclusionary Discretion over Unfairly Obtained Evidence' (1982) 31 *International and Comparative Law Quarterly* 392.

ZUCKERMAN, A. A. S., 'Illegally-Obtained Evidence—Discretion as a Guardian of Legitimacy' (1987) 40 *Current Legal Problems* 55.

—— 'Similar Fact Evidence—The Unobservable Rule' (1987) 103 *Law Quarterly Review* 187.

—— 'Procedural Fairness during Police Interrogation and the Right of Silence' (1990) 54 *Journal of Criminal Law* 499.

BOOKS

American Friends Service Committee, *Struggle for Justice: A Report on Crime and Punishment in America* (New York: Hill & Wang, 1971).

American Law Institute, *Model Penal Code: Tentative Draft No. 9* (Philadelphia: 1959).

—— *Model Penal Code: Reprint—Proposed Official Draft* (Philadelphia: 1962).

ARONSON, M., *Managing Complex Criminal Trials: Reform of the Rules of Evidence and Procedure* (Carlton South, Victoria: Australian Institute of Judicial Administration Inc. 1992).

—— and FRANKLIN, N., *Review of Administrative Action* (Sydney: Law Book Co., 1987).

—— HUNTER, J. B., and WEINBERG, M. S., *Litigation: Evidence and Procedure* (4th edn., Sydney: Butterworths, 1988).

ASHWORTH, A., *Principles of Criminal Law* (Oxford: Clarendon Press, 1991).

ATIYAH, P. S. and SUMMERS, R. S., *Form and Substance in Anglo-American Law: A Comparative Study of Legal Reasoning, Legal Theory, and Legal Institutions* (Oxford: Clarendon Press, 1987).

Australian Law Reform Commission, *Criminal Investigation* (Canberra: Australian Government Publishing Service, 1975).

—— *Evidence*, i (Report No. 26: Interim) (Canberra: Australian Government Publishing Service, 1985).

—— *Evidence*, ii (Report No. 38) (Canberra: Australian Government Publishing Service, 1987).

BARAK, A., *Judicial Discretion* (New Haven: Yale University Press, 1989).

BAREFOOT, J. K., *Undercover Investigation* (2nd edn., Boston: Butterworths, 1983).

BENNION, F. A. R., *Statutory Interpretation: A Code* (2nd edn., London: Butterworths, 1992).

BISHOP, J. B., *Criminal Procedure* (Sydney: Butterworths, 1983).

BLACKSTONE, W., *Commentaries on the Laws of England (Vol. 4)* (A Facsimile of the First Edition of 1765–9) (Chicago: University of Chicago Press, 1979).

BROWN, D., FARRIER, D., NEAL, D., and WEISBROT, D., *Criminal Laws: Materials and Commentary on Criminal Law and Process in New South Wales* (Sydney: Federation Press, 1990).

BUCKWALTER, A., *Surveillance and Undercover Investigation* (Boston: Butterworths, 1983).

CARD, R., *Card, Cross, and Jones: Criminal Law* (12th edn., London: Butterworths, 1992).

CHOPER, J. H., *Judicial Review and the National Political Process: A Functional Reconsideration of the Role of the Supreme Court* (Chicago: University of Chicago Press, 1980).

CLARKSON, C. M. V. and KEATING, H. M., *Criminal Law: Text and Materials* (2nd edn., London: Sweet & Maxwell, 1990).

CLEARY, E. W. (ed.), *McCormick on Evidence* (3rd edn., St Paul, Minn.: West Publishing Co., 1984).

Commission of Inquiry Concerning Certain Activities of the Royal Canadian Mounted Police, *Second Report*, ii. *Freedom and Security under the Law* (Ottawa: Canadian Government Publishing Centre, 1981).

COWEN, Z. and CARTER, P. B., *Essays on the Law of Evidence* (Oxford: Clarendon Press, 1956).

CRANSTON, R., HAYNES, P., PULLEN, J., and SCOTT, I. R., *Delays and Efficiency in Civil Litigation* (Australian Institute of Judicial Administration Inc., 1985).

Criminal Law Revision Committee, *Eleventh Report: Evidence (General)* (Cmnd 4991) (London: HMSO, 1972).

CROSS, SIR R. and ASHWORTH, A., *The English Sentencing System* (3rd edn., London: Butterworths, 1981).

—— TAPPER, C., *Cross on Evidence* (7th edn., London: Butterworths, 1990).

DAMAŠKA, M. R., *The Faces of Justice and State Authority: A Comparative Approach to the Legal Process* (New Haven, Conn.: Yale University Press, 1986).

DAVIS, K. C., *Discretionary Justice: A Preliminary Inquiry* (Urbana, Ill.: University of Illinois Press, 1971).

DICEY, A. V., *Introduction to the Study of the Law of the Constitution* (10th edn., London: Macmillan & Co. Ltd., 1964).

DWORKIN, R., *Taking Rights Seriously* (London: Duckworth, 1977).

—— *Law's Empire* (London: Fontana, 1986).

—— *A Matter of Principle* (Oxford: Clarendon Press, 1986).

FEINBERG, J., *Doing and Deserving: Essays in the Theory of Responsibility* (Princeton, NJ: Princeton University Press, 1970).

FELDMAN, D., *The Law Relating to Entry, Search and Seizure* (London: Butterworths, 1986).

FLETCHER, G. P., *Rethinking Criminal Law* (Boston: Little, Brown & Co., 1978).

FREEMAN, M. D. A., *The Police and Criminal Evidence Act 1984* (London: Sweet and Maxwell, 1985).

FRIEDLAND, M. L., *Double Jeopardy* (Oxford: Clarendon Press, 1969).

GALLIGAN, D. J., *Discretionary Powers: A Legal Study of Official Discretion* (Oxford: Clarendon Press, 1990).

The German Code of Criminal Procedure, trans. H. Niebler (London: Sweet & Maxwell Ltd., 1965).

GILLIES, P., *The Law of Criminal Investigation* (Sydney: Law Book Co., 1982).

GROSS, H., *A Theory of Criminal Justice* (New York: Oxford University Press, 1979).

HARRIS, D. J., *Cases and Materials on International Law* (4th edn., London: Sweet & Maxwell, 1991).

HARRISON, J. and CRAGG, S., *Police Misconduct: Legal Remedies* (2nd edn., Legal Action Group, 1991).

HART, H. L. A., *Punishment and Responsibility: Essays in the Philosophy of Law* (Oxford: Clarendon Press, 1968).

—— and HONORÉ, T., *Causation in the Law* (2nd edn., Oxford: Clarendon Press, 1985).

HEYDON, J. D. and OCKELTON, M., *Evidence: Cases and Materials* (3rd edn., London: Butterworths, 1991).

HOROWITZ, D. L., *The Courts and Social Policy* (Washington, DC: Brookings Institution, 1977).

JOWELL, J. L., *Law and Bureaucracy: Administrative Discretion and the Limits of Legal Action* (Port Washington, New York: Dunellen Publishing Co. Inc., 1975).

—— and OLIVER, D., *The Changing Constitution* (2nd edn., Oxford: Clarendon Press, 1989).

KEANE, A., *The Modern Law of Evidence* (2nd edn., London: Butterworths, 1989).

KELMAN, M., *A Guide to Critical Legal Studies* (Cambridge, Mass.: Harvard University Press, 1987).

LACEY, N., WELLS, C., and MEURE, D., *Reconstructing Criminal Law: Critical Perspectives on Crime and the Criminal Process* (London: Weidenfeld and Nicolson, 1990).

LAFAVE, W. R., *Search and Seizure: A Treatise on the Fourth Amendment* (2nd edn., St Paul, Minn.: West Publishing Co., 1987, 1991).

—— and ISRAEL, J. H., *Criminal Procedure* (St Paul, Minn.: West Publishing Co., 1985).

LANGBEIN, J. H., *Comparative Criminal Procedure: Germany* (St Paul, Minn.: West Publishing Co., 1977).

Law Commission, *Codification of the Criminal Law* (Working Paper, No. 55; London: HMSO, 1974).

—— *Criminal Law: Report on Defences of General Application* (Law Commission, No. 83; London: HMSO, 1977).

—— *Criminal Law: Codification of the Criminal Law—A Report to the Law Commission* (Law Commission, No. 143; London: HMSO, 1985).

—— *Criminal Law: A Criminal Code for England and Wales*, i. *Report and Draft Criminal Code Bill* (Law Commission, No. 177; London: HMSO, 1989).

—— *Criminal Law: A Criminal Code for England and Wales*, ii. *Commentary on Draft Criminal Code Bill* (Law Commission, No. 177; London: HMSO, 1989).

LEIGH, L. H., *Police Powers in England and Wales* (2nd edn., London: Butterworths, 1985).

—— and HALL WILLIAMS, J. E., *The Management of the Prosecution Process in Denmark, Sweden and the Netherlands* (Leamington Spa: James Hall, 1981).

—— and ZEDNER, L., *The Royal Commission on Criminal Justice: A Report on the Administration of Criminal Justice in the Pre-Trial Phase in France and Germany* (London: HMSO, 1992).

LUSTGARTEN, L., *The Governance of Police* (London: Sweet & Maxwell, 1986).

MIRFIELD, P., *Confessions* (London: Sweet & Maxwell, 1985).

MORGAN, P. and VENNARD, J., *Pre-Trial Delay: The Implications of Time Limits* (Home Office Research Study, No. 110; London: HMSO, 1989).

National Commission on Reform of Federal Criminal Laws, *Study Draft of a New Federal Criminal Code (Title 18, United States Code)* (Washington: US Government Printing Office, 1970).

New South Wales Law Reform Commission, *Working Paper on Illegally and Improperly Obtained Evidence* (1979).

—— *Criminal Procedure—Procedure from Charge to Trial: A General Proposal for Reform* (Sydney: 1986).

—— *Criminal Procedure—Procedure from Charge to Trial: Specific Problems and Proposals* (Sydney: 1987).

O'CONNELL, D. P., *International Law* (2nd edn., London: Stevens & Sons, 1970).

PACKER, H.L., *The Limits of the Criminal Sanction* (Stanford, California: Stanford University Press, 1969).

PATTENDEN, R., *The Judge, Discretion, and the Criminal Trial* (Oxford: Clarendon Press, 1982).

—— *Judicial Discretion and Criminal Litigation* (Oxford: Clarendon Press, 1990) (2nd edn. of *The Judge, Discretion, and the Criminal Trial*).

POLYVIOU, P. G., *Search and Seizure: Constitutional and Common Law* (London: Duckworth, 1982).

POSTEMA, G. J., *Bentham and the Common Law Tradition* (Oxford: Clarendon Press, 1986).

POUND, R., *Jurisprudence*, ii (St Paul, Minn.: West Publishing Co., 1959).

Report of the Canadian Committee on Corrections, *Towards Unity: Criminal Justice and Corrections* (Ottawa: Queen's Printer, 1969).

Report of the Royal Commission on Police Powers and Procedure (Cmd 3297) (London: HMSO, 1929).

Report to the Home Secretary from the Commissioner of Police of the Metropolis on the Actions of Police Officers Concerned with the Case of Kenneth Joseph Lennon (London: HMSO, 1974).

ROBERTSON, G., *Reluctant Judas* (London: Temple Smith, 1976).

Royal Commission on Criminal Procedure, *Report* (Cmnd 8092) (London: HMSO, 1981).

SKOLNICK, J. H., *Justice without Trial: Law Enforcement in Democratic Society* (2nd edn., New York: Wiley, 1975).

SMITH, J. C. and HOGAN, B., *Criminal Law* (7th edn., London: Butterworths, 1992).

STEIN, P. and SHAND, J., *Legal Values in Western Society* (Edinburgh: Edinburgh University Press, 1974).

The Supreme Court Practice 1993 (London: Sweet & Maxwell, 1992).

TAY, A. E.-S., *Human Rights for Australia* (Human Rights Commission Monograph Series, No. 1; Canberra: Australian Government Publishing Service, 1986).

THOMAS, D. A., *Principles of Sentencing* (2nd edn., London: Heinemann, 1979).

TRIBE, L. H., *American Constitutional Law* (2nd edn., Mineola, NY: Foundation Press Inc., 1988).

WAIGHT, P. K. and WILLIAMS, C. R., *Evidence: Commentary and Materials* (3rd edn., Sydney: Law Book Co., 1990).

WALKER, N., *Punishment, Danger and Stigma: The Morality of Criminal Justice* (Oxford: Basil Blackwell, 1980).

WILLIAMS, G., *Criminal Law: The General Part* (2nd edn., London: Stevens & Sons Ltd., 1961).

—— *Textbook of Criminal Law* (2nd edn., London: Stevens & Sons, 1983).

WILLIAMS, S. A. and CASTEL, J.-G., *Canadian Criminal Law: International and Transnational Aspects* (Toronto: Butterworths, 1981).

WILSON, J. Q., *The Investigators: Managing FBI and Narcotics Agents* (New York: Basic Books, 1978).

WINFIELD, P. H., *The History of Conspiracy and Abuse of Legal Procedure* (Cambridge: Cambridge University Press, 1921).

—— *The Present Law of Abuse of Legal Procedure* (Cambridge: Cambridge University Press, 1921).

Working Papers of the National Commission on Reform of Federal Criminal Laws, i (Washington: US Government Printing Office, 1970).

ZUCKERMAN, A. A. S., *The Principles of Criminal Evidence* (Oxford: Clarendon Press, 1989).

THESES

CHOO, A. L.- T., 'The Relation between Pre-Trial Executive Improprieties and the Outcome of the Criminal Trial' (D.Phil. thesis, University of Oxford, MS D.Phil. c 8701, 1990); abstract published in (1992) 41 ASLIB Index to Theses No. 41–0481.

HUNTER, J. B., 'Multiple Incriminations and Criminal Justice' (Ph.D. thesis, University of London, 1982).

MORISSETTE, Y.-M. J. R., 'Improperly Obtained Evidence other than Confessions—A Comparative Study: England, Canada, Scotland, Northern Ireland, Eire, Australia, New Zealand and the United States' (D.Phil. thesis, University of Oxford, MS D.Phil. c 2279, 1977).

Index

substantially the same offence, prosecution for 21
trial judge, determination to be by 20
'*Vandercomb* test' 24
see also greater encompassing offence, prosecution for; lesser included offence, prosecution for
police discipline 98
police perjury 92–3
pre-trial inquiries 131–6
  New South Wales 133
  United States 134–6
  Victoria 133–4
Privatbereich 90
pro-active law-enforcement techniques 148–9, 178–81
public opinion polls 102
punishment, symbolic significance of 11–12

Rechtsstaatsprinzip 90
rehabilitation, rule against double jeopardy and 18

Reinheit des Verefahrens 90
road traffic offences, prosecution for 34–6

sentencing, principles relating to 41–42, 114
speedy trial, right to, *see* delay
stay of proceedings, *see* abuse of process discretion
stay of proceedings, nature of 7

time limit for laying information, circumvention of 42–3
trial within a reasonable time, right to, *see* delay
type of trial, deprivation of right to 44–6

Verhältnismässigkeit 90
voir-dire hearings 130–1

wrongful conviction, protection of innocent from 10, 17, 71–4
  seriousness of offence, relevance of 72